The Best of
SAN FRANCISCO

The Best of
SAN FRANCISCO

*A Witty and Somewhat Opinionated
Insider's Guide to Everybody's Favorite City*

Don W. Martin
Betty Woo Martin

CHRONICLE BOOKS
SAN FRANCISCO

To Kim and Dan
You must give wings to your dreams

Printed in the United States of America.
Third Edition

Library of Congress Cataloging-in-Publication Data

Martin, Don W., 1934–
    The best of San Francisco : a witty and somewhat
  opinionated insider's guide to everybody's favorite city
  / Don W. Martin, Betty Woo Martin.
      p.   cm.
    Includes index.
    ISBN 0–8118–0611–1
    1. San Francisco (Calif.)—Guidebooks.   I. Martin, Betty Woo.
  II. Title.
  F869.S33B4653 1994
  917.94'610453—dc20   93-42284
                                                            CIP

Book Design and Production: T:H Typecast, Inc.
Cover Design: Laurie Rosenwald

Distributed in Canada by Raincoast Books,
112 East Third Avenue, Vancouver, B.C. V5T 1C8

10 9 8 7 6 5 4 3 2 1

Chronicle Books
275 Fifth Street
San Francisco, CA 94103

Contents

Introduction

I'd rather be a busted lamp post on Battery Street, San Francisco, than the Waldorf-Astoria in New York.

—Willie Britt

best *adj.* (*Superlative of* good) 1: excellent in the highest degree 2: most useful, correct, worthy, etc.

Our weathered *Webster's Dictionary* effectively sums up our reasons for offering you *The Best of San Francisco,* which we first wrote in 1986, then revised in 1989 and now again in 1994.

For decades, we've wandered the streets of this wonderful city, seeking the best it has to offer. We've consulted assorted guidebooks, tried hundreds of restaurants, and asked scores of cabbies and concierges a simple question: "Where can we find the best of San Francisco?"

That's not an easy question to answer. There are more than four thousand restaurants and just over two thousand bars in the city. The AAA's *California-Nevada TourBook* contains thirty pages of San Francisco lodgings and restaurants and another thirteen pages of activities and attractions. Dozens of other city guidebooks offer additional dozens of pounds of information. Who has time to sort through all this material?

Fortunately, we did. We decided to write a special kind of guidebook, by arbitrarily sifting through lengthy lists of attractions, restaurants, pubs, and such to offer readers only the city's very best. We wanted a book that would tell you—at the flip of a page—where to find the ten best hamburgers, the liveliest bars, the finest museums, the best fillet of sole, the most awesome ice cream ever to cool your palate on a warm September afternoon.

We wrote this book for two audiences: those who are visiting—or plan to visit—the San Francisco Bay Area, and those who live here. For both parties, we set about creating an informative and opinionated "book of lists." It covers both the obvious and the obscure, offering insight into the popular places you'll want to see, while uncovering interesting attractions, vista points, and pillow places that other books may have overlooked.

With each revision, we update and expand our listings to make the book more useful, both as an insider's guide and as a general reference source. New to this third edition are the Ten Best special places, the Ten Best things to do just because it's San Francisco, the Ten Best view cocktail lounges and restaurants, and the Ten Best breakfast places. We even nominate the Ten Best radio stations, so you can tune in your favorite noise as you drive.

In compiling material for *The Best of San Francisco,* we enlisted the aid of seven city-wise friends, asking them to prepare lists of their personal favorites.

Guided by their suggestions, we spent months in the field, sampling sundry seafoods, sushi, and soufflés, admiring each view of this handsome city, pedaling assorted bike paths.

With each revision of this book, we add new members to our panel to bring fresh insights to our research. We gather them for a tasting of the Bay Area's favorite specialty foods for our "Goodies" selection in Chapter 12. We place before the panel unlabeled samples of sourdough french bread, salami, designer muffins, gourmet ice cream, and other local delights. Then we step back quickly and watch while they nibble, chew, and gravely nod their heads.

After extended discussions, frequent loud arguments, and an occasional coin flip, we come up with *The Best of San Francisco*. Within each group of the Ten Best (except where items aren't directly related), we've picked our favorite: our personal No. 1. The other nine follow alphabetically. In this way, we have no losers among the Ten Best, only winners and runners-up.

Our selections are a mix of many new discoveries and longtime favorites. Naturally, in a city that offers so much, we were arbitrary in our final decisions. Choices were influenced by our personal interests and tastes, and these may differ from yours. If you prefer fish cooked to the consistency of an artgum eraser, or if your idea of amusement is to stroll about in a contemplative daze with a stereo cassette player plugged into your ears, you may not find this guide useful.

Incidentally, we solicited no free meals or admissions to attractions, so our selections—while opinionated—are impartial.

Come join us in rediscovering America's favorite city.

TO LEARN MORE ABOUT THE CITY Stop in at the San Francisco Visitor Information Center in Hallidie Plaza at Powell and Market streets (near the cable car turntable and Powell BART/Muni station). Hours are 9 a.m. to 5:30 p.m. Monday through Friday, 9 a.m. to 3 p.m. on Saturday, and 10 a.m. to 2 p.m. on Sunday; phone 974-6900.

GET A FAST PASS, FAST! The best way to get around the city—particularly if you plan an extended visit—is to buy a $35 Fast Pass, good for the calendar month in which it is purchased. Also available are one-day ($6), three-day ($10), and seven-day ($15) Muni Passports. The Fast Pass and Passport are good for unlimited rides on the city's bus, streetcar, cable car, and rail systems, and on BART and CalTrain within the city.

With cable car fares at $2 and basic bus fares at a dollar, the passes will quickly earn their keep. They're available from the information booth in San Francisco City Hall, the Visitor Information Center in Hallidie Plaza, the Cable Car Museum at Washington and Mason streets, and the STBS ticket office on the Stockton Street side of Union Square. Also available is a transit system route map. It's $1.50 in stores, or $2 through the mail (San Francisco Municipal Railway, 949 Presidio Avenue, San Francisco, CA 94115). For transit information and to confirm fares call 673-MUNI.

A BIT ABOUT THE AUTHORS

1 Don W. Martin has been in, out, and about the San Francisco Bay Area since 1958. With his wife, Betty, he has authored twelve guidebooks about California and other Western states. Members of the Society of American Travel Writers, they also contribute articles and photos to assorted magazines and major newspapers. A few eons ago, Don served as a U.S. Marine correspondent in the Orient, then he spent several years as a reporter and editor for various California newspapers. He was associate editor of the travel magazine of the San Francisco-based California State Automobile Association until 1988, when he left to become a full-time guidebook author.

2 Betty Woo Martin offers the curious credentials of a doctorate in pharmacy and a California real estate broker's license. But never mind that. She's also an expert in Asian cuisine, a student of culinary arts and hospitality management courses at California's Columbia College, and a free-lance writer-photographer. A graduate of the University of California at San Francisco, she's a native Californian with an extensive knowledge of the Bay Area.

...AND THE SAN FRANCISCO SEVEN

1 Charles L. Beucher, Jr. A San Francisco intimate for more than two decades, Chuck is business and production manager of *Motorland,* the California State Automobile Association travel magazine. He's also a longtime friend who has advised us on the design of our other guidebooks. He created the hiking and biking tour maps for the original edition of this publication.

2 Liz Martin A senior employee of Macy's California and a member of its buying staff, Liz has been a San Franciscan by BART commute for twenty years. She brings to our panel her expertise as Macy's former wine and gourmet foods specialist.

3 Agnes Ng Hong Kong born and Bay Area educated, Agnes is the founder of Bray & Jordan, a public relations firm representing several San Francisco restaurants and hotels. She's an active member of the San Francisco Professional Food Society and the International Association of Culinary Professionals. An avid cook who loves great food, she's always on the lookout for interesting new restaurants.

4 Shirley Fong-Torres One of northern California's leading Chinese cooking specialists, Shirley heads two local firms, Wok Wiz Chinatown Walking Tours and Cooking Company, and A Taste of Chinatown. She also finds time to conduct cooking classes and travel shows. She teaches cooking at the California Culinary Academy, and she's written three cookbooks and a travel book, *San Francisco Chinatown: A Walking Tour.*

5 Bernard A. Carver Shirley's husband, Bernie, not only manages to keep pace with the busy Wok Wiz but he's often one step ahead. He shares company chores as sales and marketing director and, as a serious San Francisco history buff, he often conducts the Wok Wiz walking tours. Catching up to the rest of the staff, he's learning to speak Cantonese—with an Illinois accent?

6 & 7 Ferdinand "Von" and Ginna Von Schlafke A friendly bear of a man, Von brings his expertise in art, museums, and galleries to these pages. Until he retired in 1989, he exhibited his skills in artistry and design as a preparator for the San Francisco Museum of Modern Art. He frequently functions as a docent for the Behring Auto Museum in Blackhawk. Ginna is a gourmet and an excellent cook, and she is also knowledgeable in art.

THANK YOU

1 Sharon Rooney and others of the San Francisco Convention and Visitors Bureau, for generously sharing their extensive knowledge of the city, providing useful information, and reviewing the manuscript.

2 Public Service Officer Diane Palacio of the Recreation and Park Department, for helping us discover the wealth of parks, museums, and other attractions administered by the city.

3 Robert Callwell of the Department of Community Affairs, San Francisco Municipal Railway, for helping us search out scenic Muni routes and for teaching us the best reason for using public transit: You don't have to look for a parking place.

4 Public Information Officer Michael Feinstein and various rangers for helping us learn about that amazing urban park called the Golden Gate National Recreation Area.

5 Harry Hamilton, director of tourism and public relations, Oakland Convention and Visitors Bureau, for helping us prove that there is a there there.

6 Robert Byrne, author of *1,911 Best Things Anybody Ever Said,* Ballantine Books, 1988. We consulted many sources for our chapter-heading quotes, and found his book to be particularly helpful—and a delight to read.

7 Malcolm Stroud, owner of Scott's Seafood Grill & Bar, Three Embarcadero Center, for providing facilities for the San Francisco Seven tasting competition.

8 Edward Benstein, owner of Contra Costa County's House of Velvet, for his assistance with the San Francisco Seven tasting.

9 ...and especially the San Francisco Seven, without whose help this book would have been considerably thinner.

Chapter 1

THE TEN BEST ATTRACTIONS IN SAN FRANCISCO

...that your other insider's guides may have overlooked

*A bay, a channel and ocean city—small in size, intense upon its hills,
haunted by fog and the bawling horns of it.*

—William Saroyan

It's not a big city, actually.

With fewer than 750,000 souls, it ranks only thirteenth in population among America's cities; San Diego, San Jose, and Phoenix are larger. Yet San Francisco is a world-class city in every sense: a delightful cosmopolitan clutter of great museums, fine restaurants, urban parks, and intriguing ethnic enclaves.

It's amazingly complex and compact, second only to New York in population density. Tucked into this 46.48-square-mile metropolis are many world-renowned attractions, and a few neat little jewels that visitors often overlook. Some of our favorite things rate only a sentence in other guidebooks or fail to make them at all.

After prowling the streets of San Francisco off and on since 1958, we've made these discoveries: our ten favorite things to see and do.

1 Watch the Surf Crash at Fort Point

*Call 556-1693 for Fort Point activities and exhibits. Fort open from 10 a.m. to
5 p.m. daily.*

Like a storm-tossed ship, San Francisco is most beautiful and exciting with the wind in her face.

When a Pacific squall surges through the Golden Gate, great waves slam into the seawall at Fort Point, sending fans of water high into the air. Above the red-brick mass of the old fort, the slender span of the bridge may disappear into the gathering storm, like a pathway to infinity. Out on the bay, Alcatraz is a huddled dark shape, like a cat caught in a downpour. Beyond, the city skyline broods under glowering clouds.

Fort Point is a nice sunny-day place, too. It draws rather light crowds even as visitors trip over one another at the Golden Gate Bridge viewpoint just above. It offers some of the city's finest vistas—panoramas of sea, bridge, city, and headland—particularly from the old cannon batteries atop its eight-foot-thick walls.

The fort is a national historic site, and park rangers dressed in period soldier suits demonstrate what army life was like a century ago: loading cannons and conducting rifle drills. You can prowl the great echoing corridors of the fort and capture stop-action glimpses of the city through its windows and gun ports.

Eight years and several million bricks were required to build this mighty bastion in the 1850s. One hundred twenty-six cannons, capable of hurling 128-pound balls two miles, were trained on the Golden Gate passage, waiting for menacing ships that never came. The armament was withdrawn around the turn of the century. Then the U.S. Army reoccupied the fort during World War II and leveled its howitzers on the narrow passage, waiting for Japanese ships that never came. Of course, those sailing through the gate today come in peace, loaded with Toyotas.

2 Amble about Alamo Square

Historic district of Victorian homes, bounded by Webster, Fell, and Divisadero streets and Golden Gate Avenue, ten blocks west of the Civic Center.

They're called the Painted Ladies: those cheerfully colored, matching Victorian row houses in the 700 block of Steiner Street. You may have seen them on postcards and magazine covers, with the city's modern skyline rising behind.

However, the Ladies are only six of several hundred Victorian-era houses still standing in this neighborhood. Indeed, slender bay-windowed homes such as these, with their ornate wooden cornices, gables, and porticoes, are scattered throughout the city. The greatest concentration extends in a several-block radius around Alamo Square, a landscaped park at Steiner and Hayes streets.

Simply by zigging and zagging through this neighborhood, you'll see dozens of these San Francisco "sticks." (See *The Ten Most Handsome Victorians* in Chapter 20 and our *Victoriana to the Haight Hike* in Chapter 21.) Most were constructed as tract homes by contractors during a building boom lasting from the 1870s through the turn of the century. Nearly all were built of redwood, which is easily milled, sturdy, and fire-resistant. Redwood trees were plentiful then, which explains why they aren't now.

The ornate trim could be ordered through catalogs—anything from a fake sunburst gable to filigree, "doughnuts," and "drips." Many architectural writers of the day scoffed at the ornamental whimsy of the homes, which they sarcastically called the Frisco-American style.

"Why the curved piece with its radiating spindles over the porch?" fussed an early critic. "Why the meaningless little columns to the attic window which we know support nothing at all, and why so much cheap detail on the frieze and in the gable's peak?"

Although the great earthquake and fire of 1906 destroyed many of the city's Victorians, the damage stopped short of the Alamo Square area. In recent years, preservation-minded folks have been buying up and restoring the surviving filigreed homes. The houses often emerge with wonderfully gaudy paint jobs, adding a kaleidoscopic brilliance to the neighborhood.

3 Inhale the Incense at a Chinese Temple

Norras Temple is located at 109 Waverly Place, Tin Hou Temple is a few doors down at 125, and Jeng Sen Temple is across the alley at 146 Waverly.

Most Chinese don't practice their religion in the Western sense of attending regular services, listening to a sermon, then dropping coins into the collection plate. They visit their temples whenever the spiritual urge moves them. They may go to send prayers to their ancestors or simply to sit quietly and reflect on their beliefs: generally a blend of Buddhism and Taoism, which venerates ancestors and the natural order of life.

The three temples we've listed sit close together in Waverly Place, a busy alley between Washington, Grant, Clay, and Stockton streets in Chinatown. They're rather small places and difficult to find, located up narrow stairways and behind nondescript doorways. They do welcome visitors; ring a buzzer and you'll be admitted. You will enter a mystical, lavishly ornate world of red (the color of good fortune), black lacquer, and gold; incense curls ceilingward from elaborate altars. After you have looked around a bit, a small contribution for the upkeep of the place will be appreciated.

4 Make It Happen at Fort Mason Center

For Fort Mason Center activities, call the 24-hour recorded information line at 441-5705. Various admission prices for museums; all are free the first Wednesday of each month from noon to 8 p.m. For general information, contact Fort Mason Center Information Office, Building A, San Francisco, CA 94123; phone 441-5706.

Make what happen?

Just about anything that culturally pleases you. Fort Mason Center is one of those "only in San Francisco" places: a gathering of galleries, museums, performing arts groups, and nonprofit organizations housed in a former waterfront army supply depot.

Members of the Fort Mason Foundation like to describe their unique enclave as a "year-round fair." Indeed, it hosts many special events in addition to housing art exhibits, music and drama workshops, and Greens, the noted Zen Buddhist vegetarian restaurant (see Chapter 8). For the casual stroller, it offers striking waterfront views and a chance to visit the restored liberty ship, *SS Jeremiah O'Brien* (see the listing later in this chapter). Note the scattered outdoor artworks, including a curious (but fading) mural of animals benignly taking over the San Francisco freeway system.

You can attend an aerobics class or a gallery opening, enjoy a music recital, sit in on a politically correct environmental seminar, fish for crab off the piers, or catch a play.

The center occupies several refurbished warehouses and piers at one corner of the former army post. Also at Fort Mason is a landscaped network of historic plantation-style army buildings housing the headquarters of the Golden Gate National Recreation Area (see Chapter 2), a still-functioning military officers' club, and a youth hostel.

The site of a Spanish garrison when San Francisco was a mission outpost in the 1770s, Fort Mason became an army embarkation depot in the 1930s. From its commodious piers, more than a million American servicemen and their supplies departed for the uncertain glories of combat in World War II and Korea. Then in a classic swords-to-plowshares move in 1972, many of the city's military facilities—including Fort Mason—became a part of the Golden Gate National

Recreation Area. The Fort Mason Foundation was established to coordinate development of this former military base into a community haven for the arts and assorted nonprofit organizations. Nearly two million people visit each year to attend its events or stroll through its galleries and museums.

5 Enjoy TGIF in a Floating Pub

Golden Gate Ferry service runs daily from 7 a.m. to 8:30 p.m. Sausalito ferry fare is $3.75 daily; Larkspur fare is $2.50 weekdays and $3.25 on weekends. Special family fare available on weekends; seniors and handicapped travel for half-fare at all times. Call 332-6600.

Tired of hanging out with the same old crowd at the same old after-work bar? For a very few dollars, you can buy a ticket aboard a pub that goes somewhere: one of the Golden Gate Bridge District's passenger ferries operating between San Francisco and Marin County.

Golden Gate Ferry's fleet runs daily to Sausalito and Larkspur Landing from a dock behind the south wing of the San Francisco Ferry Building. When the ferries were put into operation more than twenty years ago, officials decided to install a sea-going beverage and snack service to attract the commuter crowd. It's still going strong. Drink prices are reasonable, and you get all that San Francisco waterfront scenery, a close-up of Alcatraz, and a peek at the pretty Marin shoreline. What saloon can offer as much?

The thirty-minute San Francisco-Sausalito run is our favorite; we like to explore that charming community's shops and attractive waterfront after going ashore; then we catch a later ferry back. The Larkspur ferry has its appeal, too. The Larkspur Landing shopping center and a new Marriott Hotel are near the terminal, and daytime riders can walk to nearby Muzzie Marsh, a major waterfowl habitat.

We prefer boarding the ferries with the afternoon commuters rather than combating the heavy crowds of visitors on weekends. For thirsty Marin-bound commuters, it's about a two-martini crossing.

6 Shake with a Quake and Smile at a Crocodile

California Academy of Sciences, Golden Gate Park. Open 10 a.m. to 5 p.m. daily. Admission is $6 for adults, $3 for kids and seniors, and free on the first Wednesday of each month. Additional fees for planetarium and Laserium shows. Call 750-7145 (a recording) or 221-5100 for information on special exhibits. A $10 Culture Pass is good for admission to the Academy of Sciences, plus the Conservatory of Flowers, de Young Museum, Asian Art Museum, and Japanese Tea Garden.

We're recommending a science museum as a major tourist attraction? Certainly!

The California Academy of Sciences in Golden Gate Park is one of the most innovative and versatile institutions of its kind in the country. It's many good things under one big roof: a natural sciences center with stuffed creatures in realistic settings, a planetarium, a hall of human cultures that traces us from our banana-munching predecessors, and a major aquarium.

Exhibits change frequently, so there's never an excuse to stay away for more than a few months. One of the finest displays here is "Life Through Time," an entire hall devoted to the history of life on earth. It takes visitors on a three-billion-year journey through the ages, from early life in the seas to the era of giant insects to the dinosaurs epoch and into the age of mammals.

The Hall of Earth and Space Sciences teaches visitors about plate tectonics and continental drift while Plexiglas planets circle overhead, following neon orbits. You can experience a "safequake" by stepping aboard a platform that jiggles you with nearly the same intensity as the city's destructive 1906 earthquake. In Morrison Planetarium, you can lean back in special tilted seats while a five-thousand-pound star machine projects the heavens above, or you can watch a light-fantastic Laserium show.

In the Hall of Africa, recorded grunts, groans, snorts, and chirps greet visitors at a realistic African watering hole. You can stare down at a swampful of grinning 'gators in the Steinhart Aquarium, then stand inside an unusual doughnut-shaped fish roundabout, where great schools of finned critters swim about you. The academy also offers a science- and nature-oriented gift and book shop.

7 Have a Look at a Liberty Ship

The SS Jeremiah O'Brien, Pier 3, Fort Mason Center. Open 9 a.m. to 3 p.m. weekdays and 9 a.m. to 4 p.m. weekends, closed major holidays; other elements of the National Maritime Museum are generally open 10 a.m. to 5 p.m., with seasonal variations. Call 929-0202 or 556-8177.

They called them liberty ships: those hastily assembled cargo carriers that kept our fighting troops supplied with ammo and Spam during World War II. Nearly three thousand were built by legions of riveting Rosies. Each ship was hammered and welded together in a few weeks from prefabricated parts.

Only one completely intact liberty ship survives, and she sits beside Pier 3 at Fort Mason. The *SS Jeremiah O'Brien* was built in 1943 and saw action as a troop and supply carrier during the Normandy Invasion. A few years ago, she was liberated from a floating ship storage area by a group called the National Liberty Ship Memorial, restored, and put on display. The outfit has succeeded in having good old *Jeremiah* listed on the National Register of Historic Places.

You can explore her welded metal decks from bow to stern, stand in the wheelhouse, peek into seamen's cabins, and prowl along the many catwalks in the cavernous engine room. A still-operational triple-expansion steam engine once pushed the heavy cargo ship through the waves at a leisurely eleven knots. Slow and vulnerable, she was armed with ten defense guns; two are still in place.

This is more than a static exhibit. On Open Ship Weekends, held about eight times a year, the crew cranks up the steam engines and demonstrates other workings of the historic freighter. The liberty ship association also schedules annual cruises on San Francisco Bay.

The *O'Brien* is one of several yesterday ships exhibited along the city's waterfront. They're part of the National Maritime Museum, which we cover in greater detail in Chapter 2.

8 Climb the Stairs of Telegraph Hill

Greenwich and Filbert steps, below Coit Tower.

A maze of steep, often lushly landscaped stairways winds about the flanks and heights of Telegraph Hill. Many sections serve as extensions of streets that are unable to scale the near-vertical rises. Some of the homes cantilevered into the slopes are served only by these stairstep paths—great for seclusion but a pain when bringing home the bacon and other groceries. Best known of the hillside stairways is the Greenwich Steps, which begin where spiraling Telegraph Hill Boulevard enters the Coit Tower parking lot. If you follow this terraced path downhill toward the bay, you'll wind up on Sansome Street, opposite Levi's Plaza.

For another near-vertical stroll back up Telegraph Hill, head to the south end of Levi's Plaza to Filbert Street, turn back toward the hill, and pick up the Filbert Steps in a cul-de-sac. After crossing Montgomery Street at the top of the steps, the path brushes the edge of Telegraph Hill Boulevard. You can follow this back up to Coit Tower or continue downhill on the Filbert Steps, winding up on Kearny Street in North Beach.

An excellent guide to stair hikes on Telegraph Hill and elsewhere in the city is *Stairway Walks in San Francisco,* by Adah Bakalinsky, © 1992. If you can't find it in local bookstores, call Lexikos Publishing Company in Marin County at 488-0401.

9 Explore Marin Headlands' Outer Limits

Part of the Golden Gate National Recreation Area; for specifics on ranger hikes and other activities, call 331-1540.

A couple of decades ago, only a handful of people were aware of the road that climbs Marin Headlands opposite the Golden Gate Bridge. Their reward was uncrowded and awesome vistas of the city, framed dramatically by the span. However, since the creation of GGNRA, droves of people drive up there. On a sunny weekend, it's a chore to find a parking place.

But there's much more to explore in this area. If you take a right onto McCullough Road from the main headlands road (Conzelman), you'll pass through a gap in the headlands and wind up in Rodeo Valley, a much less crowded area. Fort Cronkhite is here, once an army post guarding the Golden Gate and now headquarters for the Marin Headlands portion of the GGNRA. At a small visitor center, rangers will point you to a variety of trails to follow, some old artillery batteries to explore, and several viewpoints and picture spots. Ask them about a small picnic site on a ridge where you can munch your lunch while enjoying a splendid cityscape.

Rodeo Beach, a sandbar between the Pacific and Rodeo Lagoon, is surprisingly uncrowded, even on those rare warm August and September days when you might be tempted to dip a reluctant toe into the nippy Pacific.

Another neat headlands attraction is Point Bonita Lighthouse, which has been helping steer ships through the Golden Gate since 1855. It's now automated, but it still uses the same hand-ground Fresnel lens that was installed 130 years ago.

The lighthouse occupies a dramatic niche at the tip of a razorback ridge. Visitors can reach it by walking through a tunnel and across a 120-foot-high bridge. From this vista point, the Golden Gate looms as the sea captains see it: a narrow water-way flanked by steep headlands, spanned by that magnificent bridge, and the very devil to find in a fog.

Note: The tunnel and lighthouse generally are open only on weekends. At other times, you can still enjoy the view from a walkway leading out to the tunnel entrance.

10 Shop the Produce Stands

Heart of the City Farmers' Market, United Nations Plaza near the Civic Center, Sunday and Wednesday from 7 a.m. to 5 p.m. Alemany Farmers' Market, off Alemany Boulevard south of the city, from 6 a.m. to 6 p.m. Saturday and from 7:30 a.m. to 5 p.m. Tuesday-Friday; call 558-9455 for details.

It's nice to know that in the most sophisticated city west of Chicago, you can still buy a turnip directly from the turnip grower. The Heart of the City Farmers' Market is held in United Nations Plaza, a wide promenade running from Market and Leavenworth streets to the Civic Center. Strolling past cheerful blue awnings, you can buy assorted fresh and dried fruits, vegetables, an entire tuna, honey still in the comb, and other products of soil, sea, and bee.

This market is a relative newcomer, however. The Alemany Farmers' Market started operating out of two long sheds south of the city in 1943; it's one of the oldest such markets in the state. Because of increased competition from other farmer-to-consumer marts (including downtown San Francisco's), only about a dozen stalls are busy here during weekdays. But on weekends, nearly every stall is filled.

To find the Alemany market, head south from the city on U.S. 101, take Interstate 280 toward Daly City, then catch the first Alemany Boulevard exit. You'll hit a stoplight on Alemany, and the market's just across the street.

Both marts are certified by the county agricultural commissioner, which means they can offer only commodities produced by the seller or immediate family members. California now has more than ninety farmers' markets; they're coordinated by the Direct Marketing Program of the Department of Food and Agriculture.

Chapter 2

IF YOU MUST PLAY TOURIST

Visiting the City's Most Popular Attractions

It's an odd thing that anyone who disappeared was said to be seen in San Francisco. It must be a delightful city and possess all the attractions of the next world.

— *Oscar Wilde*

Obviously, you'll want to see San Francisco's most famous attractions, and perhaps some of its lesser-known lures. Or if you've seen them all before, perhaps Cousin Ferdie is coming from Kansas, and he simply must experience Coit Tower.

It isn't necessary to compile a list of the city's most popular tourist lures. Anyone not familiar with the Golden Gate Bridge or Chinatown must be living in a Fresno fallout shelter. But they aren't much fun to visit if you have to shoulder through thick crowds and breathe tour bus fumes. And when was the last time you were able to find a parking place during a summer weekend visit to Fisherman's Wharf? (The famed wharf, ruined by developers with carnival midway mentalities, is not on our list.)

When to Visit the Ten Most Popular Attractions

We begin with the best *times* to see the city's Ten Most Popular attractions. July obviously isn't, because both the fog and visitors can become quite thick then. If you can't visit during the off-season, consider hitting the tourist high spots early in the morning or late in the day. There are no crowds, and there's a special quality to the light when the sun is low.

1 Golden Gate National Recreation Area from Dawn to Dusk, Preferably in the Fall

Details of GGNRA activities are available at the park's Fort Mason visitor center, open weekdays from 8:30 a.m. to 5 p.m. Write: GGNRA Headquarters, Fort Mason, San Francisco, CA 94123. Phone number for general information: 556-0560. Public transit serves many of GGNRA's attractions; call Muni at 673-MUNI, and 332-6600 for Golden Gate Transit schedules in Marin County.

Who would have thought that the U.S. Army would function as a major force for conservation? It did so in San Francisco—mostly by accident. A good part of the city's most beautiful terrain—beaches, headlands, and the craggy shores of the Golden Gate—were taken over by the military as sites for forts and garrisons. Military occupation, in fact, dates back to the Spanish era. In all history, no ship has ever approached the Gate in anger, so the forts rimming the entrance have never fired a retaliatory shot. And all the while, none of this land has been available for private use, so it has been spared "development."

In 1972, largely through the efforts of the late congressman Phillip Burton, much of this prime military land—along with city, state, and privately owned property—was set aside as the Golden Gate National Recreation Area. The original park was expanded in succeeding years to its present size of 114 square miles: *triple* the area of the city itself! It's the world's largest urban park and the most-visited element of the U.S. National Park system. (This is no great trick, of course; so many parts of the park rim the city and Marin County to the north that it's difficult *not* to tread on park soil.)

The GGNRA is not a solid unit but a wonderful patchwork of shorelines, viewpoints, eucalyptus groves, and history-ridden forts and buildings. Parcels include the north and south anchorages of the Golden Gate Bridge, Fort Point, most of the city's northern beaches, a collection of antique ships at Fisherman's Wharf, most of the Marin Headlands, and Muir Woods. The historic fifteen-hundred-acre Presidio of San Francisco is to become part of GGNRA when its deactivation as an army post is completed in this decade. Park boundaries even stretch north to Tomales Bay, that dramatic inland waterway created by California's notorious San Andreas Fault. The GGNRA is headquartered at Fort Mason (see Chapter 1).

The best time to enjoy the park's facilities is in the fall, simply because that's when San Francisco enjoys the clearest, most wind-free weather. So much of the park's attraction is visual: the panorama from the headlands, glimpses of the Golden Gate Bridge through Lincoln Boulevard's wind-sculpted cypresses, and city skyline views from the Coastal Trail.

GGNRA references are scattered throughout this book, since nine of its elements are worthy of national historic site status, and most of the city's best beaches are part and parcel of the park. As we said, it's difficult not to tread on GGNRA soil when visiting San Francisco. And that's just great.

2 Alcatraz on a Sunny Weekday Afternoon

Alcatraz-bound boats are operated by the Red and White Fleet, departing Pier 41 several times daily. Tickets are $8.50 for adults and teens, $7.60 for seniors, and $4 for kids from five to eleven; they're available at the pier. Call 546-2700 for ticket information and 556-0560 for Alcatraz information. Advance reservations are recommended during weekends and the peak summer tourist season.

You're no doubt familiar with the Birdman of Alcatraz: hulking Burt Lancaster tenderly chucking sick canaries under the beak. But the real-life Robert Stroud didn't do his research on bird ailments at Alcatraz; most of that took place before he got there, during his stay at Fort Leavenworth Federal Penitentiary in Kansas. But he certainly was an Alcatraz resident, along with Al Capone, killer Alvin "Creepy" Karpis, and a group of angry, disillusioned native Americans who took over the place in 1969 after it had been closed as a prison.

Alcatraz means "pelican" in Spanish; the name originally was intended for Yerba Buena Island, which links the two sections of the San Francisco-Oakland

Bay Bridge. A nearsighted mapmaker accidentally stuck the name on the large rock in the middle of the bay, which indeed pelicans had given their own personal patina. Alcatraz was an army prison from 1859 until 1933, then it became the infamous federal lockup until it was closed in 1963.

Now it's part of the GGNRA. Rangers or self-guiding audio tours will lead you through the grim cell blocks, regaling you with stories of inmates and Indians. Perhaps because of its intrigue—so close yet once so unapproachable—Alcatraz is one of the most popular units within the national park system. More than half a million people shuffle through Alcatraz in a good year.

Naturally, visiting during the off-season is advantageous, since you can wait for one of those sunny afternoons that we recommend. It can get chilly on cloudy, windy days—in other words, during normal midsummer weather. But just wait until you get out there on a sunny day and catch the view back to the city!

3 The Cable Cars at Sunrise

Cable car schedules are available by calling 673-MUNI.

All right, Andrew Smith Hallidie might have been a nice guy. However, it wasn't sympathy for horses pulling streetcars up the city's steep hills that inspired his development of the cable car. He owned a firm that manufactured wire rope (cable), which had been developed by his father in England in 1835. Obviously, cable would be a key instrument in the creation of a cable car.

It is true that he saw a team of five horses hitched to a streetcar being dragged back down Jackson Street in 1869. However, some historians say he was already at work on his invention when he witnessed that historic mishap.

Although August 1, 1873, is honored as the birthday of cable cars, Hallidie and his partners were actually a day late. He was supposed to begin operations then, under the terms of his franchise with the Clay Street Hill Railroad. However, his test run—between Jones and Kearny—wasn't made until around 4 a.m. August 2, so they backdated their records to protect their franchise. Another bit of historical trivia: A key figure in cable car development was little-known William Eppelsheimer, who invented the cable grip that is still in use. He, perhaps more than Hallidie, was responsible for most of the cable car system's technical innovations.

Public cable car service began on September 1, 1873, and the new Clay Street line was an immediate financial success. The cars have been running ever since, but only three lines remain from the twenty-two routes once operated by private companies. They're now part of the city's Muni system.

If cable cars are legendary, so are the waiting lines during peak season. They're particularly long at Fisherman's Wharf and at the famed turntable at Powell and Market. That's why we're getting up at such a ridiculous hour.

Early morning is the tranquil time for catching cable cars. They begin running at 6 a.m. We like to board the California Street line at Van Ness Avenue. The air is cool and fresh at sun-up, not yet scented with grease and diesel, and the cacophony of traffic hasn't begun. Waiting to start their first run of the day, the cable car's gripman and conductor chat with the few passengers; most are regulars.

As the Eppelsheimer Grip grabs the cable and the car lurches forward, you hear the sharp, distinctive sounds of this curious device at work: the metallic clink of wheel on rail, the whir of the cable beneath the street, the crisp clang of the bell. The car trundles along traffic-free California Street and climbs toward the sunrise as it tops Nob Hill. Soft shafts of first light burnish brick walls of the venerable Mark Hopkins Hotel and splash off Financial District towers below. It's a nice moment to be in San Francisco.

Even if you aren't moved to move out of bed so early, you can still escape lengthy prime-time queues. The California-Van Ness terminal is never as busy as the popular Powell-Market turntable. Once aboard, with transfer in hand, you can switch to a Powell Street car at California and Powell, beside the Fairmont Hotel. During peak periods, this transfer point gets pretty busy, too. But even if you have to wait a bit, it's better than standing wearily in a long line at Market Street, watching resident derelicts taking nips from their paper bags.

The funny little cars are in their second century, despite periodic efforts in the past to scuttle them. A $63.5 million restoration of the system was completed in 1984, including $10 million raised in the private sector during a "Save the Cable Car" drive. Another $4 million was spent to rehabilitate the cars.

San Franciscans fussed about this high cost, even as they fuss today about tourists crowding them off their cable cars. But they issued a collective sigh of relief, knowing that these moving monuments will be around for another century or more.

4 Chinatown Before 8 A.M.

Most early-morning activities are focused along Stockton Street, between Broadway and the Stockton Tunnel entrance.

At this point, you may have decided that this book wasn't intended for late-sleepers. Actually, I don't like rising with roosters either, but in San Francisco, the reward is generally worth the effort.

Chinatown awakens from its fitful sleep early. Merchants sweep the night's litter from sidewalks, and delivery people hurry by, pushing handcarts laden with cartons of tangerines, hairy melons, and mustard greens. At Chinatown's "produce corner"—Stockton and Broadway—diminutive housewives in quilted smocks pick through what moments before had been neat pyramids of oranges and orderly rows of bok choy. At the seafood markets, merchants smooth mounds of shaved ice that soon will glitter with freshly caught fish.

There's no other place quite like San Francisco's Chinatown, not even in China. Mainland Chinese cities tend to be low-lying and somewhat colorless. They definitely aren't choked with traffic, nor are they decorated with dragon-entwined lampposts.

Despite claims of other cities, San Francisco's Chinatown is the largest Chinese community outside the Orient, with population estimates ranging as high as two hundred thousand. That's more than one in five San Franciscans. Chinese Americans make up the city's oldest, largest, and most affluent ethnic group, and their self-contained city functions rather independently of San Francisco. It has its own chamber of commerce, banks, newspapers, and somewhat mystical service groups called benevolent associations.

Chinatown became a tourist attraction by accident. The first wave of Chinese immigrants came to California during the 1849 gold rush. Some found work near the hotels that ringed Portsmouth Square, cooking and doing laundry for macho white miners, who considered such chores to be women's work. Those early laundries and cafés laid the foundation for today's Chinatown.

Chinese were subjected to brutal discrimination, climaxed by the Oriental Exclusion Act of 1882, prohibiting further immigration. Unable to bring in brides, men turned to harlots and opium dens; bloody tong wars were fought over territorial rights, and a white slave trade thrived. Chinatown became a dark and sinister ghetto.

The 1906 earthquake and fire brought instant urban renewal, destroying the old slum. As the community rebuilt, it began attracting tourists. The Chinese opened curio shops and fancied-up their restaurants to cater to this new trade. With the addition of turned-up eaves and dragon lampposts in the 1950s and 1960s, modern Chinatown began to take shape.

It still has its scruffy side: dark but not really sinister alleys with sweatshops and mah-jongg parlors. But we hope the urban renewalists will stop trying to rehabilitate this place. Already, the Golden Arches and theme shopping centers have invaded Grant Avenue, and more are threatened. Thankfully, a wax museum that opened in the 1970s melted into oblivion.

Incidentally, go to Chinatown the way the Chinese do: aboard the "Orient Express." That's the No. 30 Muni bus that travels along Stockton Street. Never mind what you heard in Flower Drum Song; Stockton, not Grant Avenue, is the real heart of this community. A good downtown place to catch the bus is on Stockton near Sutter, just before it enters the Stockton Tunnel.

An even better way to explore this intriguing ethnic enclave is to sign up for one of Shirley Fong-Torres's "Wok Wiz" walking tours. Her guides take visitors into intimate Chinatown, through back alleys and kitchens and into artists' studios and herb shops. The three-and-a-half-hour tours are $33 with lunch or $24 without. A shorter hour-and-a-half "Yin Yang Tour" is $15. For specifics, call 355-9657.

5 The Civic Center During Business Hours

Civic Center guided tours are conducted on Mondays, and Davies Hall tours are held on Wednesdays; call 552-8338 for information.

We recommend visiting the Civic Center during business hours because that's when everything is open. Since tour buses rarely stop here, City Hall and the other buildings are never crowded, except possibly with attorneys.

San Franciscans like to boast that their city hall is taller than the nation's capitol, after which it was modeled. This is important only if you collect trivia. City Hall certainly is worth a look, with its French Renaissance columns and spired green copper dome. Step inside to admire the great rotunda and the sweeping grand stairway. Across Polk Street, in Civic Center Plaza, you can tune in on the latest protest rally or feed seagulls in the reflecting pool, while sidestepping pigeons and street folk. Beneath the plaza is Brooks Hall exhibit center and a parking garage. To the south is Bill Graham Civic Auditorium, recently renamed to honor the late rock impresario.

Opposite Civic Center Plaza is the San Francisco Public Library, which—as we write—is being replaced by a new structure next door. If the original is still intact when you visit, stride up the central stairway beneath an ornate barrel-vaulted ceiling and check out special exhibits that usually line the wide mezzanine balcony. The San Francisco Room, a mini-museum of city history, is worth a peek (see Chapter 17). Across Van Ness Avenue from City Hall are the semi-similar War Memorial Opera House and Veterans Memorial Building. All of the older Civic Center buildings are of French Renaissance design, selected by architects at the turn of the century to give the Civic Center a classic yet timeless appearance. The "Vet" houses the San Francisco Museum of Modern Art, a fine arts bookstore on the ground level, and a neat little café in the museum, worthy of a lunch stop. The Opera House—obviously—is home field for the San Francisco Opera Company, the oldest and probably the finest west of the Rockies.

Considerably less timeless and hardly classic are the new structures of the Civic Center: Davies Symphony Hall, the San Francisco Ballet headquarters, and a state office building. They all have rounded, puffy Pillsbury-doughboy looks, better suited to avant-garde hotels than to civic structures. Davies Hall, showplace of the excellent San Francisco Symphony, is indeed handsome inside, with its multitiered foyer and elegant performance hall. Its steeply raked floor, wraparound balconies, and magnificent Ruffatti organ have earned it critical praise. But the exterior—with slender columns and odd vertical fins—looks like the grille of a 1956 Buick.

Worth a look, even if you aren't an auto club member, is the eight-story green-glass San Francisco office of the California State Automobile Association at Van Ness and Hayes. Its glass skin covers the original Spanish-California facade of the structure, built in 1925. The Latin look survives on the main floor, with its lace filigree, decorated arches, and ornate atrium ceiling. If you're really observant, you'll see a bas-relief of winged Mercury—holding a steering wheel.

6 Coit Tower at Midnight

The tower is open from 10 a.m. to 6 p.m., and an elevator takes visitors to the top for $3; call 362-0808 for details.

Lillie Hitchcock Coit was a tough lady who ran around in men's clothes, smoked cigars, and chased fire engines. Fire laddies admired her spit and spirit and made her a volunteer—uh—fireperson. When she died in 1929, she left funds to build a shrine to volunteer firemen, but that isn't the famous Coit Tower. It's a sculpture of three fire fighters rescuing a woman, which still stands in Washington Square.

Her will also provided funds for "the purpose of adding to the beauty of San Francisco." From that bequest emerged the art deco Coit Tower atop Telegraph

Hill, completed in 1933. Some say the fluted column resembles a fire nozzle, but historians insist this was not the designers' intent.

An elevator whisks visitors to the top for a dazzling city panorama. Also, one can admire 1930s murals of California at work and browse through a souvenir shop on the lower floor.

We like visiting at night, even though the tower is closed. There's no bumper-to-bumper traffic jamming the curving street leading to the parking lot, and it can be very peaceful up there. For the proper nighttime approach (take a friend if you're the nervous type), start at Lombard and Hyde, drive down the squiggly "crookedest street in the world," and continue on Lombard until it blends into Telegraph Hill Boulevard.

The old fire nozzle glows warmly in the evening haze, bathed by floodlights. After dark, it's a place for lovers, locked in embrace on the leeward sides of trees; a place for dreamers standing in silence to admire the carpet of lights spread below. During quiet moments, sounds of the city drift upward like whispers in the night.

Incidentally, it isn't always that peaceful after dark. Young people often hang out in the parking lot at night, trying to blast out the windows of their low-riders with their car stereo systems. At least they scare away the muggers.

7 The Golden Gate Bridge an Hour Before Sunset

Pedestrian walkway open from 6 a.m. to 9 p.m.

Few visions in the world are more enchanting than the Golden Gate Bridge. Its architect, a little man named Joseph B. Strauss, was both an engineer and a poet: the sort of person who could create something bold and masculine, yet graceful and feminine.

The name Golden Gate was given to San Francisco Bay's narrow entrance by explorer John C. Frémont in 1846, nearly a century before the bridge was built. He apparently was moved by the golden sunsets in the open sea beyond the gate: the kind you may witness by spending a few quiet moments here late in the day. And no, the bridge isn't golden. The official name of the paint job is International Orange—picked because of its luminosity in a thick fog.

Avoid the bridge at midday when the ninth tour bus has spilled its cargo of camera-clutchers onto the viewing area near the toll plaza. The metered parking stalls will be filled, and herds of cars will be sitting at idle, waiting for someone to depart. If you want to take pictures, you'll have to wait until Martha from Madera—blocking your view of the Strauss statue—has finished grinning into her husband's Instamatic.

Go instead in the late afternoon after the others have left, when slanting rays cast shadow patterns across those lofty towers and down to the sea below. Since the pedestrian walkway is open until 9 p.m., plan to arrive an hour or so before sunset, giving yourself time to take the three-mile round-trip stroll over to the Marin County side. Stare down at the water two hundred feet below, where toy-sized sailboats weave cottony wakes as they head for safe harbor before dark. Watch the distant skyline become more sharply defined as late shadows accent the buildings.

After your bridge stroll, retrieve your car and drive across to Vista Point. When you've absorbed the view from there, cross back under the freeway, but head up to the Marin Headlands instead of returning to Highway 101. Every bend of the winding road offers a stunning new view of bridge, bay, and city. Pull off at one of the many turnouts and sit quietly with someone special. Watch as the sun slips into its own glittery path on the sea, and the lights of the city wink on like awakening fireflies. You'll understand why people are moved to write poems and books about this city and its bridge.

8 Golden Gate Park in Springtime

For information about park activities and free summer guided tours, call 750-5105.

Some flowers bloom the year around in Golden Gate Park, particularly in its wonderful century-old Conservatory of Flowers. But in springtime, the park is alive with multihued azaleas and rhododendrons. In the Japanese Tea Garden, delicate pink and white cherry blossoms timidly emerge for their brief two-week tenure from middle to late March.

A dramatic swatch of green converted from windblown sand dunes, Golden Gate is one of the world's largest man-made parks, covering 1,017 acres (larger than New York's Central Park). And it's amazingly versatile. It shelters an outstanding Academy of Sciences (about which we've already raved, in Chapter 1), the world-noted de Young and Asian Art museums (see Chapter 17), a polo field, a nine-hole golf course, a buffalo paddock, an outdoor band shell, eleven lakes, ten gardens, biking and hiking paths, and statues of people we've never heard of. John McLaren, park superintendent for more than forty years, hated those statues. Whenever city fathers erected one, he'd plant a climbing vine or bush in front of it.

San Franciscans love their park, particularly on Sundays, when the main thoroughfare, John F. Kennedy Drive, is closed to vehicles. It becomes a happy highway of cyclists, skateboarders, roller bladers, Frisbee flippers, runners, and power walkers.

Some park attractions not covered elsewhere in this book:

JAPANESE TEA GARDEN *Martin Luther King Jr. Drive, open daily from 9 a.m. to 6:30 p.m. March-September, 8:30 a.m. to 6 p.m. October-February; $1 for all ages.* Famed for its spring cherry blossom display, the Japanese Tea Garden is a prettily landscaped complex of pools, pagodas, and quiet walkways, plus a teahouse and a gift shop.

STRYBING ARBORETUM *Ninth Avenue at Lincoln Way; free; guided tours at 10:30 a.m. and 1:30 p.m.; horticultural library open weekdays from 8 a.m. to 4:30 p.m. and weekends and holidays from 10 a.m. to 5 p.m.* The arboretum sprouts six thousand plants from around the world, and it offers a Garden of Fragrance for the blind.

THE DUTCH WINDMILL *Near the Great Highway.* One of two built early in this century to pump the park's water supply, the windmill was restored in 1981 after sitting bladeless for decades. Officials hope to raise funds to renovate the nearby Murphy Windmill.

CHILDREN'S PLAYGROUND AND CAROUSEL *Near Kezar Drive; carousel, food stand, and gift shop hours 10 a.m. to 5 p.m. daily in summer and 10 a.m. to 4:30 p.m. Thursday-Sunday the rest of the year; rides are $1 for adults, 25 cents for kids, and free for tots; 611-9130 or 759-5884.* The playground features the exquisitely restored 1912 Hershel-Spillman carousel, a gift shop, and innovative play equipment.

9 Mission San Francisco de Asis During Celebration of the Eucharist

Dolores Street at Sixteenth Street; museum hours 9 a.m. to 4:30 p.m. May-October and 9 a.m. to 4 p.m. the rest of the year. Museum admission is $1, which goes to the Maintenance and Education Fund. Call 621-8203 for times of religious services and special events.

The simple adobe mission isn't just an isolated curiosity and popular tour bus stop. It's part of a busy Catholic parish, although most activities are centered in the large basilica next door.

You'll enjoy sitting beneath the painted wooden beams of the old chapel during a service. You can sense the pace of life as it was before the gold rush, when this was the church of the little pueblo of *Yerba Buena*—the good herb. Currently, the only service regularly conducted in the chapel is eucharist, celebrated every morning at 7:30, and at 5 p.m. Saturdays. After morning eucharist, you can tour the grounds and see relics of the city's Spanish mission era in the museum.

After exploring the museum and its brilliantly flowered cemetery garden, step into the lofty sanctuary of the basilica. Soaring Moorish-Corinthian spires overshadow the little adobe chapel; some visitors think the basilica is the mission. Gaze upward into the unusual vaulted and domed ceiling. Admire the stained glass windows depicting the twenty-one missions that led to the state's settlement.

San Francisco's history began in 1776, when Father Francisco Palou established California's sixth Spanish mission in a simple brushwood shelter on the banks of *Arroyo de los Dolores* (the stream of sorrows). He offered up the first Mass on June 29, just five days before American independence was declared in faraway Philadelphia. The fledgling mission was named for St. Francis of Assisi, founder of the Franciscan order. It's more popularly known as Mission Dolores. The present chapel, completed in 1791, is two blocks from the original site, which is at the intersection of Guerrero and a scruffy residential alley called Camp Street. No monument marks the spot.

10 San Francisco Zoo During Mealtime

Sloat Boulevard near Forty-fifth Avenue; daily from 10 a.m. to 5 p.m. Admission $6.50; seniors and kids twelve to sixteen, $3; kids six to eleven, $1; under six free. Children's Zoo admission $1. Phone 661-2023 for special activities.

We mean the animals' mealtime, not yours. The lions are liveliest when they're being fed (daily at 2 p.m. except Monday); call for schedules of other animal mealtimes.

San Francisco's zoo has evolved in recent years into an excellent zoological complex; it's rated among the six finest in the nation. Particularly noteworthy is the Primate Discovery Center, with its nocturnal gallery where day and night are reversed so visitors can watch nighttime prowlers in action, and special exhibits telling you all you ever wanted to know about simians. Other realistic habitats have been constructed to give critters and visitors a feeling of place. Among these theme areas are Koala Crossing, with Australian flora and fauna; Musk Ox Meadows, for dwellers of the Alaskan tundra; Gorilla World, the world's largest gorilla habitat; and Wolf Woods, for North American mammals. Naturally, the penguin habitat is called Tuxedo Junction.

More than a thousand furred and feathered creatures call the zoo's seventy acres home, including rare snow leopards and a white tiger. A quick way to see it all is aboard the Zebra Zephyr train. Ever felt the urge to pet a grasshopper? The Children's Zoo has an animal petting yard, nature trails, and an insect zoo where youngsters can get curious about creatures with six or more legs.

The Next Ten Most Popular Attractions

The next Ten Most Popular attractions are listed alphabetically, with no attempt at rating, since one visitor's curiosity is another tourist's yawn. (Other specialty museums are featured in Chapter 17.)

1 Battery Lowell A. Chamberlain

At Baker Beach, part of the GGNRA; open weekends only; phone 556-0560 for hours.

Tracing two centuries of fortification of the bay entrance, this intriguing mini-museum is built into a coastal battery's thick concrete bunkers. It exhibits historic photos, sketches, a rare "disappearing rifle" artillery piece, shells, and other military regalia.

2 Cable Car Museum

1201 Mason Street (at Washington). Open daily from 10 a.m. to 5 p.m.; free; call 474-1887.

Housed in the 1887 cable car barn and powerhouse, the museum offers an intimate look at this wonderfully archaic transit system. From a viewing gallery, visitors can see the machinery that powers the cables that pull the little cars halfway to the stars. Exhibits also include historic photos and cable car artifacts. The museum was completely redesigned during the 1982-84 rehabilitation of the cable car system.

3 Cliff House and Musée Mechanique

Great Highway at Point Lobos Avenue; 386-1170. Museum open weekdays 11 a.m. to 6 p.m., weekends 10 a.m. to 7 p.m.; free.

A Cliff House has clung to the rough coastal promontory above Seal Rocks since the 1860s; versions have been alternately destroyed and rebuilt. The current edition houses an information center of the GGNRA, a viewing platform for the seals of Seal Rocks, several restaurants, and a bar. Musée Mecanique features one of the world's largest collections of old-time nickelodeons, music boxes, and historic mechanical art. Take along some change and watch these Rube Goldberg devices do their thing.

4 Exploratorium

Behind the Palace of Fine Arts (enter at Bay and Lyon). Open daily in summer 10 a.m. to 5 p.m. (until 9:30 p.m. Wednesday); the rest of the year 10 a.m. to 5 p.m. Tuesday-Sunday (with extended Wednesday hours); 561-0360. Adults $8, children $4; first Wednesday of each month is free day.

Called the "best science museum in the world" by *Scientific American,* the Exploratorium is a wonderful hands-on museum with more than seven hundred scientific exhibits happening right in front of you. This "interactive museum of science, art and human perception" will intrigue both adults and children. Make your own personal lightning bolt, create a phosphorescent impression in the Shadow Box, or learn about thermodynamics. Exhibits change whenever the museum's creative staff comes up with another way to bring science alive, so repeated visits definitely are recommended.

5 Grace Cathedral

1051 Taylor Street (at California, atop Nob Hill); visitors welcome and guided tours given; call 776-6611.

Grace Cathedral is a virtual gallery of religious art, as well as one of the oldest cathedrals in America, established in 1863. Seat of the Episcopal Bishop of California, the present neoclassic edifice was completed in 1964.

6 Museum of the City of San Francisco

Third floor of the Cannery, between Leavenworth, Beach, and Columbus; 928-0289. Wednesday-Sunday 10 a.m. to 4 p.m.; free; donations appreciated.

Opened in the summer of 1991, this small museum traces the city's history from the mission to the gold rush through two earthquakes up to—but certainly not including—the departure of Joe Montana to the Kansas City Chiefs. Among its appeals are a 1913 coin-fed player piano that will be activated at your request, hand-tinted photos of old Chinatown, and relics from the days when the Cannery was the Del Monte Canning Company. Look up and you'll see an unusual conical coffered ceiling pilfered from a thirteenth-century Spanish palace by agents of San Francisco newspaper baron William Randolph Hearst.

7 Palace of Fine Arts

Baker Street at Marina Boulevard; open during daylight; free.

Built in 1915 for $750,000 and restored in 1965 for ten times that amount, the Palace of Fine Arts is the last survivor of the 1915 Pan-Pacific Exposition celebrating the opening of the Panama Canal. The dramatic beaux arts rotunda is as tall as a ten-story building. A reflecting pool and small park attract dozens of ducks and duck feeders; watch where you step.

8 Presidio of San Francisco

Reached by continuing west on Lombard Street beyond the "motel row" area.

The Presidio dates to 1776, when the Spanish set up a military garrison to protect the nearby mission. The fifteen-hundred landscaped acres, once headquarters for the U.S. Sixth Army, become part of the Golden Gate National Recreation Area when the military base is deactivated in this decade. Its winding, tree-shaded streets are popular with strollers and cyclists, providing impressive views of the city and the Pacific. The Presidio Officers' Club, originally the Spanish commandant's headquarters, is the city's oldest building.

9 Randall Museum

199 Museum Way (off Roosevelt Way in the upper Market Street area); 554-9600.
Tuesday-Saturday 10 a.m. to 5 p.m.; animal room hours 10 a.m. to 1 p.m. and
2 p.m. to 5 p.m.; model train hours 1 p.m. to 5 p.m. second and fourth Saturday
of each month; free.

A real find for both visitors and residents, this innovative youth-oriented museum exhibits more than forty native animal species, and it has a petting area, permitting city kids to become acquainted with California wildlife. It also features scientific exhibits, and it offers arts and crafts displays and classes, and special programs for families. Parking is free; another bonus is an awesome city and bay view from its hillside location. The museum is run by the San Francisco Recreation and Parks Department.

10 San Francisco Maritime National Historic Park

The maritime park has several elements, all near Fisherman's Wharf: Hyde Street
Pier at the foot of Hyde, admission $2 (kids under seventeen and seniors free),
daily from 10 a.m. to 5:30 p.m.; National Maritime Museum at the foot
of Polk, free, daily from 10 a.m. to 5 p.m.; and the World War II submarine
USS Pampanito at Pier 45, admission $3 for adults, $2 for juniors, and
$1 for kids and seniors, daily from 10 a.m. to 5 p.m. Phone 929-0202
for park details.

The assorted elements of the maritime historic park remind us of those days when lusty men—and women—went down to the sea in ships, or off to war.

Hyde Street Pier features America's largest collection of vintage ships, including a century-old lumber schooner, a San Francisco Bay ferryboat, and the square-rigged *Balclutha*, which once sailed around Cape Horn. The Maritime Museum, in a building shaped like the superstructure of an art deco ship, exhibits dozens of model vessels, paintings, photos, and other aquatic artifacts. The *Pampanito* at Pier 45 offers visitors the opportunity to crawl around the compact innards of a battle-scarred World War II submarine. It sank six Japanese ships and damaged four others. Exhibits and a self-guided audio tour help explain the sub's complexities. (See Chapter 1 for details on another element of the park, the World War II liberty ship *Jeremiah O'Brien*.)

The Ten Best Special Places

Every city has its hidden corners, appealing enclaves that often are missed by visitors and even by residents. San Francisco is particularly rich in these little-known locales. Ironically, the city's abundance of major lures tends to distract people from the lesser ones. We begin with a good example: Chinatown swarms with visitors, yet most of them miss one of the largest Japanese cultural centers outside the Orient.

1 Japan Center

Two city blocks between Geary, Post, Laguna, and Fillmore streets; 922-6776.

Nihonmachi, or Japantown, is a large Asian community about a mile from downtown. It's easy to find; just follow Geary Street west from Union Square, cross Van Ness Avenue, and look on your right for the oriental architecture of the Miyako Hotel and the Peace Plaza pagoda. *Nihonmachi's* focal point is Japan Center, two covered malls separated by the Peace Plaza. Although the huge buildings are rather austere from the outside, they're a shoppers', browsers', and diners' delight from within. It's Japan in a can, with eighteen Asian restaurants, including nine sushi bars, a Japanese spa, more than thirty shops, and two art galleries. The east end is anchored by the stylish Miyako Hotel, featuring both Japanese and American rooms and the new Elka seafood restaurant.

Among Japan Center's more interesting attractions are the Ikenobo Ikebana Society gallery, with its striking flower arrangements; the Kintetsu Restaurant Mall, fashioned like a Tokyo side street; the Webster Street Bridge, lined with shops (supposedly the first of its kind in America); and the five-tiered, one-hundred-foot Peace Pagoda. One feature of Japan Center that's particularly appealing to many of us: The entire premises are nonsmoking. Also, there's relatively inexpensive parking right under the complex.

Teeing into Japan Center is Buchanan Street Mall, a landscaped, cobbled pedestrian way lined with more shops and restaurants. The center and mall become visions of old Japan during the annual *Sakura Matsuri,* or Cherry Blossom Festival, in April; call 922-6776 for dates and details.

Nihonmachi is one of America's largest urban Japanese enclaves, with a population topping twelve thousand. Its roots go back to the 1906 earthquake, when Japanese families burned out of their downtown homes retreated to this "western addition" to rebuild. After World War II, when Japanese-Americans were released from those awful detention camps, many came here to pick up the pieces of their disrupted lives. Japan Center, part of a major urban renewal project, was opened in the spring of 1968.

2 St. Dominic's Catholic Church

2390 Bush Street (at Steiner); 567-7824. Open daily from 7:30 a.m. until early evening.

Missed by most visitors and many residents, St. Dominic is one of the city's most imposing churches, a grand edifice of gray cut stone with a classic square

Gothic tower. Inside, stained glass windows soar heavenward to a vaulted arch ceiling. St. Dominic's stations of the cross are particularly impressive, done in marble *bas-relief.* The quiet, cavernous interior with its saints in niches, glittering bays of votive candles and imposing altar brings to mind the noble sanctuaries of Europe.

A Save St. Dominic's drive is under way to raise funds for the restoration and preservation of this magnificent structure. If you're moved to contribute, drop a note to: St. Dominic's Church, 2390 Bush Street, San Francisco, CA 94115.

3 Embarcadero Promenade and South Beach Marina

South of the Ferry Building, along the Embarcadero.

A short walk south of the Ferry Building takes you to an often-overlooked slice of the waterfront. While most of the visitor traffic is focused north, toward Fisherman's Wharf, the south side has its appeal as well. As part of the rehabilitation of the south waterfront, the San Francisco Port Commission has constructed a bayside promenade with multilevel risers, just to the right of the Ferry Building. It's a great place to admire the arching contours of the Bay Bridge ahead and the city skyline behind. Between the promenade and the Ferry Building is Ferry Plaza, with more places to stroll and sit. You can catch Golden Gate Ferries from here, chat with fishermen who like to dangle their bait over the railing, or pause for food and drink at the stylish Gabbiano's Restaurant, with a sunny cocktail lounge and café under an imposing greenhouse roof. Nearby is another fine view restaurant, Sinbad's, with an outdoor cocktail patio.

A stroll beyond the promenade takes you along the waterfront to South Beach Marina, a modern marina opposite a new housing complex. Walk to the far side of the marina and stroll to the end of a concrete pedestrian pier. You'll enjoy fine views through a forest of masts to the Bay Bridge and city skyline. Near the marina is the Sailing Ship Dolph Rempp Restaurant (listed in Chapter 8), built into the hull of a 1908 three-masted gaff-rigged schooner that once hauled lumber and spices. Step aboard for a cocktail or dinner.

4 Ferryboat Santa Rosa

Pier 3 (off the Embarcadero); 394-8900. Public access to the dock 9:30 a.m. to 6 p.m. weekdays; ferryboat access 9:30 a.m. to 4 p.m. Monday-Saturday.

Once a member of San Francisco's car ferry fleet, the *Santa Rosa* now serves as headquarters for Hornblower Dining Cruises (see Chapter 8); the car deck has become a floating nightclub (see Chapter 13). Visitors may go aboard and explore this fine old craft, which has been meticulously restored and declared a city historic site.

The 242-foot *Santa Rosa* was built across the bay in Alameda in 1927. She ferried commuters and their cars between the Ferry Building and Sausalito until completion of the Golden Gate Bridge put her out of business. She worked for Washington State Ferries for two decades, then languished in dry dock until she was rescued and restored at a cost of a million dollars. The work was completed in 1989. Although technically afloat, she's anchored to the pier and doesn't go anywhere.

5 Historic Levi's Factory

250 Valencia Street (two blocks south of upper Market near Duboce Avenue); 565-9153. Ninety-minute tours Wednesdays only, at 10:30 a.m. and 1 p.m. Reservations required; should be made well in advance.

This is both a historic place and an intriguing tour. Every serious jeans aficionado knows that Levi Strauss got his start in San Francisco, making britches for gold miners from tent canvas. From this simple beginning in 1853 has emerged the world's largest apparel company, with factories worldwide. The oldest existing factory—and the only one where Levi's are still made by hand—is housed in a bright yellow building just off upper Market Street. The operation moved here in 1906, after the earthquake and fire destroyed the original headquarters near the waterfront. The only product here is the classic Levi's 501 button-fly jeans, and you must sign up for a tour to watch the nimble-fingered tailors guide the denims through the stitching machines.

Ironically, you can't buy a pair of these handmade Levi's. The factory's entire output is shipped to Japan, where Nippon yuppies pay a lot of yen (triple the normal price) for a fabric of American history.

6 Fairmont Hotel Lobby

950 Mason Street (at California); 772-5000.

The Fairmont is one of the city's most storied and attractive hotels, and its lobby is stunningly elegant. Pause to admire its marbled columns, rococo friezes, gilt-edge mirrors, rich dark wood paneling, and elaborate coffered ceilings. The carpets are so plush that one has the sensation of walking on cushions. Continue through the lobby to the arcade of shops, containing some of the most fashionable boutiques in the city.

One of only forty-nine lodgings in America to carry the AAA Five Diamond Award, the Fairmont remains as splendiferous as it was during its glorious early years. The family of Nevada silver baron James G. "Bonanza Jim" Fair started building the hotel in 1902, but it was destroyed by the 1906 earthquake before completion. Opened in 1907, it has hosted several presidents and foreign leaders, from William Howard Taft to Soviet Union President Mikhail Gorbachev. The Fairmont also was the site of the drafting of the United Nations Charter in 1945. Fanciful history has occurred here, too. This was the "St. Gregory" of TV's "Hotel" series. The Fairmont appeared in Alfred Hitchcock's 1957 classic, *Vertigo*, and it was "destroyed" in the 1974 movie *Towering Inferno*. It also has been featured in a score of other movies, plus TV's "Lifestyles of the Rich and Famous" and "Murder, She Wrote."

7 Garden Court of the Sheraton Palace Hotel

Two New Montgomery Street (at Market); 392-8600.

Still glistening from its recent renovation, this imposing dining court with its monumental glass dome could be the city's most splendid indoor setting. Plan a lunch or dinner, or catch the elaborate Sunday brunch (see Chapter 8). Or just step inside between meal service to study the marble columns, rococo trim, sparkling crystal chandeliers and potted palms, all bathed in light from that great dome. Rivaling the Fairmont in early San Francisco splendor, the Palace Hotel was built in 1875. Originally called the Grand Court, this majestic space was described by an early critic as the world's most beautiful restaurant. Like the Fairmont, the Palace perished in the 1906 fire; it was reopened in 1909. Under Sheraton ownership, it was completely refurnished early in this decade.

8 Monadnock Building Courtyard

685 Market Street (between New Montgomery and Third Street).

No rival to the Fairmont or Sheraton Palace, this quiet courtyard is still a special place. The venerable Monadnock office building, dating from the turn of the century, is one of the few surviving structures built around an enclosed courtyard. It's dressed in potted trees, modern sculptures, and old-fashioned lion head fountains. Step through the building's entrance and note the unusual barrel-arch ceiling with a Greco-Roman balcony scene. Then continue into the courtyard, where you'll find instant refuge from the clamor of Market Street. Upstairs on the second floor is the fine American Indian Contemporary Art Gallery, which we discuss in detail in Chapter 17.

9 Canton Bazaar

616 Grant Avenue (between California and Sacramento) in Chinatown; 362-5750. Daily 10 a.m. to 10:30 p.m.

Bazaar indeed! If Chinatown is a shoppers' paradise, then Canton Bazaar is paradise found. Hundreds of carvings, antiques, and artwork from mainland China and elsewhere in the Orient are stuffed into four crowded floors. Browse among the monumental wood carvings, huge cloisonné vases, carved chests, lacquered and inlaid tables, teakwood stands, and rose chinaware.

10 Ten Ren Tea Company

949 Grant Avenue (between Jackson and Washington) in Chinatown; 362-0656.

If you're intrigued by an incredible selection of teas, Ten Ren's is your cup. Based in Taiwan, it's the world's largest tea company, operating five tea factories and fifty-four stores around the world. In its large San Francisco shop, you can sample savories such as hibiscus tea and purchase everything from basic black or green tea to jasmine, oolong, strawberry-spiced, chamomile, cinnamon-spiced, and assorted ginseng teas. Former president George Bush stopped by here for a ceremonial sip during a San Francisco visit.

The Ten Best Things to Do
Just Because It's San Francisco

In a survey conducted several years ago by a national travel organization, San Francisco was selected as the city most Americans would like to visit. Why? Among other things, it offers many things that are distinctively—if not exclusively—San

Franciscan. We present herewith, in no particular order, the Ten Best things you must do to absorb the total San Francisco experience.

1 Have an Irish Coffee at the Buena Vista

2765 Hyde Street (at Beach); 474-5044. Open 9 a.m. to 2 a.m. Monday-Friday and 8 a.m. to 2 a.m. weekends. No credit cards.

Local pubs have been noted for their Irish coffee since 1952. The fad started when the late *San Francisco Chronicle* columnist Stan Delaplane told Buena Vista café owner Jack Koeppler of a tasty hot drink he'd enjoyed at Ireland's Shannon Airport. Koeppler experimented extensively to perfect this blend of whiskey, coffee, and thick cream; he even flew to Shannon to fine-tune the recipe.

Many places now serve Irish coffee, although the original Buena Vista version is still the best. It's made with Irish whiskey, a couple of cocktail cubes of sugar, and moderately strong coffee, topped with lightly frothed whipping cream. (Some pretenders use—good grief!—whipped cream from aerosol cans.) The Buena Vista imports and labels its own Irish whiskey (Tillimore Dew) and sells bottles to the faithful, along with a free recipe folder.

2 Take a Walk with a Walk-Away Shrimp Cocktail

Available at several Fisherman's Wharf takeouts.

Many coastal cities now offer walk-away seafood cocktails, although the practice originated at San Francisco's Fisherman's Wharf. When we came here decades ago and had our first shrimp cocktail (pretty exciting stuff for a kid from Idaho), the going rate was fifty cents. It's now $2.50 to $2.75, slightly more for crab, although little else has changed. You get a blop of meat splashed with red sauce, which quickly begins dissolving its cardboard carrier, plus a plastic spoon and a tiny envelope of oyster crackers. The new walk-away item at the wharf is hot clam chowder in a sourdough bread bowl for about $3.50. Don't set it down near a seagull.

3 Queue Up for a Cable Car at Fisherman's Wharf

Cable car turntable near Aquatic Park, at Hyde and Beach streets.

Earlier in this chapter, we told you how to avoid the long cable car queue at Fisherman's Wharf. However, at least once during your visit, you should get in line with the rest of the folks and enjoy the leisurely wait for the world's most famous transit car. You'll fall into easy conversation with others in line (the city is noted for its friendly natives and visitors), and you'll likely be serenaded by street musicians. At least one wandering minstrel is stationed alongside the queue on most days. You may prefer this waiting line to the one at Powell and Market, where panhandlers and shouting preachers of the gospel are more likely to be your companions.

4 Drive Down Squiggly Lombard Street

Start at the intersection of Lombard and Hyde streets.

A block-long section of Lombard Street between Hyde and Leavenworth has been terraced, landscaped, and squiggled to earn the title of "crookedest street in the world." Everyone who visits the city—except those with large RVs and trailers—should take this twisting descent, just to have done it. Most visitors follow Lombard east across Van Ness, but there's often a waiting line to start down the squiggle. This leaves drivers stalled on an uphill tilt below the crest of Hyde Street. For a more intelligent approach, follow Pine, California, or Sacramento street from downtown, turn right onto Hyde, drive a dozen blocks or so to the top of Hyde Street hill, then turn right down crooked Lombard.

5 Meet Someone Under the Clock in the St. Francis Lobby

St. Francis Hotel, Powell and Geary streets, downtown.

The large, ornate 1856 Magneta clock in the lobby of the Westin St. Francis Hotel has been a traditional meeting place for decades. For the true San Francisco aficionado, "Meet me under the clock" is sufficient instruction to set up a rendezvous. If you're alone in the city, go there anyway. The opulent lobby with its elaborately carved and coffered ceilings and grand black marble columns is a treat for the eyes. Further, this is a great people-watching place. It is said that every San Francisco resident and visitor at one time or another passes through the St. Francis lobby.

6 Enjoy a Sunset Cocktail at the Top of the Mark

Mark Hopkins Inter-Continental Hotel, California at Mason; 392-3434. Cocktails 4 p.m. to 1:30 a.m.

After you've met someone under the clock, adjourn to the Mark Hopkins Hotel atop Nob Hill. Topping off the nineteenth floor, the Top of the Mark is the city's oldest skyroom, dating from 1939. Although other skyrooms are newer and higher, this remains a traditional gathering place. With an almost 360-degree view of city and bay, it's a fine viewpoint for enjoying the changing shadows of sunset.

When it was first opened, patrons gathered to watch the glitter of the Golden Gate International Exposition on Treasure Island in the middle of the bay. During World War II, it was popular with servicemen passing through the city, headed for the Pacific. It became a tradition for GIs to spend their last evening of liberty here with their sweethearts before shipping out. Later, the wives or girlfriends would gather in the skyroom's northwest corner to watch the troopships steaming out of San Francisco Bay. Old-timers still call that alcove Weepers' Corner.

7 Join Crowds at Twin Peaks Viewpoint

Off Twin Peaks Boulevard in the upper Market Street area.

In Chapter 3, we nominate an obscure place called Tank Hill as the city's best viewpoint since it's lower and provides a closer vista than the traditional Twin Peaks Viewpoint. However, Twin Peaks, easier to find, offers an ideal introduction to Bay Area topography, since you can enjoy a dramatic sweep from the Golden Gate, across to the East Bay, and down the San Mateo peninsula. For an even better view, climb one of the Twin Peaks themselves. They're right behind you, a brief walk from the vista point parking area. Railroad-tie steps set into the slope simplify the short climb.

8 Eat an It's-It

Available in store freezer sections throughout the city.

What on earth is an It's-It?

It's an only-in-San Francisco ice-cream sandwich, invented (if that's the word) in 1928 and served at the "It Stand" at Playland-at-the-Beach on the Great Highway. Playland is long gone, replaced by condos, of course. However, It's-It survives and thrives, still produced in San Francisco and available in the ice-cream section of every civilized grocery store. This unique treat consists of a generous dollop of ice cream wedged between a pair of oatmeal cookies and laminated with chocolate.

Oatmeal? And inventor George Whitney probably didn't know a thing about cholesterol suspension.

9 Have a Hot Fudge Sundae at Ghirardelli Chocolate Factory

*Ghirardelli Square, 900 North Point; 474-1414. Sunday-Thursday 10:30 a.m.
to 11 p.m., Friday-Saturday 10:30 a.m. to midnight.*

Italian-born Domingo Ghirardelli arrived in San Francisco during the peak of the gold rush in 1852 and opened his first confectionery, from which the Ghirardelli Chocolate empire was born. The factory at Ghirardelli Square, occupying the same site since 1895, serves lush ice cream and chocolate treats that will have you avoiding the bathroom scales for weeks. Best of the lot is the traditional hot fudge sundae. With all the trimmings and toppings, it's a hefty $5.50. Dietary sin has its price.

10 Read Herb Caen and "Farley" in the *Chronicle*

The *Chronicle* is the city's morning newspaper. Sacramento-born Herb Caen, the leading liberal voice of San Francisco, has been writing his daily column of wit, gossip, and political commentary since 1938. The column is required reading for residents, and it provides insightful humor for visitors. Cartoonist Phil Frank originally syndicated a successful comic strip called "Travels with Farley," chronicling the adventures of a wanderer. A few years ago, he settled his hero in a San Francisco bay-windowed Victorian with a wisecracking crow and put him to work as a reporter on the *Daily Demise*. To properly parody the true spirit of the city, Frank withdrew his strip from syndication and runs it exclusively for northern California readers.

Chapter 3

WHERE TO STARE ON A CLEAR DAY

The Ten Best City Views

> *Oh God, I was afraid it would be this beautiful!*
> —*New York author Gail Sheehy, standing on Telegraph Hill*

Built on seven hills perched on a peninsula, flanked by sea cliffs, San Francisco is a city of vistas. When columnist Walter Winchell visited here half a century ago, he claimed the best view was from the men's room on the twenty-second floor of the 111 Sutter Building. My research did indeed uncover a male rest stop there, but it's windowless. So much for legends.

However, we have discovered hundreds of other great places from which to admire this special city. Here are our ten favorites.

1 THE BEST OVERALL VIEW OF SAN FRANCISCO
Tank Hill

End of Belgrave Street, off Seventeenth Street.

Tank what? That's right, not Twin Peaks, but Tank Hill, a promontory just beneath the famous pair of peaks. We prefer it for two reasons: It's practically deserted and provides a serene setting for eyeing the city, and it's a bit lower in elevation, offering a closer but equally impressive vista. You can see the entire cityscape from here in one slow-motion sweep.

To find this little-known lump, drive up Market to Castro, and veer slightly to the right onto Seventeenth Street; follow this to Stanyan Street, turn left, and go up a steep grade to Belgrave Street. Go left again and—still climbing—drive a few blocks to the end of the street. Before you, on the left side of the street, is a trail sloping upward to Tank Hill. The best viewpoint is from a rocky promontory to your left. Just to your right, you'll discover the concrete base of an old water tank that gave this place its inelegant name.

When you reach the top of Tank Hill, the great sweep of the city is unveiled suddenly. It reminds us of the sensation experienced in a helicopter flight that tops a ridge to reveal a hidden panorama.

Reach for your camera and your adjectives. This is the place.

2 THE BEST VIEW OF THE CITY SKYLINE
Treasure Island

View point just outside Treasure Island Naval Station.

From a vista point near Treasure Island's main gate, you look flat across San Francisco Bay, and the skyline seems to rise from its choppy waters. Technically, many of the high-rises do that, for they're built on bay fill.

This viewpoint is easy to find. Just take the Treasure Island exit from the Bay Bridge, and drive to a parking area just outside the naval station. Many people, assuming that entry to Treasure Island is restricted, bypass this spot. You do have to be a member of the military or have official reasons to enter the station itself, but the public has access to the parking area outside the gate. The Treasure Island turnoff is marked from either direction on the bridge.

3 THE BEST VIEW OF THE RESTLESS SEA
3 GGNRA's Coastal Trail

Off Lincoln Park, just north of the Palace of the Legion of Honor.

Many people are familiar with the Golden Gate Promenade, a pedestrian trail that extends from Aquatic Park near Fisherman's Wharf to Fort Point. Less known and probably more dramatic is GGNRA's Coastal Trail. (Both are suggested hikes in Chapter 21.)

A section of this trail just off Lincoln Park Golf Course offers wonderful vistas of the Pacific and its rocky shoreline. Often, such views are filtered through veils of Monterey cypress. It's difficult to believe that you're in a major city—until you glance to your right and see the Golden Gate Bridge and buildings of the nearby neighborhoods.

The Lincoln Park section of the Coastal Trail begins to the right of El Camino del Mar, just after it emerges from the exclusive Sea Cliff residential area. Look for the Welcome to the Golden Gate National Recreation Area sign. A path skirts the edge of the golf course and takes you to the Coastal Trail. Stroll in either direction on this wilderness-trail-in-a-city and enjoy the scenery.

4 THE BEST VIEW OF THE WATERFRONT
4 Coit Tower

Tower elevator hours are 10 a.m. to 5:30 p.m. daily; elevator fee is $3.

Certainly this is an insider's guide, full of hidden discoveries, but we can't always avoid the obvious. There's no quarrel that the best viewpoint for the city's waterfront, with its pier fingers reaching out into the bay, is from Coit Tower atop Telegraph Hill.

The view is very appealing from the circular parking area below the tower, and the higher you go, the better it gets. So ignore our advice in Chapter 2 about coming here at night; plan a visit when the tower elevator is still operating.

During summer or any sunny weekend, avoid the bumper-thumper traffic by walking up to Telegraph Hill; it's only a ten-minute stroll along a shady pedestrian path. The trail starts where Lombard Street blends into Telegraph Hill Boulevard. Catch Muni's 39-Coit bus and get off here before it, too, gets stuck in the jam.

5 THE BEST VIEW OF THE BAY BRIDGE
5 Embarcadero Promenade

Just south of the Ferry Building.

This concrete promenade, nominated in our *Ten Best Special Places* in Chapter 2, is a great place from which to admire the bay. From this point, the San Francisco-Oakland Bay Bridge stands boldly in front of you, with little in the foreground to clutter your vision.

6 THE BEST VIEW OF THE GOLDEN GATE
Marin Headlands

North headlands of the Golden Gate, just across the bridge and to the west.

We keep coming back to this ridge, but it does offer the most spectacular images of the Golden Gate Bridge and the city skyline. Vistas of all varieties present themselves as you wind up the narrow road. Pause at the first turnout at Battery Spencer, where the bridge's north tower filters a cityscape through its suspension cables. Climb farther and you see its entire length below you, cradling the skyline in its curved main cables. Gazing at the center span, you may find it hard to believe that this slender reach of steel is a mile long.

If you think this is a beautiful viewpoint on a sunny day, hurry up there when cottony tufts of fog roll over the hills to caress those towers, or at night when the city glimmers beyond the gate.

7 THE BEST VIEW OF SAILBOATS AT PLAY ON THE BAY
Fort Point Pier

Off the Golden Gate Promenade, between Fisherman's Wharf and Fort Point.

What are those little sailboats doing out there on the bay all day? Having fun, mostly. If you watch closely, you'll note that many of them are racing. Several sailing clubs stage weekly regattas, using buoy markers and landfalls to chart their liquid courses around the bay.

The best place to watch these races—and to get an eyeful of city, shoreline, and bridge—is from the end of Fort Point Pier. It's not actually at Fort Point, but about half a mile east, along the Presidio shoreline. You can follow the Golden Gate Promenade from the fort, or follow signs to the Crissy Field parking area and walk toward the old L-shaped pier, near a coast guard station.

This vista point is just a few hundred feet from a buoy marking one of the race courses. Boats sailing toward the Golden Gate (usually against the wind) must tack sharply toward the buoy, leaning precariously as they work against the stiff breeze. You can hear their sails pop as they change tack, heel around the marker, and head downwind. Some unfurl their spinnakers like giant colored balloons and run with the spirited breeze toward the finish line.

8 THE BEST VIEW FROM ON HIGH
A Left Window Seat on United Airlines Flight 553 to Seattle

This daily flight leaves San Francisco International Airport at 4:10 p.m. and normally turns inland just over the bay. Left-seaters get a great glimpse of the city crowded onto its small peninsula; details are accentuated by late-afternoon shadows.

Air travelers often miss the best views because the airport is south of the city and most routes go south, west, or east. Isn't flying to Seattle a rather costly way to get a good aerial vista? Well, there's always United's Flight 1452 to Medford.

9 THE BEST OVERALL VIEW OF THE BAY
Grizzly Peak Boulevard

Berkeley hills, above University of California campus.

Grizzly Peak follows the Berkeley hills ridge line, offering pretty pictures of the entire northern end of San Francisco Bay, from San Mateo to the Golden Gate to Belvedere. Several turnouts along this winding, forest-cloaked route invite you to stop and admire the entire San Francisco peninsula and much of the Bay Area; it's like studying a living topographic map. The best viewpoints are in Tilden Park, just above the University of California campus. Any good Oakland-Berkeley map will get you up there.

10 THE BEST VIEW OF THE SUNSET
The Captain Phineas T. Barnacle

Cliff House, 1090 Point Lobos (at Ocean Beach); 386-3330.

The P. T. Barnacle is a made-to-look-funky Cliff House pub that provides a picture window vision of Seal Rocks and the Pacific. It faces westward so you get the full grandeur of the sun sizzling into the sea. The trick here is to get a window table, because a lot of other folks agree with us and most spots are taken as sundown approaches.

There are many other view areas around the Cliff House, including an assortment of terraced walks and a trail down to the site of the old Sutro Baths. (Be wary of the surf here; the stones can be slippery and dangerous if you try to work your way out toward Seal Rocks.)

If the Barnacle is full and you really must have a glass in hand to appreciate the sunset, walk up to Louis' Restaurant at 902 Point Lobos; maybe the people there can find room for you.

Chapter 4

WHERE TO POINT YOUR PENTAX

The Ten Best Photo Spots

> *"What is the use of a book,"* thought Alice, *"without pictures?"*
> —*Lewis Carroll, Alice's Adventures in Wonderland*

Remember those "Kodak picture spots" scattered around Disneyland? They're supposed to make it easier for novice photographers to take better snapshots. In the same spirit, we offer you San Francisco's Ten Best picture spots.

Bear in mind that popular vista points don't necessarily produce the best photos. Skyline views usually are too shallow to photograph well, and high viewpoints tend to flatten out the scenery. A good scenic photograph should have an interesting foreground, middle ground, and background. Sometimes it's nice to frame your subject with a twig or bright flower.

If you want Aunt Irma in the photo, dress her in something bright; yellows, reds, and oranges are good. And don't force her to squint into the sun. Photograph her with the sun behind you but to your right or left. The angle will add shadow detail to her face and she won't look like she just ate a bad pizza. Also, ask her to interact with the scenery instead of just staring morosely into your lens.

Time of day also is important for photography. During early morning and late afternoon, shadows are sharper, bringing out more detail—particularly in buildings. Often, the atmosphere has a subtle golden quality late in the day, giving warm tones to subjects. At midday when the sun's rays shine straight down, objects look flat and uninteresting.

Dozens of professional photographers have taken hundreds of San Francisco photos that are more dramatic than anything we might produce. But by following our simple hints and finding some interesting viewpoints, you'll be able to take home some images that are substantially better than the average snapshot.

What follows are the Ten Best vista points from which to shoot some of the city's most popular settings. You can use an ordinary adjustable 35mm camera; a 35mm to 80mm zoom lens couldn't hurt. Even a simple fixed-focus camera will give you acceptable results, although you can't frame the setting as precisely as you can with a zoom.

1 BEST SHOT OF BRIDGE AND CITY
From Kirby Cove

At the base of Marin Headlands, across the Golden Gate.

The Golden Gate Bridge is the most photographed manmade object in the world. We can understand why. Like a beautiful woman or a handsome hunk, the bridge looks good from any angle. It's difficult to take a bad picture of it—although thousands of people succeed every year.

For our favorite photo, we're returning you to Marin Headlands. Instead of heading for the heights, hike down a dirt road from Battery Spencer (the first fortification you encounter on the headlands road) to Kirby Cove. A short walk through a campground takes you to Kirby Beach, and that beautiful cityscape reappears. This time, it's under the bridge span.

The composition is elegant: the beach in the foreground with some tree limbs for framing, the surf and bridge in the middle ground, and the city beyond. It's a late-afternoon horizontal shot; use a 28mm to 35mm lens to get the full expanse of the bridge. Shoot around sunset, when lights begin to twinkle in the city and the last rays of Old Sol highlight the bridge and paint the ocean a gunmetal gray. The results can be stunning.

2 BEST SHOT OF ALCATRAZ
From the Aft Gun Deck of the *Jeremiah O'Brien*

If the Golden Gate Bridge is the most photographed subject in the city, Alcatraz must be a close second. We found an unusual angle aboard the old liberty ship *SS Jeremiah O'Brien* anchored at Fort Mason's Pier 3 (see Chapter 1). By framing the scowling old prison island under the barrel of a deck gun on the ship's stern, you can create a rather sinister-looking composition.

This photo can be either a vertical or a horizontal; the gun is movable, and its position might have changed since we were there. Your lens length can vary from 35mm to 80mm. Photograph the ship as close to opening (9 a.m.) or closing (3 p.m.) hours as possible, to get those distinct shadows we've been talking about.

3 BEST SHOT OF THE BAY BRIDGE
From Yerba Buena Island

Midway across the Bay Bridge, adjacent to Treasure Island.

You've probably seen this handsome view, with the San Francisco–Oakland Bay Bridge in the foreground and the familiar cityscape beyond. But from where was it taken?

That's the problem. This classic San Francisco scene can be captured only from an overpass just above the tunnel that passes through Yerba Buena Island, which is navy property. Strolling around isn't encouraged, says the Treasure Island Public Affairs Office. This is a narrow road with no sidewalks and no place to park. Professional shutter-clickers can contact Public Affairs and be escorted up there, but the office understandably can't handle requests from the general public.

The solution? Have someone with a light foot drive you by slowly while you get a nice shot or two out the car window. To get there, take the Treasure Island turnoff from the Bay Bridge, drive down to the parking area outside the main gate, then turn around and go back up the road, following signs to Oakland. That takes you across the overpass and you—as the passenger—will be on the proper side of the car to get the shot. The best angle is just beyond the overpass, placing the span between you and the city skyline. Please don't stop or block traffic, or we'll hear about it from the navy.

The format is horizontal and it's a morning picture, using a 55mm to 80mm lens. Take it on a weekend, when the traffic is light.

4 BEST SHOT OF THE CITY'S PAINTED LADIES
From Alamo Square
Steiner Street, between Fulton and Hayes.

Once little known, this photo angle of six matching Victorian homes with a modern city skyline beyond has become very popular. Good grief, the area is now on the tour bus route.

The Painted Ladies are opposite a hillside park called Alamo Square. To get your picture, walk up the sloping lawn of the park until you line up the Ladies with the city skyline. We like to shoot under a small evergreen to frame our shot in foliage.

This is a midafternoon photo, best as a horizontal; use an 80mm lens. Don't wait until too late in the day, or tree shadows will start obscuring the Ladies' bright makeup.

5 BEST SHOT OF MISSION DOLORES
From the Mission Cemetery-Garden
Dolores Street at Sixteenth Street.

It's a challenge to get an effective photo of Mission Dolores from the street because of parked cars—and frequently, tour buses—that distract from the historic aura of the old adobe. We found a nice angle from a back corner of the cemetery, which is planted in brilliant mums and other flowers.

This view picks up the ancient grave markers, a side of the mission with its old tile roof, and the twin spires of the basilica beyond. We shot it vertically with a 28mm lens in midafternoon.

6 BEST SHOT OF THE CITY SKYLINE
From South Beach Marina
About half a mile south of the Ferry Building, off the Embarcadero.

Most skyline photos aren't interesting unless you have something in the fore-ground to give the picture depth. And what better than a forest of masts in a city surrounded by water? South Beach Marina (identified as South Beach Harbor on some maps) is a new development along the Embarcadero, less than a mile south of the Ferry Building. The masts of pleasure boats provide a fine foreground filigree.

You can shoot this early in the morning or late in the afternoon, since the view is north and the sun is generally behind you. Any length of lens will work, depending on how large a skyline slice you desire. We like to shoot it as a vertical, capturing reflections of pleasure boats in the water at our feet.

7 BEST SHOT OF YESTERDAY AND TODAY
Transamerica Pyramid and Sentinal Building from the Winchell's Donut Sign on Columbus Avenue

Columbus Avenue near Pacific, in North Beach.

A wonderfully ugly little old structure called the Sentinal Building stands on the corner of Columbus and Kearny, and the Transamerica Pyramid towers behind it.

The skinny, wedge-shaped Sentinal Building, constructed in 1907, houses Francis Ford Coppola's Zoetrope Studios. If you step into the street just opposite the Winchell's Donut sign at 145 Columbus, you can capture a nice wide angle—about 35mm—of old and new architectural extremes. Late afternoon is best; make sure a passing car doesn't run over your foot.

8 BEST SHOT OF COIT TOWER
From 807 Francisco Street

Francisco Street, off Hyde.

We should have at least one simple little photo in our collection, and we found it with a nice, clean angle of Coit Tower, taken from Francisco Street. After crossing Hyde Street, Francisco bumps into a cement wall above Leavenworth. Just short of the wall, at 807 Francisco, a bonsai-shaped pine tree leans into the street and forms a frame around Coit Tower, several blocks away. As we said, it's a simple shot: just the tower and the tree border. Take it in late afternoon, or in the morning if you want the tower silhouetted. This is a vertical, best photographed with an 80mm lens.

9 BEST SHOT OF THE FERRY BUILDING AND THAT UGLY FOUNTAIN
From Justin Herman Plaza

Opposite Embarcadero Four, below Clay and Drumm streets.

You either love the Vaillancourt Fountain in Justin Herman Plaza or you hate it, right? If you want to capture it on film, you might include the Ferry Building, because I can't think of anyone who doesn't like that.

The best vantage point is from the north side of the plaza near Los Chiles Café, in front of Four Embarcadero Center. If you can't tell which is north, it's the side toward Fisherman's Wharf. Now that the Embarcadero Freeway has been torn down, you'll have a clear shot, with the square-jointed fountain in the foreground and the Ferry Building beyond. A tree offers a pleasant frame for the Ferry Building's clock tower. And watch out for that garbage can near the fountain on your left. This is an afternoon vertical; shoot it with a 55mm lens.

Incidentally, most folks know that Armand Vaillancourt is an artist with a curious sense of form, but who was Justin Herman? He was head of the San Francisco Redevelopment Agency and was largely responsible for waterfront area improvements. Originally called Embarcadero Plaza, this spot was renamed in his honor in 1974, three years after he died.

10 BEST NIGHT SHOT OF THE CITY
From the Treasure Island Naval Station Entrance

Viewpoint just outside station entrance.

This is the same spot that we recommended in Chapter 3 for the best view of the city skyline. At night, cityscape colors glitter and ripple in the waters of the bay, offering creative photo opportunities. Also, those striking garlands of lights on the cables of the Bay Bridge provide a nice dimension. The area is paved, so you've got level terrain for your tripod. Arrive just before sundown, so you can shoot under varying conditions as the light fades. Night photos are best when a bit of light still lingers in the sky, helping silhouette the skyline. This is generally shot as a horizontal, with light ripples in the water to give the photo depth.

Chapter 5

DINING: THE INSIDE GUIDE

The Ten Very Best Restaurants

One cannot think well, love well, or sleep well if one hasn't dined well.
—*Virginia Woolf*

As a restaurant town, San Francisco has no equal in America. There are more than four thousand eating establishments here—something like one for every 180.9 residents. The city has more cafés per capita than any other in the world except Hong Kong.

Statistics say that San Franciscans dine out two-thirds more often than other Americans and that they spend twice as much on restaurant food as New Yorkers. Of course, the city's dining spots draw people from throughout the Bay Area as well as tourists from all over the world, so the per-capita figures are distorted somewhat. Still, by every measure, the city is the nation's dining-out mecca.

Several factors contribute to this bounty. San Francisco is one of the world's most ethnically rich cities, and the nearby Pacific Ocean and the great San Joaquin Valley farm belt provide chefs with a variety of fresh ingredients. From this largess, a contemporary American fare has developed, called California cuisine. It's based on innovative combinations of simply prepared, interestingly spiced dishes using fresh, local ingredients. The movement got its start across the bay in Berkeley, with Alice Waters's now-legendary Chez Panisse, and quickly spread to San Francisco's Stars, Square One, Zuni Café, and others. The chef-owners of Stars and Square One, in fact, are Chez Panisse graduates.

For the next several chapters, we offer you the results of the most pleasant part of our research, dining out in San Francisco. We didn't get around to all four thousand of the city's restaurants, but Betty and I or the San Francisco Seven have tried every one mentioned in the pages that follow. We dined out nearly two hundred times to research the first edition of this book, then we tried many new places in researching the revisions. We thus gained quite an insight into the San Francisco dining scene.

Also about fifteen pounds each.

Naturally, we have to be brazenly arbitrary to nominate a few restaurants out of thousands. Some of our choices are old hangouts where we've eaten for years; others are new discoveries. Our criteria are simple: consistently good food, prepared as requested, served at the proper temperature, in interesting surroundings.

In terms of prices, our selections run the gamut from some of the city's most expensive places to some of the cheapest. Our judgment is not based on the bottom line on the check, but on value received.

As we mentioned in the introduction, we've selected a No. 1 restaurant as our favorite and listed the rest alphabetically, with no further ranking. Credit card abbreviations are obvious: MC/VISA for MasterCard and VISA (which virtually always appear together), AMEX for American Express, DC for Diners Club, and DISC for the Discover card. "Major credit cards" indicates the two bank cards plus two or more of the others.

Our price guidelines work this way: Expensive: $30 or more per person for soup or salad and dinner entrée (not including dessert, beverage, or gratuity); moderately expensive: from $20 to $29; moderate: from $10 to $19; and inexpensive: under $10.

Thanks primarily to the efforts of former supervisor Carol Ruth Silver, an ordinance was passed in 1987 requiring eating places to set aside separate sections for nonsmokers. (If clean air is an important part of your meal, remember to ask for seating in the nonsmoking section.) In recent years, many restaurants have become entirely smoke-free.

Incidentally, if you can't tear yourself away from a rerun of "Gunsmoke" on your hotel TV set, you can order complete meals from any of several San Francisco restaurants by calling one of two food delivery firms. Waiters on Wheels (252-1470) and Dine-One-One (928-3278) will whisk piping-hot fare to your room or home at the touch of a few buttons. Call for one of their thick brochures, which list menus from fifty or more restaurants, or pick one up from your hotel concierge.

We begin our dining chapters at the top, with the Ten Best restaurants in San Francisco.

1 Ristorante Donatello

501 Post Street (at Mason); 441-7182. Regional Italian; expensive; full bar. Open 7 a.m. to 10:30 a.m. and 5:30 p.m. to 11 p.m. daily. Reservations essential; major credit cards. Jacket and tie for lunch and dinner.

When we wrote the first edition of this book, we selected Donatello as San Francisco's finest all-round restaurant. Then when we compiled San Francisco's Ultimate Dining Guide, based primarily on surveys of people who work with the restaurant and travel trades, it was given the highest rating of any establishment in its price range.

The city's best must pass several tests. The food must be both interesting and superlative, the setting pleasant, and the service attentive. Since we Westerners have little patience with stuffiness, it must meet all these criteria without pretension.

Donatello continues to succeed in every measure. Further, all dining areas are smoke-free. Part of the Donatello hotel (see Chapter 19), this exquisite restaurant is divided into two intimate dining rooms, each simply decorated, but with elegant touches such as Fortuny silk wall coverings and delicate Venetian glass lamps. The setting enhances the food instead of competing with it. Service is efficient, alert, and congenial.

The regional Italian cuisine is imaginative, delicious, and artfully presented; its flavors are complex yet subtle, not overwhelmed by thick sauces or heavy spicing. The menu is changed frequently, and it's not limited to Italian fare. Strong hints of California cuisine appear, and the accent is on lightly cooked, fresh ingredients.

Donatello has a feature we'd like to see other establishments adopt: a table d'hôte with a different wine to complement each of four courses. Buon appetito!

2 Alejandro's Sociedad Gastronomica

1840 Clement Street (at Nineteenth Avenue); 668-1184. Latin; moderate; full bar.
Open 5 p.m. to 11 p.m. Monday-Thursday, 5 p.m. to midnight Friday and Saturday,
4 p.m. to 11 p.m. Sunday. Reservations; major credit cards.

Alejandro's is one of those rare restaurants capable of turning an evening into an absolute delight. Patrons are greeted by a pleasing south-of-the-border eclectic decor: hand-painted Mexican tile, carved high-backed Peruvian chairs, Spanish mirrors, and walls busy with all sorts of bright and cheery objects. A mellow-voiced troubadour strolls among the diners, creating the perfect mood for sampling the intriguing menu.

Chef-proprietor Alejandro Espinosa describes his fare as Peruvian-Spanish-Mexican, but he stirs in a lot of Espinosan creativity. Try deep-fried Alejandro pastries with cheese, mild chilies, and egg; a cold cooked cactus and shredded lettuce salad; tapas (spicy Spanish hors d'oeuvres); and entrées such as paella valenciana (rice with mussels and cracked crab) or trout wrapped in dried ham. Alejandro serves the best flan in town.

In case you're curious, Sociedad Gastronomica is an association of Latin epicures that convenes at the restaurant from time to time to pass judgment on the fare. Menu items with the initials S.C. have earned its highest ratings.

3 Big Four

1075 California Street (in the Huntington Hotel, at Taylor); 474-5400.
Contemporary Continental; moderately expensive; full bar. Breakfast daily 7 a.m.
to 10 a.m., lunch weekdays 11:30 a.m. to 3 p.m., and dinner nightly 5:30 p.m.
to 10 p.m. Major credit cards. Jackets requested at dinner.

This is one of the city's preeminent restaurants, offering attentive service and creative cuisine in an atmosphere of quiet elegance. The stylish decor of warm woods, historic prints, and artifacts celebrates the city's glory days, from the gold rush to the railroad barons—for whom it is named.

Should you wonder, four Sacramento merchants—Leland Stanford, Charles Crocker, Mark Hopkins, and Collis P. Huntington—made quick fortunes as the financial and political brawn behind the transcontinental railroad. These and other post-gold rush "nabobs" and Nevada silver barons built their mansions atop these heights, thus inspiring the name Nob Hill. (And now you know why it's never spelled Knob Hill.) However, we've come to dine, not to discuss historical trivia.

The restaurant reflects the opulence of its Nob Hill location, with rich oak paneling, high-backed leather banquettes, rams horn wall sconces, a polished copper bar, and railroading memorabilia. It may be, in fact, the most comely example of 1880 restaurant decor in the country.

Amidst this grandeur, the food is contemporary and innovative. Wild game—actually farm-raised—is a specialty. The changing menu ranges from wild boar cutlets with green peppercorn butter and brandied apples, and spicy duck sausage with greens and ginger-mango vinaigrette, to sautéed petrale sole over spinach with a sweet corn and sun-dried tomato butter sauce. We like to end our meals with dessert and coffee in the stylish nineteenth-century bar, warmed by a cheery fire and mellowed by a tinkling piano. The dining room is smoke-free.

4 Fleur de Lys

777 Sutter Street (at Jones); 673-7779. French; expensive; full bar. Open 6 p.m.
to 9 p.m. Monday-Thursday and 5:30 p.m. to 9:30 p.m. Friday-Saturday.
Reservations essential, well in advance; major credit cards. Jacket and tie requested.

For decades, the city has been noted for its wonderfully posh French restaurants. But many remain in a culinary time capsule, still serving cholesterol- and calorie-rich haute cuisine despite the trend to lighter fare. Fleur de Lys broke out of this capsule a few years ago with the arrival of a new partner, French-born chef Hubert Keller. He quickly restored it to a premier position among the city's finer dining establishments. Chef Keller describes his cuisine as "haute nouvelle." It's frankly French, yet with light, innovative touches and curious uses of seasonings such as cilantro and ginger—curious at least for cuisine de France. The menu, incidentally, includes some vegetarian selections.

Keller's three-star creations are served under a canopy of old-world elegance; the cascading fabric ceiling and lavish Continental decor provide a lush setting for a pleasing evening.

Fleur de Lys was selected as the city's best restaurant in our poll of restaurant executives and celebrity chefs for our earlier book, San Francisco's Ultimate Dining Guide, and it was voted the Bay Area's best French restaurant in San Francisco Focus magazine's 1992 restaurant review. Keller was voted Chef of the Year by Focus in 1988.

5 Harris'

2100 Van Ness Avenue (at Pacific); 673-1888. American (primarily steaks and
ribs); moderately expensive; full bar. Lunch from 11:30 a.m. to 2 p.m. Wednesdays
only; dinner nightly, from 6 p.m. Monday-Friday and from 5 p.m. Saturday-Sunday.
Reservations essential; major credit cards. Jackets requested for dinner; tie optional.

When this handsome, plush, and spacious restaurant opened on Van Ness Avenue several years ago, it quickly became—and remains—the best place in the Bay Area to get excellent beef.

The American-style menu features fresh fish and Maine lobster as well, although we go for the wonderful pepper steak and rare prime rib. Seasonal vegetables arrive properly crisp, and the decadent desserts are to die for. With its oak paneling, brass chandeliers, and large, deeply upholstered booths, the place has a warm, clubby feel, and the friendly staff contributes to a congenial atmosphere.

6 Kuleto's

221 Powell Street (at Geary); 397-7720. California-Italian; moderate; full bar. Open from 7 a.m. to 11 p.m. daily. Reservations accepted; all major credit cards.

Opened in 1987, Kuleto's rose quickly through the ranks of the city's leading restaurants and has become something of an institution. It is today one of the city's most versatile and consistent culinary venues. The dining arm of the Villa Florence Hotel, Kuleto's serves creative omelets to early rising stockbrokers, California cuisine lunches, and a mix of classic Italian and other Continental fare for dinner.

It's a stylish and cheerfully bright place: a pleasing blend of marble, copper, brass, and mahogany glowing under a striking vaulted plaster ceiling. The interior work was done by Pat Kuleto, set designer for Corona Bar and Grill and the smart new McCormick & Kuleto's at Ghirardelli Square. He fashioned his namesake place working in partnership with hotelier Bill Kimpton, who created the adjacent Villa Florence.

7 Moose's

1652 Stockton Street (at Filbert); 989-7800. Italian-Mediterranean; moderate; full bar. Monday-Thursday 11:30 a.m. to 11 p.m., Friday-Saturday 11:30 a.m. to midnight, and Sunday 10 a.m. to 11 p.m. Reservations advised; major credit cards.

Some years ago, Ed and Mary Etta Moose created a legend—and a media hangout—with the Washington Square Bar and Grill in the heart of North Beach. In late 1992, they crossed the square, hoping to begin a new culinary chronicle. If the Victorian-accented WSB&G was classic San Francisco, then Moose's is classic San Francisco moderne. It's an appealing space of brightness and light, with subtle art deco touches, high ceilings, walnut accents, and white napery. Like the WSB&G, which still thrives under different ownership, Moose's is a place of happy tumult; a tinkling piano is barely heard above the dinner din.

A focal point is the open kitchen, and we like to perch at its counter, intrigued by the controlled chaos of food preparation. From this kitchen, commanded by bright young chef Lance Dean Velasquez, emerges Mediterranean nouveau creations such as ragout of fish with red pepper and leek, and chicken breast with chestnut dressing and cherry chutney. The menu changes daily, although a few items are standard, such as perfectly seared "Mooseburgers" with Gorgonzola cheese, and personal-sized pizzas that emerge from a ceramic oven.

Although we were reluctant to elevate a new restaurant to our Ten Best list, all that happy hubbub suggests that Ed and Mary Etta's place will be around for a while.

8 Square One

190 Pacific Avenue Mall (at Front); 788-1110. Mediterranean-international; moderately expensive; full bar. Lunch 11:30 a.m. to 2:30 p.m. weekdays; dinner nightly from 5:30 p.m. Reservations essential; major credit cards.

Joyce Goldstein, nominated as San Francisco Focus magazine's 1992 Chef of the Year, says she goes back to "square one" every day to create things tasty in the nouvelle style.

Her eclectic menu dances around the "robust and sensual" foods of the Mediterranean, ranging from Spanish paella to North African couscous. She also reaches beyond the Med for Russian shashlik, Brazilian churrasco, and Indonesian satay. She bases her often-changing menu on whatever fresh, interesting ingredients are available. Daily specials may include linguine with grilled tuna, saffron, onions, and sun-dried tomatoes; grilled chicken in an oriental five-spice marinade with orange, ginger, garlic, and hot pepper; and vegetarian entrées such as cracked-wheat pilaf, grilled eggplant with cumin-tomato sauce, and green beans with basil and walnuts. Everything is prepared in-house, from breads and ice creams to chutneys and mustards.

All this creativity occurs in an expansive, modern brick structure near the Golden Gateway just off the Embarcadero. Sitting opposite Sidney Waldon Park, it's a study in architectural nouveau with brass, glass, natural woods, and warm fall colors. An open kitchen, the essential ingredient for trendy restaurants, issues its pleasant aromas to waiting diners. A high waffled ceiling softens the clang and clatter.

9 Stars

150 Redwood Alley (off Van Ness Avenue between McAllister and Golden Gate); 861-7827. California cuisine; moderately expensive; full bar. Lunch 11:30 a.m. to 2:30 p.m. weekdays; dinner 5:30 p.m. to 10:30 p.m. Monday-Saturday and 5 p.m. to 10 p.m. Sunday; Sunday brunch 11 a.m. to 2:30 p.m. Reservations essential; MC/VISA, AMEX.

The home of the power lunch continues to thrive. Opened in 1984 by Jeremiah Tower, Stars has become an institution. So has Tower; he won the James Beard Award for the Best California Chef in 1993. Stars remains the favorite haunt of power brokers, local celebrities, and faithful followers of Tower's creative California cuisine.

Green awnings and a neat little neon star are the only clues that a busy restaurant lurks in Redwood Alley; the more obvious entry on Golden Gate is the back door. Decor in the barnlike interior is upscale rudimentary: brass railings, wood paneling, French posters, celebrity photos, and walls immodestly filled with framed awards, accolades, and clippings. It is in the huge open kitchen that creativity really thrives. The daily changing menu features an innovative mix of new California creations with strong international accents.

The entrées are complex and handsomely presented; ingredients are impeccably fresh. Examples are sautéed chicken breasts over fried polenta with rosemary hollandaise; grilled scallops on shredded chilies, cilantro, and ginger with black bean sauce; and, for dessert, rich and creamy hazelnut parfait.

Next door is Stars Café, serving a similar quality of food at lower prices, and in a more casual setting.

10 Tommy Toy's Haute Cuisine Chinoise

655 Montgomery Street (at Clay); 397-4888. Chinese-French; expensive; full bar. Lunch weekdays 11:30 a.m. to 3 p.m.; dinner nightly 6 p.m. to 9:30 p.m. Reservations essential; major credit cards. Jacket and tie requested.

Critical comments on Tommy Toy's lavish dining palace range from "exquisite" to "Chinese excess." The food has been flawless during our several visits, and we like dining amidst elegance, even when it's almost overdone. Toy, who earned his marks as a restaurateur with his Imperial Palace in Chinatown, opened this "elegant nineteenth-century palace" in the heart of the Financial District in 1985.

The restaurant brims with Chinese art and affluence—a museum-quality collection of rare paintings in sandalwood frames, lacquered carvings, and blue porcelains. Booths and chairs are brocaded silk, and tables are set with delicate little porcelain Chinese bridal lamps.

Toy's menu is upscale Cantonese and Mandarin with strong French accents. The food is served European-style, in individual and beautifully presented entrées. Examples include Szechuan lamb, Maine lobster in ginger sauce, and a wonderfully crispy Peking duck. For more of a Chinese-style "sampler" feast, try an eight-course prix fixe dinner.

Chapter 6

DELIGHTS FROM THE DEEP

The Ten Best Seafood Restaurants

> *I like my oysters fried;*
> *That way I know my oysters died.*
>
> —*Roy G. Blount, Jr.*

A city surrounded on three sides by water had better offer good seafood restaurants, and San Francisco certainly does. It's not just the water-bound topography that has created this abundance of chowder houses. Fish was a dietary staple for two of our earliest immigrant groups, the Italians and Chinese, and they opened many of the city's first cafés.

Fisherman's Wharf, for instance, has been a focal point for Italian seafood restaurants for decades. However, we feel that many of them have become complacent, catering more to tourist traffic than culinary creativity. Only one—Tarantino's—makes our list of the Ten Best fish spots. We've found more interesting restaurants with more innovative menus elsewhere.

Incidentally, many of San Francisco's large seafood houses with extensive menus may serve frozen as well as fresh fish, so always ask what's just been landed. We usually get a frank answer, although some waitpeople use that wonderful self-canceling response: "Well, it's freshly frozen." About the only things frozen at our favorite fish venue are some of the desserts.

1 Hayes Street Grill

324 Hayes Street (at Franklin); 863-5545. Moderate to moderately expensive; full bar. Lunch 11:30 a.m. to 3 p.m. weekdays; dinner 5 p.m. to 10 p.m. Monday-Thursday, 5 p.m. to 11 p.m. Friday, and 6 p.m. to 11 p.m. Saturday. Reservations essential; MC/VISA.

Although Hayes Street Grill is a bit out of the way, on the outer fringe of the Civic Center, the faithful have been making a path to it since 1979. Only fresh fish is served, and you have a choice of preparation: mesquite broiled, pan fried, or whatever. It's always lightly done, and it's offered with an interesting selection of sauces, served on the side so you can nip at them carefully before committing your entire fish.

A California-oriented wine list features several full-flavored yet dry wines by the glass, selected with fish in mind. The daily changing menu is written on a blackboard, saving you the need to memorize a waiter's long incantation. A few meats and even an excellent burger and fries are included on the large menu; but essentially, this is the place for fresh, simply prepared seafood.

2 Aqua

252 California Street (near Battery); 956-9662. Moderate to moderately expensive;
full bar. Lunch weekdays 11:30 a.m. to 2:30 p.m., dinner Monday-Thursday
5:30 p.m. to 10:30 p.m., Friday-Saturday 5:30 p.m. to 11 p.m. MC/VISA, AMEX.

Chef-owner George Morrone's starkly attractive new seafood place in the
heart of the Financial District has been reeling in impressive numbers of locals and
visitors since it opened in 1992.

An aficionado of the *nouveau* school, Morrone experiments boldly with
intriguing blends of spices and other new-wave ingredients in his faultlessly fresh
seafood fare, and most of his experiments work. You'll enjoy your tuna *foie gras*
and accompaniments in a bright and lofty space of high ceilings held up by square
columns, indirect lighting, and floral arrangements in large urns. Plush seating and
white napery add final touches to the simple elegance of this place.

Was the location of Aqua next door to the venerable Tadich Grill a coincidence
or a challenge? No matter; both were crowded when we last stopped by for lunch.

3 Bentley's Seafood Grill & Oyster Bar

185 Sutter Street (at Kearny); 989-6895. Moderate; full bar. Lunch Monday-
Saturday 11:30 a.m. to 3 p.m.; dinner Monday-Thursday 5 p.m. to 9:30 p.m. and
Friday-Saturday 5 p.m. to 10:30 p.m. Reservations advised; major credit cards.

The dining arm of the art deco Galleria Park Hotel, Bentley's combines a
handsome 1920s look with a trendy seafood menu. If you've grown weary of
basic fillet of sole, try intriguing dishes such as monkfish roasted with endive,
chanterelles, and fried Jerusalem artichokes; linguine with cracked pepper and
roasted tomatoes; Dungeness crab, simmered in vodka; or blackened prawns with
green onions and papaya bits. Entrées come with tasty house-baked corn muffins.
The menu changes weekly to feature curious new kitchen creations; although the
fare is primarily seafood, a few meat dishes are offered.

The place pleases the eye as well as the palate. The entrance is particularly
striking: a twenty-five-foot-high glass portal etched with seafood designs. The
interior is done in salmon pink with shell wall sconces and black-and-white
photos of Roaring Twenties scenes. A raw bar, a lively booze bar, and dining tables
occupy the main floor; a more intimate dining area is tucked into a second-floor
balcony.

4 Maye's Steak and Oyster House

1233 Polk Street (at Sutter); 474-7674. Inexpensive to moderate; full bar.
Open Monday-Saturday 11:30 a.m. to 9:30 p.m., Sunday 2 p.m. to 9:30 p.m.
Reservations accepted; MC/VISA, AMEX.

Venerable Maye's, in business since 1867, is the second-oldest restaurant in the
city. New owner James S. Han has spruced up the interior, adding lighter touches
to the old wainscoting and dark woods. But the old-fashioned deep, comfortable
booths and crisp white linens remain, along with remarkably modest prices;
Maye's is one of the city's least expensive seafood places.

The kitchen has been updated as well, offering mesquite-grilled seafood and steaks, along with the traditional crab casseroles and steamed clams. We compliment Han's wisdom in buying a dining landmark, then—to quote that old Kenny Rogers song—knowing what to throw away and knowing what to keep.

5 McCormick & Kuleto's Seafood Restaurant

Ghirardelli Square (Beach and Larkin); 929-1730. Moderate to moderately expensive; full bar. Lunch and dinner daily from 11:30 a.m. to 11 p.m.; food service in Crabcake Lounge until midnight. Reservations accepted; major credit cards.

The aquatic culinary creativity of McCormick & Schmick's of Portland and the dazzling design work of Pat Kuleto have combined to create one of the city's smartest new seafood cafés.

Several restaurants have occupied this sterling location with its fine bay vistas, but none so handsomely as the present tenant, with its light woods, boat-shaped tortoise-shell fixtures, brass and glass, and picture windows. Diners can choose between the *nouveau moderne* main dining room or the ship-shape Crab Cake Lounge above.

The focus is on fresh seafood, either mesquite grilled, sautéed, or pan fried and often prepared with creative sauces, herbs, and spices. Among the interesting offerings are a dinner of three kinds of salmon with tarragon butter sauce, ahi tuna with chilies and almonds, and thresher shark with coriander-peanut sauce and fried leeks. Or are you ready for halibut in raspberry butter sauce? The changing menu is huge, with thirty to fifty entrées on a given day, including pastas, meat, and poultry. If you're adventurous, try the seafood pizza in the Crab Cake Lounge; it also serves fresh crab and other shellfish.

6 Pacific Heights Bar & Grill

2001 Fillmore Street (at Pine); 567-3337. Moderate; full bar. Lunch Wednesday-Sunday from 11:30 a.m., dinner Sunday-Thursday 5:30 p.m. to 9:30 p.m., and Friday-Saturday 5:30 p.m. to 10:30 p.m. Reservations accepted; major credit cards.

Owners Susan and Craig Bashel claim their restaurant has the largest raw bar on the West Coast, offering twelve to sixteen varieties of oysters daily. We didn't know those awful-looking things *came* in a dozen different types. But there they were, flashing crooked grins from their bed of shaved ice: blue points, golden mantels, quilcenes, appalachicolas, yaquina bays, and even New Zealand green-lipped mussels. The courageous can try them with an assortment of sauces, from sour cream dill to tomato herb salsa.

Those who don't care for such slippery fare can pick from a bistro-style menu that goes beyond seafood to include pastas, chicken, steaks, and salads. The oft-changing menu may wander from sautéed chicken breasts with artichoke hearts to honey-mustard glazed pork tenderloin or spicy barbecued prawns and sea scallops served on a roasted corn tortilla. In-house breads and desserts are specialties.

Opened in 1984, the place is contemporary California in style, with cool pastel colors, brick accent walls, oak trim, and lots of mirrors. It's housed in a venerable Victorian along Fillmore Street's growing restaurant row. The raw bar set in the front window and the long liquor bar are popular with locals, and the place can get noisy on Friday and Saturday nights. But the volume wasn't excessive when we visited, and the service was excellent.

7 Scott's Lombard

2400 Lombard Street (at Scott); 563-8988. Moderate to moderately expensive; full bar. Open 11:30 a.m. to 10:30 p.m. daily. Reservations accepted; major credit cards.

Scott's was one of the first major seafood restaurants located away from downtown and the waterfront. It was erected along the city's "motel row" in 1976. One of the original partners later returned to the bay front to open the Embarcadero Center Scott's, which is next on our list.

We like the original Scott's stylish Cape Cod-Victorian atmosphere, with lots of brass, warm woods, and glass. The fine kitchen specializes in locally caught fish and assorted mollusks, and it serves an outstanding fisherman's stew, one of the better in this seafaring city. The versatile menu changes frequently, offering as many as a dozen fresh fish entrées, plus steaks and chops, several appetizers, a couple of pastas, and tasty in-house desserts.

8 Scott's Seafood Grill & Bar

Three Embarcadero Center, 981-0622. Moderate; full bar. Monday-Thursday 11 a.m. to 10 p.m., Friday-Saturday 11 a.m. to 11 p.m., Sunday 4:30 p.m. to 9:30 p.m. Reservations advised; major credit cards.

The Financial District/waterfront edition of Scott's offers great balance—a bright and pleasing environment and a contemporary, innovative kitchen where fresh seafood is merged with seasonal ingredients and light spices in creative combinations.

The menu changes daily, ordained by what's currently fresh and available. You might encounter charbroiled salmon with wild rice and herb butter, or Cajun-spiced prawn and Andouille sausage with pasta in tomatoes. If they're available, don't pass up the small, sweet aqua gem clams, flown in from Washington's Puget Sound.

Everything works in concert here, from the enterprising entrées and extensive California wine list—mostly white—to the in-house desserts and rich cappuccino for a finale. The look of the place is pleasingly simple: open and airy, with large windows, white napery, bentwood chairs, and pastel prints of fish species on the light walls.

9 Tarantino's

206 Jefferson Street (above the boat basin at Fisherman's Wharf); 775-5600. Moderate; full bar. Open 11 a.m. to 11 p.m. daily. Reservations accepted; MC/VISA, AMEX.

We've been ordering fresh fish from Tarantino's since the 1950s, watching the place change with the times by lightening up on its sauces while maintaining its role as both a tourist lure and a comfortable haven for regulars. It has kept its dignity amid the growing tackiness of the wharf.

Perhaps we favor the place because it was founded by a couple of Irish lads. When Gene McAteer and Dan Sweeney opened their restaurant in 1946, they gave it an Italian name, since the area was dominated by the sons of Italy. The tip-off to Tarantino's genealogy is the green bow ties worn by the servers and green trim on the busboys' jackets.

Tarantino's second-floor location over a corner of the Jefferson Street Boat Basin provides one of the best views on the wharf; seating is tiered so all diners can share the vista. The seascape is equally appealing from a handsome little cocktail lounge.

10 The Waterfront

Pier 7 (Embarcadero at Broadway); 391-2696. Moderate to moderately expensive; full bar. Open 11:30 a.m. to 10:30 p.m. daily. Reservations accepted; major credit cards.

Combining fresh seafood, an elegant old San Francisco decor, and a great bay view, Al Falchi's place has become the waterfront establishment for power lunches, first-rate dinners, and Sunday brunch.

The menu changes daily, focusing on seasonally fresh fish—local and flown in from afar. Specials include red abalone, scampi, Dungeness crab, and more than eighteen varieties of oysters. Beef and homemade pasta also find a spot on the menu. The food is served in a pleasing environment of brass, natural woods, potted foliage, and crisp white linens.

All this ambiance is housed in a sturdy old masonry building on the waterfront, with a glass-walled view of the Bay Bridge and Treasure Island. The dining room is steeply terraced so that everyone can enjoy the vista. To further fortify his niche among the city's Ten Best, Falchi offers a great wine selection, with more than a hundred California vintners represented.

Chapter 7

FARE WITH AN INTERNATIONAL FLAIR

The Ten Best Ethnic Restaurants

Nachman's rule: when it comes to foreign food, the less authentic the better.

— *Gerald Nachman*

Few people can agree on the authenticity of ethnic foods. What Americans consider Mexican cuisine has been altered by generations of Mexican-American cooks. On the other hand, many Chinese dishes retain their traditional style and are even superior to the original fare in China. Why? Because fresher ingredients are more available in our affluent society, and because Chinese farmers in the San Joaquin Valley grow the same hairy melons and long beans that are staple veggies of the old country.

However, the issue here is not authenticity, but variety. San Francisco probably has a greater range of international restaurants than any other city in the world.

How is it possible to choose the best from among the scores of ethnic places? Which of the several hundred Chinese restaurants—Cantonese, Hunan, Szechuan, Mandarin, Hakka—deserve top honors? Can one pot of properly prepared pasta really be more perfect than another? How does one decide among the many elegant little French restaurants where candles glimmer on white-clothed tables and mysterious sauces simmer in back kitchens?

An impossible task, you say?

Obviously.

We therefore rely on the divination that has served us so well in the past: personal preference. In arriving at our ethnic Ten Best, we applied criteria similar to those used in our earlier selections: good food, service, and value.

We also made some arbitrary decisions, both in price range and style. Since the French produce the world's most elegant fare, we focused on upscale restaurants featuring *haute cuisine.* From Italy, we sought hearty *trattorias,* which are typical of San Francisco's Italian community—although we hastily add that some of the city's most elegant restaurants are Italian as well. Our Chinese selections reflect classic old-country cooking, not San Franciscanized chop suey. Since Chinese restaurants represent the largest group in the city and their cuisine is quite divergent, we've divided them into two broad groups: Cantonese reflects the cooking style of Canton and adjacent Hong Kong with its fresh, lightly seasoned fish and vegetables; and Mandarin is our catchall category covering the spicier cooking of the rest of China, including Szechuan and Hunan.

In limiting ourselves to ten types of ethnic restaurants, we are unable to mention many of the foreign cuisines that can be savored in this city. We apologize to the Afghanistan, Brazilian, Czechoslovakian, Korean, Nicaraguan, Philippine, Polish, Salvadoran, Turkish, and many other ethnic restaurants that failed to make the list. Those that have made it are tallied alphabetically.

1 THE BEST CANTONESE RESTAURANT
Hong Kong Flower Lounge

5322 Geary Boulevard (between Seventeenth and Eighteenth avenues); 668-8998. Inexpensive to moderate; full bar. Weekdays 11 a.m. to 2:30 p.m. and 5 p.m. to 9:30 p.m., weekends and holidays 10 a.m. to 2:30 p.m. and 5 p.m. to 9:30 p.m. MC/VISA.

With the recent influx of residents from Hong Kong, who are dubious about the pending Chinese takeover of their city-state, we've witnessed a major change in San Francisco's Asian dining scene. The city's small cafés, often run by family cooks with no formal training, have been overshadowed by large and professionally staffed restaurants financed by Hong Kong money. A fine example downtown, for instance, is the opulent Harbor Village at Four Embarcadero Center, easily one of the city's finest Asian restaurants. Another—our new Cantonese favorite—is way out there on Geary Boulevard.

We'd heard about the Flower Lounge before it came north, when it was building a reputation in Millbrae as the best Chinese restaurant on the peninsula. When a branch opened in the city, we hurried to give it a try. We weren't disappointed.

Chef Alice Wong leaves no Chinese culinary stone unturned, offering everything from an extensive *dim sum* menu to perfectly seasoned fresh vegetable and seafood dishes. She even goes slightly Cajun with wok-charred prawns or black codfish. For those needing spice in their life, a few peppery northern China dishes are included on the large menu, in addition to the more mildly flavored Cantonese fare. For wonderfully fresh fish or shrimp, order something from the live tank—and expect to pay significantly for the privilege.

Readers of *San Francisco Focus* magazine selected the Flower Lounge as their favorite Chinese restaurant for two years running. We find no fault with their judgment.

2 THE BEST FRENCH RESTAURANT
Masa's

648 Bush Street (at Powell); 989-7154. Expensive; full bar. Tuesday-Saturday 6 p.m. to 9:30 p.m. Reservations essential, well in advance; major credit cards. Jackets required, ties optional.

Masa's is the most opulent and expensive French restaurant in San Francisco and one of the finest west of the Mississippi, and perhaps west of the Seine.

"Contemporary subdued elegance" is manager John Cunin's description of this posh restaurant, founded in 1983 by the late Masataka Kobayashi. Present chef Julian Serrano and owner Bill Kimpton have successfully carried Masa's banner of excellence. Cost is no object, for it is passed on to eager diners, who cheerfully pay to be fed and pampered by a serving staff that outnumbers the guests.

The fare is classic Gaelic, which is curious, since the founder was Japanese and the present chef is Italian. Yet the food is faultlessly French, with its rich sauces, served in a hushed environment of burgundy and gray, with textured wallpaper, gold-rimmed mirrors, a paneled ceiling, and subdued lighting. Smoking is not permitted, so you smell only those savory sauces.

With only a dozen or so tables to attend, alert waiters are at your side at the slightest arch of an eyebrow, but they never hover. Masa's remains the ultimate venue for special occasions and quiet celebrations.

3 THE BEST GERMAN RESTAURANT
Schroeder's

240 Front Street (between California and Sacramento); 421-4778. Moderate; full bar. Weekdays 11 a.m. to 9 p.m., weekends 4:30 p.m. to 9 p.m. Major credit cards.

One of the city's dining legends, Schroeder's has been serving ample portions at modest prices since 1893. The place has aged gracefully. With its wood paneling, plate rails lined with beer steins, and murals of Bavaria, it has the look and feel of a carefully maintained old German club.

The sign says Continental although the menu is mostly German-Bavarian. Start your meal with Schroeder's legendary German potato salad, then follow with typical Bavarian fare such as smoked pork loin with sauerkraut, red cabbage, and potatoes or sauerbraten with potato pancakes. One of our favorites is paprika *schnitzel*—breaded veal cutlet with a creamy paprika sauce. Daily specials, always excellent buys, include such yesterday fare as pigs' knuckles and oxtail sauté.

4 THE BEST INDIAN RESTAURANT
Gaylord

Ghirardelli Square, 900 North Point, 771-8822; also at One Embarcadero Center, 397-7775. Moderate to moderately expensive; full bar. Lunch noon to 2 p.m.; dinner 5 p.m. to 11 p.m. nightly. Reservations suggested; major credit cards.

This handsome restaurant's roots reach back to British colonial India, when the Gaylord family started its first dining palace in Bombay. Branches have since opened in a few other major cities, although the chefs are still India-trained.

Gaylord typifies the quiet elegance of fine Indian restaurants with a mix of old European and Eastern decor. A bonus at the Ghirardelli location is a striking view of the bay.

The two restaurants specialize in the *tandoori* cooking of northern India instead of the hot curries typical of southern India. Meats are rubbed with light seasonings, then cooked at a high temperature in round clay *tandoor* ovens to preserve their juices. Your meal should be accompanied with *kulcha*, a bread made of wheat, yogurt, and onion. It's whomped against the side of the *tandoor*, where it is quick-baked, and brought to your table still radiating that tantalizing aroma.

5 THE BEST ITALIAN RESTAURANT
Basta Pasta

1268 Grant Avenue (at Vallejo); 434-2248. Inexpensive to moderate; full bar. Open 11:45 a.m. to 2 a.m. daily. Reservations accepted; MC/VISA, AMEX.

Picking the city's best Italian restaurant is as frustrating as selecting the top Chinese place; there are too many choices. However, we'll stay with our longtime favorite. Basta Pasta was founded in 1977 and reopened in late 1988 with a sleek new look: off-white walls accented by green and burgundy ceramic tile strips and set off by dark wood trim. A ceramic tile wood-fed pizza and calzone oven is a focal point of the open kitchen downstairs. Upstairs, folks can dine beneath a skylight.

Only a bathtub painted with comic caricatures survives from the old, funkier Basta Pasta. The versatile menu and long hours remain; we like to wander into this cheerful place at midnight and order a plate of predictable pasta. Although the menu lists hearty southern Italian fare such as fresh-made pastas, veal dishes, pizza, and calzone, its choicest entrées are fish, literally fresh off the boat. Proprietors Bruno Orsi and Lorenzo Petroni are part owners of a fishing boat. So if you seek really fresh seafood, ask what the *North Beach Star* brought in that morning.

6 THE BEST JAPANESE RESTAURANT
Yoshida-Ya

2909 Webster Street (at Union); 346-3431. Moderate; full bar. Sunday-Thursday 5 p.m. to 10:30 p.m., and Friday-Saturday 5 p.m. to 11 p.m. Reservations advised; major credit cards.

Japanese are masters at understated decor. Yoshida-Ya captures this in the simple, clean lines of its upstairs dining room with its tatami floor, shoji screens, and artfully placed folk art and ceramics. Entrées are part of this pretty picture, stylishly presented in handsome ceramics and lacquerware.

The kitchen excels at light, crisp tempuras and other traditional dishes of Nippon. It also likes to experiment, offering such curiosities as a dinner of shrimp prepared in seven different styles. And it features skewered delicacies called *yakitori,* common in Japan but not always available here. Unlike the larger Middle Eastern-style kabobs, *yakitori* is rather delicate: small, tender bits of marinated meat, seafood, and vegetables threaded onto slim bamboo skewers and broiled over a charcoal fire.

In addition to the traditional tatami rooms, the restaurant offers conventional seating for those unwilling—or unable—to enjoy leisurely dining with their legs wadded beneath them. And it offers a sleek, modern sushi and appetizer bar downstairs. A final touch: The tea accompanying the meals has a rich, nutty flavor, accomplished by mixing browned rice with the tea leaves.

7 THE BEST MANDARIN RESTAURANT
Brandy Ho's

217 Columbus Avenue (at Pacific); 788-7527; also at 450 Broadway, 362-6268. Inexpensive to moderate; wine and beer (full bar at Broadway location). Open 11:30 a.m. to 11 p.m. daily (to midnight Friday and Saturday). MC/VISA, AMEX.

Can a noisy place plastered with NO MSG signs really be the best Hunan-style restaurant in the city? It's certainly one of the liveliest, and we like the fact that Brandy S.C. Ho's spicy entrées are free of that cloying monosodium glutamate. We also like the hustle, rustle, and clatter of this place.

This is a raucous marriage of Chinese cuisine and American marketing; the food is excellent, and the servers are unusually helpful at steering Caucasians through the menu. But this is no Chinatown tourist trap; the place brims daily with local Chinese patrons and office workers from the nearby Financial District.

Although the well-prepared dishes are amply laced with those mouth-searing bits of dried red peppers, you can ask that the kitchen go easy on the hot stuff. The menu also offers more mildly spiced dishes, including some excellent steamed fish and a really fine sizzling rice soup.

If the clamor is too much, try the new, more sedate, and classy place on Broadway. "Spent lots of money, but I'm keeping prices within reason," Brandy tells us.

8 THE BEST MEXICAN RESTAURANT
Corona Bar and Grill

88 Cyril Magnin (at Ellis Street); 392-5500. Moderate; full bar. Sunday-Thursday 11:30 a.m. to 10 p.m., Friday-Saturday 11:30 a.m. to 11 p.m. Reservations accepted; major credit cards.

With many diners losing their enthusiasm for air-dried tomatoes and other nouveau condiments, Corona has come half-circle and switched its menu from Southwestern to upscale Mexican. Since the city's numerous smashed-beans-and-rice places tend to be tortilla-wrapped clones, we've forsaken them in favor of Corona's culinary creativity.

Corona still has its appealing Southwestern look, with the requisite salmon, black, and turquoise Navajo paint job. However, the menu has shifted south of the border to feature grilled chicken breast with black beans and tomato salsa, shrimp enchiladas, spiced lamb on corn *masa,* and such. If you've traveled south of San Diego or the Rio Grande, you know that fine *restaurantes* in Mexico feature seafood, and you'll find some excellent examples emerging from Corona's kitchen. Some of the Southwestern *nouveau* remains on the menu; the Petaluma duck burritos with corn *pasitas,* avocado, and red chili salsa are curiously tasty.

9 THE BEST MIDEASTERN CAFÉ
The Grapeleaf

4031 Balboa Street (at Forty-first Avenue); 668-1515. Moderate; full bar.
Dinner 6:30 p.m. to 10:30 p.m. Wednesday-Saturday; 5:30 p.m. to 9:30 p.m.
Sunday. Reservations accepted; MC/VISA, AMEX.

When we feel the need to party, we gather a group of friends, adjourn to the Grapeleaf, and put ourselves in the capable hands of Gabe and Suzy Michael.

They cover our table with spicy Lebanese and other Mideastern delicacies and keep the wine flowing. They'll begin the banquet with a *mezza* appetizer tray of tiny *dolmas,* chick-peas, and spicy bits of meat and vegetables, then follow with kabobs of seasoned lamb or spiced fish, accompanied with marinated vegetables rich enough to serve as entrées. Between bites, we pause to study the aerobics of the resident belly dancer as she squiggles past, inviting us to tuck dollar bills into her skimpy waistband.

Diners can enjoy quiet evenings here as well; dancers don't perform every night, and the lantern-lit courtyard can be quite cozy and intimate. Incidentally, the Grapeleaf is one of the least expensive Mideastern restaurants in the city.

We once spent a month traveling through Turkey and came away delighted by the good-natured, warmhearted people and their great array of rich foods. The Grapeleaf, with its Mediterranean courtyard decor and Middle Eastern ambiance, beams us right back there.

10 THE BEST SOUTHEAST ASIAN RESTAURANT
Straits Café

3300 Geary Boulevard (at Parker); 668-1783. Inexpensive to moderate; full
bar. Daily 11 a.m. to 10 p.m. Reservations accepted; MC/VISA, AMEX.

It was difficult to make a selection among the scores of Vietnamese, Thai, Indonesian, Malaysian, and other Southeast Asian restaurants in the city. Then we discovered an appealing little place that covers virtually all of these cooking styles.

Straits Café takes its name from the Strait of Malacca at the tip of Singapore. At this international crossroad, the food reflects the culinary cultures of China, Malaysia, Indonesia, Thailand, and India. Peanut sauce, lemon grass, basil, and hot chilies make themselves heard in this cuisine.

Chef-owner Chris Yeo's ethnic roots are Malaccan—Chinese who settled in Singapore two centuries ago—and that cultural link is evident in his restaurant's fare. Try the *hai nan* chicken with ginger-chili sauce, showing a north China influence; lamb *korma* with white curry sauce, which exhibits strong Indian accents; or *nonya daging redang* beef with sweet-and-sour citrus sauce, whose spicy hot roots reach into Malaysia. This intriguing variety is served in a pleasing space. Above the small, airy dining room, Yeo has created a mini Southeast Asia village scene, with a facade of shuttered windows and clothes hanging from bamboo poles.

Should you like to try preparing Malaccan food at home, he has authored a cookbook, *The Cooking of Singapore,* on sale at the restaurant.

Chapter 8

SAVORING SOMETHING SPECIAL

The Ten Best Specialty and Curiosity Restaurants

Eat, drink and be merry, for tomorrow ye diet.

—*William Gilmore Beymer*

San Francisco's dining largess is exceeded only by its variety. In addition to the scores of different types of ethnic restaurants, the hungry and the inquisitive will find places to satisfy virtually every culinary curiosity, from restaurants devoted to garlic to fancy dining parlors that float.

The Ten Best Specialty Restaurants

The following selections were compiled from extensive personal taste-testing; they are listed in no particular order.

1 THE BEST BUSINESS LUNCH RESTAURANT
Jack's

615 Sacramento Street (at Montgomery); 986-9854. Moderate; full bar.
Lunch weekdays 11 a.m. to 3 p.m., dinner Monday-Saturday 5 p.m.
to 9 p.m. Reservations accepted; AMEX only.

Long before the city's power brokers began gathering at Stars and other trendy places, Jack's was the quintessential business lunch venue. To many in the Financial District, it still is. In fact, it's one of the city's oldest restaurants, dating back to the gold rush and functioning in the same simple masonry building since 1864.

To lunch at Jack's is to retreat to that era of elegant simplicity. This is classic no-nonsense early San Francisco, a place of stern decor and straight-up martinis, efficient and not-quite-aloof black-jacketed waiters, and American-Continental fare bathed in buttery sauces. Your sole *meunière* will arrive not with *polenta* or air-dried tomatoes, but with a single small potato, peeled and boiled, adrift in the rich sauce that bathes the fillet. The tea is Lipton; a request for something herbal likely would earn you a blank stare. The wine list is excellent and stylishly overpriced. A glass of good burgundy will nudge $5.

The interior is early-day stark, with warm woods, a simple rococo frieze, bentwood chairs, and greatcoat hooks still lining the walls. The rooms upstairs, I understand, are a bit more elaborate. However, mere guidebook authors are not invited to these private dining havens of the city's real power brokers.

Although it's noted primarily as a lunch place, Jack's serves an excellent *prix fixe* dinner for under $20.

2 THE BEST SAN FRANCISCO SUNDAY BRUNCH
The Garden Court at the Sheraton Palace Hotel

*639 Market Street (at New Montgomery); 392-8600. Moderate; full bar.
Sunday brunch 10:30 a.m. to 2 p.m.; breakfast, lunch, and dinner the rest
of the week. All major credit cards.*

Other hotel brunches are equally lavish and tempting, but none is offered in a more handsome setting than the Garden Court, with its soaring spaces beneath a domed skylight. White-clothed tables are arrayed with alluring displays of goodies, all bathed with warm amber light from the dome.

This opulent room, known as the Grand Court when the hotel opened in 1875, was described by one critic as the world's most beautiful restaurant. It's a study in Victorian opulence with its great glass dome, marble Ionic columns, elaborate chandeliers, and statues in scalloped corner niches. Completely renovated in the early 1990s, it sparkles with new paint and polish—as splendiferous as it was more than a century ago.

3 THE BEST DIM SUM RESTAURANT
Harbor Village

*Four Embarcadero Center (off the Embarcadero); 781-8833. Moderate; full bar.
Dim sum lunch 11 a.m. to 2:30 p.m. weekdays, 10:30 a.m. to 2:30 p.m.
Saturday and 10 a.m. to 2:30 p.m. Sunday; dim sum also available during
evening meal service, 5:30 p.m. to 9:30 p.m. daily. MC/VISA.*

Dim sum means "little hearts" or "to touch the heart" in Chinese. That's a nice way of describing an array of tasty morsels, usually three to a plate, served by waiters and waitresses who hurry by your table with temptingly laden carts. (A *dim sum* dining tip: If a cart is nearly empty, wait for the next one to come, for the food may have cooled.)

The city's *dim sum* restaurants rival its sushi bars in number, and we've sampled most of them. Although many cafés specialize in these morsels, our favorite *dim sum* venue is an attractive full-service Hong Kong-based restaurant in Embarcadero Center. When Harbor Village opened a few years ago, it gained quick fame for its creative, skillfully prepared Hong Kong/Cantonese fare. In menu and appearance, it's a far cry from the ordinary mom-and-pop cafés of Chinatown. Overlooking Justin Herman Plaza, this light and airy restaurant has an appealing mix of modern and traditional Chinese decor.

Its extensive *dim sum* selection ranges from classic items to savory new creations. They're served on the traditional carts during lunch and are available as individual orders with dinner. Among our favorites are the excellent baked pork buns with wonderful glazed crusts and spicy fillings, rich shrimp puffs, steamed tofu stuffed with crab, and sweet rice dumplings with chicken fillings. For a spicy departure from the conventional, try the curried calamari. Although most of the traditional fare is always available, specialty selections change daily. All *dim sum* items are prepared and assembled on the premises. On a busy weekend, cooks and their assistants will shape and wrap as many as fifteen thousand dumplings by hand.

4 THE BEST JOE-STYLE RESTAURANT
Original Joe's

144 Taylor Street (at Turk); 775-4877. Italian-American; inexpensive to moderate; full bar. Daily 10:30 a.m. to 1:30 a.m. MC/VISA.

What, you may query, is a Joe-style restaurant? It's a San Francisco creation, dating from 1934. Entrepreneur Frank Venturi decided to build a new kind of Italian *trattoria* with an open kitchen, where diners could watch their food being prepared. However, he had a problem common to most of us: insufficient capital. Nightclub owner Joe Morelio offered to stake him; in gratitude, Venturi named his place New Joe's. He was so successful that he sold out in 1937 and opened a larger café, called Original Joe's. This was a more stylish joint with a dining room in addition to the open kitchen area, and the waiters wore tuxedos.

Joe restaurants have spread far and wide, and the open kitchen concept has been copied in recent years by trendy nouveau places. Original Joe's survives— which is surprising, since it sits on the edge of the Tenderloin, the city's scruffiest downtown area. However, the neighborhood is gradually improving, mostly through the hard work of Vietnamese immigrants.

Little has changed at Joe's, including some members of the staff who have been here more than forty years. The basic Italian fare is generous and quite good, and the prices are great, since the mortgage was paid decades ago. For instance, you can get pasta dinners for $6 to $8 and half a fried chicken for $9. Original Joe's also serves an excellent hamburger—an imposing chunk of beef wedged into a slab of french bread.

You don't have to tell them "Joe sent me" to gain admission, although you might have to brush past a panhandler outside. Inside, the look is well-kept thirties, with plush curved booths, wood paneling, and the celebrated open kitchen. It fills the place with good smells of garlic and olive oil.

5 THE BEST PLACE FOR RIBS
Bull's Texas Café

25 Van Ness Avenue (at Oak, just above Market); 864-4288. Inexpensive to moderate; full bar. Monday-Saturday 11 a.m. to 11 p.m., Sunday 3 p.m. to 9 p.m. Major credit cards.

This Civic Center haven for urban (if not urbane) cowboys is the proper place for tasty ribs done over a wood-fired barbecue. Select from a menu featuring huge portions of pork ribs, brisket of beef, or barbecued chicken, all slathered in a savory sauce that's just an inch from being too rich. You have a choice between mild or spicy. Texas-style beans 'n' biscuits, coleslaw, or mashed potatoes with rural gravy are suitable accompaniments. Very good hamburgers and Tex-Mex fajitas and nachos also appear on the menu.

The place has physical as well as Texas-culinary appeal. It's Hard Rock Café gone country, with cactus, pitchforks, plank floors, allergy-free hay bales, rough-hewn wooden furniture, and Waylon Jennings wailing on the jukebox.

6 THE BEST FIFTIES CAFÉ
Mel's

2165 Lombard Street (at Fillmore), WA 1-3039; also at 3355 Geary Boulevard (at Parker), EV 7-2244. Inexpensive; wine and beer. Open 6 a.m. to 1 a.m. Sunday-Thursday and 6 a.m. to 3 a.m. Friday-Saturday. No credit cards.

The fifties-sixties nostalgia wave has swept a pair of American Graffiti drive-ins back into San Francisco. Steven Weiss, whose father created California's original Mel's, opened a shiny new version on Lombard in 1986, followed by another on Geary the next year.

These aren't done to decorators' excess, like many of the new, contrived nostalgia diners. They're reasonable facsimiles of Dad's original, with jukebox outlets on Formica tables and green-trimmed vinyl booths. They return me to the fifties, when I tooled around southern California in my pre-war Chevy, flirting with carhops in their doily-sized aprons. However, with parking at a premium, the new versions don't offer carhop service.

The menu is from my past, too, offering lemon Cokes, banana splits, Mel Burgers, and—good grief—they even brought back the fried egg sandwich. Will chicken-fried steak and lime phosphates be next?

7 THE BEST PIZZA PARLOR
Pizzeria Uno

2200 Lombard Street (at Steiner), 563-3144; also at 2323 Powell Street (near Fisherman's Wharf), 788-4055; and Two Embarcadero Center (podium level) 397-8667. Inexpensive; full bar. Open 10 a.m. to 11:30 p.m. Monday-Thursday, 11 a.m. to 12:30 a.m. Friday-Saturday, and noon to 11:30 p.m. Sunday; hours may vary at some locations. MC/VISA.

Hard choices faced us here; we've had excellent pizzas at Vicolo Pizzeria (Ghirardelli Square, and 201 Ivy near the Civic Center), Basta Pasta (1268 Grant), and the new Moose's (1652 Stockton). However, after a new round of taste-testing, Uno still leads our pepperoni parade, with its deep-dish Chicago-style pizza.

Our victor was the Uno Special; we were impressed by its rich herbal flavor and thick thatch of fresh melted cheese, tomatoes, onions, green peppers, and mushrooms over the pepperoni-sausage-tomato sauce filling. The crust is wonderfully crunchy. With its abundant topping, you get about twice the mileage from an Uno as from a conventional pizza. It's served steaming hot from the oven in its own personal metal pan. These are handmade pizzas, so plan on a fifteen- to twenty-minute wait.

We also like the cheerful decor of the three Uno branches, with their wood-paneled, upbeat 1800s Chicago look.

8 THE BEST VEGETARIAN RESTAURANT
Greens at Fort Mason

Building A, Fort Mason Center; 771-6222. Moderate; wine. Lunch Tuesday-Thursday 11:30 a.m. to 2 p.m., Friday-Saturday 11:30 a.m. to 2:15 p.m.; café dinners Tuesday-Thursday 5:30 p.m. to 9:30 p.m.; prix fixe dinners Friday-Saturday 6 p.m. to 9:30 p.m.; Sunday brunch 10 a.m. to 2 p.m.; bakery counter Tuesday-Saturday 8 a.m. to 4:30 p.m. and Sunday 9:30 a.m. to 3:30 p.m. Reservations accepted; MC/VISA.

When this spacious restaurant opened in a Fort Mason warehouse in 1979, its rich vegetarian dishes created a sensation amongst local dining wags. Reservations were required weeks in advance, even for lunch. A day or so is sufficient these days, although it still gets crowded on weekends.

Food quality hasn't suffered during the passing years; perhaps it has even improved. This is an "only in San Francisco" place: a Zen Buddhist restaurant serving vegetarian dishes in a former U.S. Army supply depot. The chefs do a remarkable job of showcasing their culinary talents. When their ragouts, pastas, and mesquite-grilled brochettes emerge from the kitchen, you'll swear they aren't vegetarian dishes. Entrées are so hearty and full-flavored that you'll forget they're meatless, fishless, and chickenless.

This former cargo shed is eye-appealing, with natural wood risers, pony walls, and potted plants to offset the warehouse look of its thirty-foot ceilings. And the view across the bay is imposing. The Zen Center also operates an outlet of its Tassajara bakery and take-out counter here, offering wonderfully hearty breads, muffins, and desserts. Incidentally, the restaurant recently released a new vegetarian cookbook by Annie Somerville called *Fields of Greens*.

9 THE BEST SAN FRANCISCO HOFBRAU
Lefty O'Doul's

333 Geary Street (at Powell); 982-8900. Moderate; full bar service. Food service daily 7 a.m. to 11 p.m. No credit cards.

Of the dozen or more hofbraus that once thrived in the city, only two good ones survive: Lefty's and Tommy's Joynt (see *The Ten Most Unusual Restaurants* later in this chapter). Lefty's and its founder are part of the San Francisco legend. Lefty O'Doul was a local baseball hero a few generations ago, first as a star with the minor league San Francisco Seals, then as a major leaguer, and finally as the Seals manager. He opened this place in the fifties to serve his fans good, honest, and inexpensive slabs of spit-roasted beef, pastrami, corned beef, french dip, and ample salads. Lefty departed this vale in 1969, although his legacy survives.

This is one of downtown's least expensive diners. It's also a virtual museum of sports memorabilia. Walls brim with glossies of Lefty in action or posing with other sports greats such as San Francisco's own Joe DiMaggio. Look for the photos of the Giants coming to town from New York (to think that we almost lost them!), Willie Mayes standing in front of Seals Stadium, and—rather touching—a reproduction of a 1954 Norma Jean DiMaggio ID card.

10 THE BEST PLACE FOR DESSERT
Just Desserts

*248 Church Street (at Market), 626-5774; Three Embarcadero Center
(at Davis and Sacramento), 421-1609; 836 Irving Street (at Tenth Avenue),
681-1277; 3735 Buchanan Street (at Marina Boulevard), 922-8675.
Moderate; no alcohol. Hours vary, but are generally from 8 a.m.
to midnight. MC/VISA.*

Save room for dessert at Just Desserts. These are pleasant little cafés specializing in wonderfully rich pies, cakes, pastries, cookies, and muffins, accompanied with teas and assorted espresso drinks.

Quality is not compromised, yet a slice of decadently rich pecan tart or chocolate fudge cake, with a cinnamon-dusted caffé latté, is less expensive than dessert and coffee in a fine restaurant. Also, the pies, cakes, and cheesecakes can be purchased *en toto.* These are cheerful and upbeat places, popular with breakfast crowds and night owls. Our favorite is the 248 Church Street outlet just off upper Market, with a landscaped patio out back.

The Ten Most Unusual Restaurants

San Francisco has never been short on the curious and the cutesy, and that's certainly reflected in its restaurants. Blessed with an excess of individualists and interior decorators, the city offers a good assortment of unusual places to eat. Want to dine beside an outlaw motorcycle or in a greenhouse? How about aboard a ship that doesn't go anywhere, or would you prefer one that does? This is the place.

1 Hornblower Dining Yachts

*Pier 33, The Embarcadero (near Sansome); 788-8866. Continental cuisine on
floating restaurant yachts; expensive; full bar. Nightly dinner cruises depart at
7 p.m.; weekday lunch cruises at 11:30 a.m.; and Sunday champagne brunch
cruises at 10:30 a.m. Reservations essential; MC/VISA, AMEX.*

What could be more unusual—and romantic—than a candlelit dinner while cruising about the bay? Hornblower dining yachts, luxury restaurant ships built for on-the-bay dining, easily top our list as the city's most unusual restaurant. Most cruises are aboard the 183-foot *California Hornblower,* newly built and styled after an opulent turn-of-the-century steamer; and the *Empress Hornblower,* fashioned as a Mississippi paddle wheeler. The M/V *Monte Carlo* is a floating nightclub with buffet meal service, dance music, live entertainment, and a charity casino using Nevada-style gaming equipment.

As you sip your champagne and nibble your entrée, your sailing salon offers an ever-changing view, never following the same itinerary twice. The main dining room is as posh as a luxury liner's, with fine china, crystal, and silver set on crisp white linen. Before and after your meal, you can wander about the ship and perhaps stop by the wheelhouse to watch the skipper guide his craft through Raccoon Strait or perhaps up the Oakland Estuary. Or linger in the dining room, where a combo plays dancing music.

We've taken the dinner cruise several times through the years, and always felt it was worth the price: around $50 a person (more on weekends), including a multicourse meal, hors d'oeuvres, and entertainment. Luncheon and weekend champagne brunch cruises also are offered. Although scores of meals must be served simultaneously, the on-board kitchen and serving crew do a good job of presenting your entrées hot, on time, and properly cooked.

2 California Culinary Academy

625 Polk Street (at Turk); 771-3500. Continental; moderate; full bar. Open weekdays only; main dining room: lunch sittings at noon and 12:30 p.m. and dinner sittings at 6 p.m., 6:45 p.m., and 7:30 p.m.; Brasserie: lunch 11:45 a.m. to 1:15 p.m.; Academy Grill: lunch 11:30 a.m. to 2 p.m. and appetizers 3 p.m. to 9 p.m. Reservations essential for dinner; no reservations for lunch; major credit cards.

Dining at the California Culinary Academy can be a bit of a gamble, since you're relying on the skills of students to create a properly prepared breast of pheasant. All preparation, cooking, and serving are done by academy pupils.

Of course, they work under the watchful eyes of master chef-instructors, so most of our experiences here have been rewarding. And the setting is certainly impressive. Several years ago, the school moved from limited quarters on Fremont Street to the great open spaces of old Germania Hall (renamed California Hall during World War II), a historic landmark building at Polk and Turk.

Three restaurants are operated by the academy in the vintage structure. The main dining room occupies the lofty Grand Hall, where students serve à la carte lunches and *prix fixe* full-course dinners. Expanses of glass allow diners to watch the students stirring their sauces in the kitchens. The Brasserie offers international lunches, and the Academy Grill, a comfortable old basement bar, serves light lunches and evening appetizers.

The focus here—particularly in the main dining room—is on the classic cuisines of Europe, and the prestigious cooking school has graduated some of the country's leading chefs.

The academy also operates a Culinary Shoppe and Café, selling the students' baked goods, pastries, salads, and pâtés; hours are 8:30 a.m. to 6 p.m.

3 Caribbean Zone

55 Natoma Street (between First and Second streets, south of Market); 541-9465. Caribbean/tropical; moderate; full bar. Lunch Monday-Friday 11:30 a.m. to 3:30 p.m., dinner Monday-Thursday 5 p.m. to 10 p.m., Friday-Saturday 5 p.m. to 11 p.m., and Sunday 5 p.m. to 9:30 p.m. Reservations accepted; major credit cards.

Fancy this: Your battered old DC-3 Gooney Bird crash-lands on a jungle island so, like those guys in the beer truck commercial, you turn it into a lively restaurant.

Herb Caen calls this place a must see, and we agree. Housed in a corrugated shack in alley-like Natoma Street, it's a happy blend of tropical vegetation, water-falls, and cozy booths in Gunite grottoes. The Gooney Bird fuselage offers bar seating and—a nice gimmick—the windows are video terminals. Don't let the deliberately scruffy look fool you, however. This place is right out of a restaurant management school designer's manual. If you gotta have a gimmick, it's a good one.

The menu is predictably Caribbean/Cajun, featuring food such as spicy jerked chicken, conch fritters, and ground steak wrapped in plantains (stubby little bananas). A range of steaks and seafood is offered as well, plus seafood salads with interesting accoutrements such as toasted cashews and papaya dressing. For dessert—key lime pie, of course.

4 The Gold Spike

527 Columbus Avenue (at Green); 421-4591. Italian; inexpensive; full bar. Open 5 p.m. to 10 p.m. Sunday, Tuesday, and Thursday; 5 p.m. to 10:30 p.m. Friday-Saturday, closed Monday and Wednesday. Reservations for six or more; MC/VISA, DISC.

The wonderfully cluttered Gold Spike dates back to Prohibition, when the Mechetti family opened the Columbus Candy Store here. Natalina peddled lico-rice whips up front while Paul stirred spaghetti sauce and bathtub gin in the back.

The licorice whips are gone, and gin comes from bottles lining the busy old bar, but not much else has changed. Walls and ceilings drip with war souvenirs (pick your war), corsets, moose heads, faded photos, and about ten thousand busi-ness cards. It looks like a pioneer museum that exploded. The menu is small, and the food's remarkably good; we've enjoyed such Italian standards as veal *par-migiana* and *scampi,* with lots of pasta and sourdough bread. The price for a full dinner is around $12.

We've eaten here a dozen or more times and have always waddled away happy. I recall one evening when service was curiously slow; it's usually moder-ately prompt. The waitress came over to apologize: "Sorry, but we had to redo your scampi. The cook dropped the first batch on the floor."

You have to like this place.

5 Hard Rock Café

1699 Van Ness Avenue (at Sacramento); 885-1699. American Graffiti menu; moderate; full bar. Open 11:30 a.m. to 11:30 p.m. daily. No reservations; MC/VISA, AMEX.

This certainly qualifies for our list of unusual restaurants; it's a wild and wacky melee of fifties and sixties excess. Like many of the city's overdone nostal-gia cafés, the focus is more on the outlandish decor than on the menu. Perhaps the management should start charging admission and give the food away.

Actually, the food has improved since we last reviewed the place, from ordi-nary to not bad. And generally, you can get inside these days, although crowds of eager teenagers sometimes spill onto Van Ness Avenue. However, go for the look more than the food. Struggle into your old letterman's jacket, pick up a glass of wine at the island bar, and wander around saying things like: "Wow, catch this! Hey, neat, man!"

Study the candy-apple red 1959 Cadillac convertible emerging from a wall, the Elvis posters, the plastic dairy cow, Waylon Jennings's guitar, the outlaw motorcycle atop the bar, and the football helmets dangling from the high ceiling of this former auto dealership.

Like, you're really gonna dig it.

6 Isobune Sushi

1737 Post Street (in Japan Center); 563-1030. Sushi and sashimi; moderate; beer, wine, and sake. Open 11:30 a.m. to 10 p.m. daily. No reservations; MC/VISA.

We were skeptical when we first tried this place. A restaurant that serves sushi by launching it on little boats that float past diners? A Tokyoesque tourist gimmick, right? But Betty, who has an excellent sushi palate, confirms that it's as tasty and fresh as most of the other sushi served in the city. Prices are comparable to other places (which isn't cheap, if you can put away as much sushi as my wife can).

Actually, it's kind of fun, watching two sushi chefs deftly shaping bits of rice and seafood and setting them afloat in the narrow mini-moat that surrounds the oval seating counter. You merely pluck your selections from the little wooden barges as they pass. Pricing is simple, too, based on the design of the plates you've plucked; the waitress totals your stacked-up dishes and presents your bill.

7 Sailing Ship Dolph Rempp Restaurant

Pier 42, China Basin; 777-5771. Seafood; moderately expensive to expensive; full bar. Pre-arranged luncheons available; dinner 6 p.m. to 10 p.m. Tuesday-Saturday. Reservations advised; major credit cards.

Dolph Rempp's Sailing Ship doesn't sail around the bay with the Hornblower dining yachts; it's firmly dry-docked at Pier 42. But it's equally opulent inside, and the food is usually excellent. It serves an assortment of American regional cuisine, often with Continental accents.

Built in 1908 as a gaff-rigged three-masted schooner, the ship carried lumber and spices between the North Atlantic, Africa, and the South Seas. Now it carries a small cargo of diners through a very stylish lunch or dinner. A few years ago, Dolph converted the menu from seafood modest to Continental expensive, creating a classy environment with tables set as elegantly as any of the city's other fine restaurants. The lower deck houses a lively cocktail lounge.

8 San Francisco Brewing Company

155 Columbus Avenue (at Pacific); 434-3344. Pub grub; inexpensive; wine and beer. Open 11:30 a.m. to 12:30 a.m. Monday-Wednesday, 11:30 a.m. to 1:30 a.m. Thursday-Friday, and noon to 1:30 a.m. Saturday-Sunday. AMEX.

This is San Francisco's first brew pub, a place that produces its own beer and offers suitable pub grub to match its frothy offerings.

Opened in 1986 by brewmaster Allan Paul, it's housed in the old Albatross Saloon space, with the famous belt-driven horizontal ceiling fan rig still in place. Historians claim that Jack Dempsey was once a bouncer here and that Baby Face Nelson was nabbed in a back room by the Feds during Prohibition. Paul has refurbished the 1907 mahogany bar and retained much of the character of the old place, while sprucing it up. Think of it as a grand old saloon with the addition of gleaming copper brew kettles.

Paul serves home-brewed beers with names like Emperor Norton Lager and Albatross Lager, made with malted barley and whole-leaf hops in the hearty style of European beers. He offers other boutique brews, including San Francisco's Anchor Steam, of course. Accompaniments include grilled sausages, sandwiches, fresh gumbo, assorted salads, and a chili with his special brew as one of the ingredients. Diners and quaffers also can arrange a tour through the copper kettle finery of his brewery.

9 The Stinking Rose

325 Columbus Avenue; 781-ROSE. Northern Italian and contemporary Californian; moderate; full bar. Daily 11 a.m. to 11 p.m. Reservations accepted; MC/VISA, AMEX.

What a wonderfully inelegant name for such an appealing restaurant. Garlic-lovers of the world, grab your Binaca and unite! This Italian café, opened in 1991, is your mecca. Beneath garlands of garlic, you can dine on garlic chicken, pork chops with garlic, fresh pepper Atlantic salmon with garlic, plus conventional ravioli, lasagna, and other pastas, which—incidentally—are seasoned with garlic.

This shrine to the stinking rose is a very attractive place: Italian moderne with black-and-white floor tiles and marble tabletops. You probably won't be surprised to learn that there is a garlic shop at the entrance. Nor should you be alarmed by the establishment's slogan: We Season Our Garlic with Food.

10 Tommy's Joynt

1101 Geary (at Van Ness Avenue); 775-4216. Hofbrau; inexpensive to moderate; full bar. Open 11 a.m. to 2 a.m. daily. Major credit cards.

If you think this legendary place with its wonderful old San Francisco murals is only a tourist trap, check the necktie-clad crowd of bureaucrats and businessmen at lunchtime. Locals have been crowding into Tommy's hofbrau for decades for his thick pastrami sandwiches, corned beef and cabbage, and buffalo stew.

Tourists love it too, of course; they're drawn here by the bright old San Francisco mural on the exterior, then they stand dutifully in the serving line with the rest of us. While the white-aproned cook is slicing pastrami and dipping your sourdough bun in its juices, examine the cluttered interior of this place. Like the Gold Spike, it's a scatter of old posters, curios, and artifacts. At a long, old-style carved-wood bar, diners can choose from a long list of domestic and international beers.

Sunup with a Flair:
The Ten Best Breakfast Places

We've suggested in other chapters that San Francisco is best seen in early light, before the crowds and exhaust fumes have gathered. Obviously, such an advanced start requires fueling. To qualify for our list of the Ten Best early morning diners, an establishment must open its doors at least by 8 a.m., and preferably before. We're talking breakfast here, not brunch.

1 Doidge's Kitchen

2217 Union Street (at Fillmore); 921-2149. Daily from 8 a.m. Moderate; MC/VISA.

This popular breakfast haunt, a culinary fixture for a quarter of a century, tops our breakfast list. Start your San Francisco morning with rich, bountiful, and often innovative entrées. Although food is served through lunch, the menu is basically morning fare, featuring honey-cured ham, cinnamon french toast, buttermilk pancakes, house-baked scones, and baked poppy seed toast. Our favorite is a tasty breakfast casserole of diced new potatoes, green onions, spicy Italian sausage, and fresh-cooked tomatoes, topped with a dollop of sour cream or a poached egg.

Select from an assortment of omelets, including a peach-and-walnut-chutney number that tastes as good as it sounds. A soup of the day is added to give the egg-oriented menu a noontime tilt, and you can order wines by the glass.

Doidge's is a simply decorated little storefront café with seasonal prints lining white walls, captain's chairs pushed under burgundy tablecloths, and classical music sighing in the background. You can sit at a counter and watch breakfast happen or retire to a small nonsmokers' dining room.

2 Brother Juniper's Bread Box

1605 Sutter Street (between Larkin and Hyde); 771-8929. Monday-Friday 7 a.m. to 2 p.m., Saturday 7 a.m. to 12:30 p.m., closed on the Sabbath. Inexpensive to moderate. No credit cards.

Brother Juniper has become something of a whole earth celebrity chef, noted for his wholesome *straun* bread and hearty organic breakfasts. Try the Brother Juniper special of avocado, cream cheese, bacon, tomato, and sprouts or the Happy Hermit club sandwich with turkey, ham, Swiss and cheddar cheese on roasted three-seed bread. Breakfast isn't too early for dessert, so finish your sunrise meal with his Hollywood cheesecake or excellent carrot cake.

You have a second motivation for dining here. Proceeds from his homey little café go to the support of the Raphael House, which shelters San Francisco's homeless.

3 Caffé Roma

414 Columbus Avenue (at Vallejo); 391-8584. Daily from 7 a.m. Inexpensive to moderate; MC/VISA.

Morning is a wonderful time for strolling along Columbus Avenue in North Beach. The exhaust fumes haven't yet accumulated, and you may hear an aria from an Italian opera, drifting from a bay-window apartment—or at least a street musician playing a wailing sax. Our preferred North Beach breakfast stop is the venerable Caffé Roma, with its pastel cherubic murals, marble tables, and bent-wood chairs—a vision from a side street in Rome.

This long-established Italian café is noted mostly for pastas, although the menu has a strong breakfast focus. Try the Roma omelet with salami, scallions, mushrooms, and peppers; vegetarian omelet; spinach and sour cream omelet; or create one of your own. Cappuccinos and espressos provide caffeine fuel to get your system started.

4 Chinatown Breakfast

Golden Dragon takeout at 833 Washington Street (between Grant and Stockton), 398-4550, daily from 8 a.m.; MC/VISA; New Ping Yuen at 1125 Stockton Street (between Jackson and Pacific), 433-5571, opens at 5:40 a.m., no credit cards; Sandy's Restaurant 1040-A Stockton Street (between Washington and Jackson), 989-0477, opens at 7 a.m., no credit cards. All three inexpensive.

Chinatown is another great place to start your day, as we pointed out in Chapter 2. The busy community wakes from its fitful sleep as merchants sweep away yesterday's litter, fashion vegetable displays in perfect geometry, and shape mounds of shaved ice, preparatory to displaying fresh fish.

Although *dim sum* is certainly popular in Chinatown, that's more of a mid-morning to lunch repast. A more traditional Chinese breakfast is *jook,* a curiously bland rice gruel, which is enlivened with sliced mushrooms, green onions, and bits of other vegetables, meat, poultry, or fish.

You may feel more comfortable having your breakfast *jook* at the neat and tidy Golden Dragon takeout, across the street from the main restaurant. It has a dining area, so you don't have to slurp your *jook* on the street. For the more adventurous, try a taste of old Chinatown at New Ping Yuen (new it certainly isn't), a scruffy place on busy Stockton Street. Be advised that you'll likely be the only non-Asian in the place, and you may be sharing a littered table with old men puffing on stubby cigarettes. The *jook,* however, is excellent—reasonably priced and served in huge portions. Try the fish Five Precious for $3.70, or the pork, kidney, or liver combos for a bit more than $2. Slightly less tatty than New Ping Yuen is Sandy's Restaurant, noted for its excellent glazed duck (those naked, golden brown birds you see hanging in Chinatown windows). It's a tiny cellar place with a few tables, also frequented mostly by locals.

Fried crullers the size of mini-baguettes, sometimes called Chinese doughnuts, are proper companions to *jook,* and it's okay to dunk. New Ping Yuen doesn't serve them, but the Golden Dragon and Sandy's do.

5 Diller's Delicatessen

348 Pine Street (corner of Leidsdorf alley); 391-5650. Awake at 5:15 a.m., whether you are or not. Inexpensive; no credit cards.

Stockbrokers hit the city's Financial District with the first tick of a Wall Street ticker, and several deli cafés rise with the roosters to provide breakfast. Oldest of the lot is Diller's, which has been serving scrambled eggs with ham or bacon since 1908. Breakfast croissants, pastries, and bagels reside in the deli counter, waiting to be washed down with Peerless coffee.

Diller's is housed in an ancient masonry structure, held up by fluted columns and adorned by high coffered ceilings. It's a pleasing island in time amidst the modern high-rises of the Wall Street of the West.

6 Eagle Café

Pier 39 (at the Embarcadero); 433-3689. Open at 7:30 a.m. Inexpensive to moderate; MC/VISA.

This appealing old survivor, a San Francisco fixture since 1928, was moved lock, stock, and weathered siding to Pier 39 from its original location in 1978. It was moved because it lay in the path of the Embarcadero Freeway. We're pleased to report that the Eagle has outlived that roadway, which was demolished after the 1989 Loma Prieta earthquake.

Sitting just off the Embarcadero on the second deck of Pier 39, it's a popular breakfast stop for Fisherman's Wharf-bound visitors. Our favorite here is home-made corned beef, and the eggs Benedict are excellent as well. The usual eggs, pancakes, omelets, and thick french toast also appear on the menu. During pleasant weather, you can adjourn to a balcony and admire the view across Fisherman's Wharf to the distant Golden Gate Bridge. Or stay inside and admire old waterfront photos and other early day memorabilia.

7 Eppler's Bakery

760 Market Street (corner of Grant and O'Farrell), 392-0101, Monday-Saturday from 6 a.m. and Sunday from 9:30 a.m.; 90 New Montgomery Street (between Market and Mission), 546-4166, Monday-Saturday from 6 a.m. and Sunday from 7 a.m. Inexpensive; no credit cards.

These two outlets for San Francisco's oldest bakery, dating from 1884, are full-scale cafés. The Market Street branch, sitting on the Grant Avenue and O'Farrell Street wedge, is a fine place for watching downtown come alive.

Load up on pastries, breakfast croissants, and other savories, then hit the coffee/tea bar and find a table beside one of the big picture windows. If you really enjoy lingering and people watching, you'll be pleased to know that refills are only 25 cents.

8 Lou's Pier 47

300 Jefferson Street (Fisherman's Wharf); 771-0377. Daily from 6 a.m. Moderate; MC/VISA.

Ticky-tacky Fisherman's Wharf enjoys its best moments early in the morning, before the wax museum opens and the tour buses hit. Come smell the steamy aroma of the crab boilers and watch the fishing boats return with their silvery cargo. And come for breakfast, either at the Buena Vista Café at Hyde and Beach (listed in Chapters 2 and 14) or at Lou's Pier 47.

Although neat little Pier 47 is noted primarily as a jazz joint featuring "cool music and hot food," it's also a worthy breakfast stop. Further, it's pretty much ignored by the tour groups, who crowd into the larger restaurants nearby. When you pull up a morning chair at Lou's, you're greeted by a gratis dish of fresh fruit. You might follow this with eggs Neptune (crab and egg on an English muffin), steak and eggs, or a shrimp and crab omelet. Breakfast is served in an Ascot interior of black and white, with checkered tablecloths to complete a simple yesterday scene.

9 One Market Restaurant

One Market Street (at Steuart); 777-5577. Breakfast weekdays from 7 a.m. to 10 a.m., Sunday brunch 10 a.m. to 1:30 p.m. Moderately expensive; major credit cards.

Chef Bradley Ogden, who put Campton Place on the culinary map, recently opened one of the city's most stylish restaurants. It has gained quick acclaim as a business lunch venue and upscale dinner restaurant. Since it opens at 7 a.m. weekdays to serve morning fare to the commute crowd, it earns a spot on our breakfast list.

Sit among Financial District shakers and start your day with a "power sunrise drink"—kefir, orange juice, banana, wheat germ, date bits, and bee pollen. Butter-milk yeast waffles with blueberry-honeycomb *beurre* are awesome. Or try lemon pancakes with fresh strawberries, or a cornmeal waffle smothered under apple but-ter. The farmer-style omelet is hardly bucolic; it's made with cured shaved ham, roasted peppers, red onions, and jack cheese. All of this is served in a light, soaring space, with picture window views of an awakening waterfront. And it's all smoke-free.

10 Seal Rock Inn

545 Point Lobos Avenue (at Forty-eighth Avenue); 386-6518. Daily from 6:30 a.m. Moderate; major credit cards.

If you drive away from the sunrise, far out on Geary Boulevard, the route curves into Point Lobos Avenue, just short of the ocean. Seal Rock Inn restaurant is tucked into that corner, with picture windows offering Pacific vistas filtered through wind-bent cypresses. It is certainly one of the city's better spots for a view breakfast.

The simple, family-style café gets serious about the morning repast, offering omelets of Spanish, Hellenic, Italian, Hawaiian, and Swedish origin, plus assorted American versions. The sour cream, shredded carrot, and banana omelet, called the Sunrise, is curiously refreshing. Eggs Benedict and homemade muffins also are menu features.

Down around the corner, Louis' Restaurant (902 Point Lobos Avenue, 387-6330; open from 6:30 a.m.) offers a better view of Seal Rocks from its basic For-mica dining room. However, the breakfast menu is rather ordinary.

Vittles with a Vista:
The Ten Best View Restaurants

We won't send you up an express elevator or down to the water's edge to enjoy a great view while tolerating mediocre food. We've dined at all of these places and determined that the fare, if not as good as the view, is at least a close second.

1 The Carnelian Room

Atop Bank of America, 555 California Street (at Montgomery); 443-7500. Continental; expensive; full bar. Open 6 p.m. to 10:30 p.m. daily; Sunday brunch from 10:30 a.m. Reservations suggested; all major credit cards. Jacket and tie requested.

Even without the view, the Carnelian Room is one of the city's better restaurants. And since it serves fine food at the city's loftiest perch, we have an easy winner. The vista from this fifty-second story is spectacular; you look *down* on most other skyrooms. When not gazing out the windows, you can admire the French antiques, exquisite tapestries, and crystal chandeliers. It's truly a handsome place, inside and out.

The menu is eclectic Continental, with tasty entrées such as Pacific baby abalone with lemon *beurre blanc,* rack of lamb with broiled marinated sweet peppers, and hot smoked sturgeon sautéed with wild mushrooms. Further, it has one of the largest wine cellars in the city. We like to arrive early to enjoy a drink—and a different view—in the adjacent cocktail lounge before adjourning to dinner.

2 Alioto's

Eight Fisherman's Wharf; 673-0183. Seafood and Italian; moderate; full bar service. Lunch and dinner daily from 11 a.m. to 11 p.m. Reservations accepted; all major credit cards.

Perched over the boat basin at Fisherman's Wharf, this longtime family-owned restaurant offers a mix of seafood and Sicilian cooking, along with an excellent picture window vista of the fishing fleet. Also providing a fine boat basin view, listed among our best seafood places in Chapter 6, is Tarantino's on the corner of the wharf and Jefferson.

3 The Cliff House

1090 Point Lobos Avenue (at Ocean Beach); 386-3330. American, mostly seafood; moderate; full bar service. Daily 9 a.m. to 4 p.m. and 5 p.m. to 11 p.m., Sunday brunch 9 a.m. to 2 p.m. Reservations accepted; major credit cards.

While it hasn't won any culinary raves of late, the Cliff House Food and Beverage Company does offer the area's best Pacific Ocean vistas. The downstairs restaurant is attractively decorated in busy, ornate Victorian patterns with *linquesta* ceilings, polished woods, and brass.

The upstairs dining room is less formal, with a slightly higher viewpoint for a slightly better view of Seal Rocks and the Pacific beyond. The downstairs P.T. Barnacle cocktail lounge, as we said in Chapter 3, is a great place to watch the sunset, and it serves light fare.

4 Fairmont Crown Room

Atop the Fairmont Hotel, 950 Mason Street (at California); 772-5131. Buffet; moderately expensive; full bar service. Monday-Saturday 11:30 a.m. to 2:30 p.m. and nightly 6 p.m. to 10 p.m., Sunday brunch 10 a.m. to 2:30 p.m. Major credit cards.

With its Nob Hill perch, the twenty-fourth-floor Crown Room offers the second loftiest dining venue in the city, after the Carnelian Room. It offers buffet dining only, and you can catch slices of the nearly 360-degree view as you move about the center serving tables. For a preview of this sky-high vista, take the Sky Lift outside elevator to the top.

5 Franciscan

Pier 43½ (at Fisherman's Wharf); 362-7733. Seafood; moderate to moderately expensive; full bar service. Sunday-Thursday 11 a.m. to 10 p.m., Friday-Saturday 11 a.m. to 10:30 p.m. Reservations accepted; major credit cards.

While neighbor Alioto offers a view of the boat basin, the Franciscan allows its diners to scan the bay, Alcatraz, Angel Island, and the waterfront. The menu, while not particularly innovative, offers a proper assortment of seafoods and pastas. They're served in an attractive nautical dining room with floor-to-ceiling windows to maximize the view.

6 Gabbiano's Restaurant and Oyster Café

One Ferry Plaza (just south of the Ferry Building); 391-8403. American, mostly seafood; moderate to moderately expensive; full bar service. Lunch Monday-Friday 11:30 a.m. to 2:30 p.m., dinner Wednesday-Sunday 5:30 p.m. to 9:30 p.m., Sunday brunch 10:30 a.m. to 2:30 p.m. Downstairs Oyster Café open Monday-Saturday 10 a.m. to 3 p.m. Reservations accepted upstairs; major credit cards.

This cheerfully sunny establishment, done up in brass and pastels, provides fine bayside views in the upstairs dining room, looking north toward the Golden Gate. An imposing glass-roofed cocktail lounge and café downstairs provides views east across the bay, along the south waterfront, and heavenward.

The restaurant menu gallops from seafood to steaks and a few chops; lighter fare is served downstairs. For those with an architectural curiosity, Gabbiano's is built over the ventilation shaft for BART's transbay tubes. Sketches and blueprints on a wall illustrate its configuration.

7 Julius' Castle

1541 Montgomery Street (at Union); 362-3042. Continental; moderately expensive; full bar service. Dinner nightly 6 p.m. to 10 p.m. Reservations accepted; major credit cards.

Wedged high into the slope of Telegraph Hill, this turreted castle offers picture window vistas of the city at its feet and the bay beyond. Refurbished a few years ago, it features an interior to rival the views, with Victorian high-backed chairs, rich wood paneling, and glittering chandeliers. The food is contemporary

European. The "castle" was built as an elaborate mansion by one Julius Roz in 1922; it later functioned as a private club before its 1980s conversion to a restaurant.

8 Neptune's Palace

Pier 39; 434-2260. Seafood; moderate to moderately expensive; full bar. Open 11 a.m. to 11 p.m. daily. Reservations advised during summer; major credit cards.

Most Pier 39 restaurants offer something of a view, since this tourist trap wharf thrusts into the bay. Perched at the far end, Neptune's provides the finest vistas, and it's easily the best restaurant out here. The handsome early San Francisco Victorian dining rooms rise above the tackiness of the rest of the pier. (It earned a niche as one of the city's Ten Best seafood restaurants in earlier editions of this book.)

The kitchen keeps pace with cooking trends, offering lightly done, subtly sauced seafood dishes. One of the original Pier 39 restaurants, Neptune's has survived where others have failed. With consistently good food at the pier's best view, it should continue to thrive.

9 The Rotunda

In Neiman-Marcus at 150 Stockton Street (at Union Square); 362-4777. American-Continental; moderately expensive; full bar. Lunch Monday-Saturday 11 a.m. to 5 p.m. Reservations accepted; AMEX.

The view here is mostly inward. This distinctive circular balcony restaurant is suspended beneath the opulent leaded-glass dome of Neiman-Marcus; old-timers such as ourselves remember it as City of Paris.

Diners can gaze up at the canopied dome's seafaring scene, down at the stylishly tiered shopping floors, or out across Union Square. This high-class cutesy café offers safe haven for shoppers who've exhausted their feet and their credit cards. The fare is predictably upscale, and lightened for lunch. It ranges from roast rack of lamb and scallop *piccata* to lobster club sandwiches and smoked chicken *carbonara*.

10 Victor's

In the Westin St. Francis, 335 Powell Street (at Geary); 956-7777. Contemporary American; expensive; full bar. Dinner nightly 6 p.m. to 10 p.m. Reservations accepted; major credit cards.

One of the city's more regal restaurants, Victor's doesn't need its thirty-second-floor perch atop the St. Francis tower to draw patrons. The view—downtown and to the south—is a bonus in this opulent dining room. Floral drapes, oriental carpeting, massive chandeliers, and other upscale decorator touches provide an equally pleasing visual impact.

The American nouveau menu is excellent, if pricey. A five-course "California dinner" goes for $55, or you can choose creatively prepared and interestingly spiced entrées ranging from medallions of venison to breast of free-range chicken.

For the uninitiated, a free-range chicken is a cluck that flew the coop.

But not for long.

Chapter 9

THE LUNCH BUNCH

Lists of the Ten Best Places to Enjoy Noontime Nibbles

Fry one, hold the mayo!
—Any waitress in any Chicago diner

The Ten Best Burger Lunches

If you were to pick the traditional All-American lunch, it probably would be the hamburger. So it's not unusual to find assorted publications in earnest quest for the best burger in captivity. However, what's the use of a wonderful hamburger if the accompanying shoestring potatoes have the consistency of shoelaces? Or if the wine you ordered to complement your noontime nibble is so tannic it could be used to preserve lab specimens?

What we seek, therefore, is the Ten Best burger *lunches*. And by burger, we mean a cheeseburger. A hamburger without cheese is incomplete, like pasta without the sauce. Our lunches also include fries, the condiments that accompany the burger, and a glass of red: whatever the establishment pours as its basic house wine. We weren't looking for economy here, but for the best burger lunch that money could buy. Predictably, none of the fast-food heat-lamp places survived the cut, although we gave them a fair test.

Our burger standards are simple but unyielding. The patty must be cooked as ordered (medium rare in our case), and the bun should be toasted inside to fend off the soggies. We like skins-on, thick-cut fries; shoestrings are acceptable if they're properly crisp and not greasy. The burger should be presented open-faced, with condiments on the side. This gives one the option of creating a gloppy Bumsteadburger or eating the lettuce, pickle, tomato, and whatever as a small salad. That's our preference. Why smother good, hot beef with clammy, cold lettuce?

A twenty-point system was devised to measure the key elements of a burger lunch: the patty and cheese, the bun in which they arrived, condiments and fries, wine, and finally the atmosphere of the place. Since we have specific scores, we've listed winners in the order of finish. Prices include fries and a glass of house wine.

An Aside to the Health-Conscious: Yes, we *know* cholesterol-rich hamburgers are currently out of favor. However, since recent studies show that red wine lowers cholesterol, perhaps having a hamburger with wine constitutes offsetting penalties. (This, of course, is a totally unscientific observation.)

1 Moose's

1652 Stockton Street; 989-7800. Full bar. Monday-Thursday 11:30 a.m. to 11 p.m., Friday-Saturday 11:30 a.m. to midnight, Sunday 10 a.m. to 11 p.m. Major credit cards. Score 18; burger lunch price $12.70.

When Ed and Mary Etta Moose sold their Washington Square Bar and Grill and later moved across the square to open this new place, they obviously brought their hamburger recipe along. Not only does the Mooseburger place in our Ten Best, it climbs all the way to the top, barely edging out another newcomer, Harpoon Louie's. Again, we seem to be proving that the best hamburgers in San Francisco don't emerge from hamburger houses.

Moose's thick chunk of ground beef was perfectly seared, arriving on a toasted bun, with a choice of cheddar, jack, or Gorgonzola cheese. The fries were shoestring, skins on, tantalizingly salty, and perfectly crisp, fried in seasoned oil. Condiments, served on the side as they should be, consisted of lettuce, seasoned sweet pickles, and shredded red onion. The wine was a light cabernet, served in a generous-sized glass.

For ambiance, Moose's is an easy winner. The light and airy new restaurant with its open kitchen and subtle art deco touches is one of the city's more attractive cafés. It also earned a spot among our Ten Best restaurants in Chapter 5.

2 Harpoon Louie's

55 Stevenson Street (off Third Street, just south of Market); 543-3540. Full bar. Lunch 11 a.m. to 3 p.m. MC/VISA, AMEX. Score 17.5; price $11.95.

This busy lunch spot has the look of old San Francisco, with its ornate bar, dark woods, white napery, and brick-wall interior, yet it's relatively new. We were tipped by another publication to try Louie's hamburgers, and we weren't disappointed.

The meat was broiler-seared, topped with a choice of cheddar, Swiss, or jack cheese and served on a sesame bun. The fries were excellent—thick cut and skins on. The medium-bodied burgundy was ideal for the burger. Condiments were conventional—tomato slice, onion slice, dill pickle, and limp lettuce. With its rough-brick and polished-wood look, Louie's scored high in ambiance.

3 Balboa Café

3199 Fillmore Street (at Greenwich); 922-4595. Full bar. Daily 11 a.m. to 11 p.m. MC/VISA. Score 17; price $10.75.

A Marina-area institution since 1914, Balboa Café also is new to our list of select burger places. It won a nomination after we received a tip that the Balboa burger was worth a trip across town.

It certainly was. The seared, blood-rare patty arrived on a wonderfully crunchy french roll, with a choice of Swiss, jack, or cheddar cheese melted therein. Fries were shoestring, slender, and nicely brittle, with a hint of seasoning in the oil. Condiments were ordinary—a slice of red onion on the side and a tomato installed on the bun. The house red was mellow, quite pleasant if a bit light for a hamburger.

Like the first two winners, Balboa scores high on ambiance, with its old-style drop lamps, large oak bar, and an occasional potted palm. It's primarily a lively saloon with a café attached. In addition to the $8.25 Balboa burger, you can get a $5.75 Bar Burger which—curiously—is served only at the bar.

4 The Holding Company

Two Embarcadero Center (between Davis and Front streets); 986-0797. Full bar.
Lunch 11 a.m. to 3:30 p.m. Monday-Friday; dinner 5 p.m. to 10 p.m. Monday-
Thursday, 5 p.m. to 11 p.m. Friday. Major credit cards. Total points: 16.5;
price $9.75.

This popular lunch spot for the lower Market Street white-collar crowd placed fourth in our competition. The burger is a hefty thing, a half-pound patty on either a crusty bun or a sourdough roll. Cheese choices are cheddar, jack, or Swiss. Our thick, juicy patty had a nice smoky flavor, accompanied with the usual lettuce, tomato, and a formidable dill pickle wedge. Fries were excellent, thick cut with the skins on and perfectly crispy. For wine, you have choices of several by the glass; we found the Mark West pinot noir to be the ideal burger associate.

The Holding Company is an attractive place with an upscale yet comfortable look: dark paneling, beveled mirrors, and bentwood chairs. It offers the option of outdoor seating under green canvas during warm weather. The view of the surrounding office towers is imposing, if you're moved by urban vistas.

5 Hamburger Mary's Organic Grill

1582 Folsom Street (at Twelfth Street); 626-5767. Full bar. Daily 10 a.m.
to 1:30 a.m. MC/VISA, AMEX. Score 15.5; price $11.81.

Mary's has leaped from tenth to fifth place since our last revision of this book. Those soggy sprouts that turned the Maryburger into a disintegrating mess have been replaced by lettuce. The thick burger arrives sliced in half, either to improve handling or to ensure that the cow died. Although no cheese choice is offered, the whole-milk cheddar is quite good. Condiments consist of chopped lettuce and tomato aboard the burger, plus a green chili on the plate.

If this were a french fries competition, Mary's would be the undisputed winner. The thick-sliced and chili pepper-dusted "home fries" are outstanding. You also have a choice of conventional fries, coleslaw, or cottage cheese. The house wine is ordinary but quite drinkable.

The look is fun; Mary's scores high for *un*-ambiance. It's a clutter of posters, pictures, doodads, curios, and knickknacks plastered over weathered wood. The music is predictably loud and the punk-rocker types who serve you are not only harmless, they're remarkably efficient and friendly.

6 Eddie Rickenbacker's

133 Second Street (at Minna); 543-3489. Full bar. Lunch 11 a.m. to 3 p.m.
MC/VISA, AMEX. Score 14; price $12.

A virtual museum of World War I memorabilia, Rickenbacker's is a popular downtown business lunch spot, so you might want to call for reservations. Check out the old-timey flying regalia, uniformed mannequins, and other displays as you work through your burger.

The large patty is served on an equally large bun, with a selection of cheeses; jack is our burger cheese of choice. Our patty was perfectly seared, with the cheese properly melted over. The fries were shoestrings—not our favorite, but these were nicely crisp. Red onion and tomato slices, and lettuce arrived on the side. The wine was one of the best on our list—a nice, mellow burgundy.

7 Hot and Hunky

1305 Polk Street (at Bush); 931-1004; 4039 Eighteenth Street (at Castro), 621-6365; and 1946 Market Street (at Duboce), 621-3622. Wine and beer; full bar adjacent to Polk Street outlet. Sunday-Thursday 11 a.m. to midnight and Friday-Saturday 11 a.m. to 1 a.m. No credit cards. Score 13.5; price $7.31.

Hot and Hunky specializes in "square meals in a round bun," so one has an extensive choice of hamburgers. We selected the Double Hot and Hunky Cheese, which most closely paralleled the competition. The double patties arrived medium rare despite their thinness—the work of an extremely alert cook. Two slices of American cheese on a toasted bun were installed around the burger. Since Hot and Hunkys are walk-up burger stands, you add your own accoutrements at a condiment station, and the selection is extensive, including relishes, onions, and the usual mustard and ketchup. The wine was ordinary, but quite drinkable.

The decor at these places is simplistic fifties, consisting mostly of Marilyn Monroe posters and photos.

8 Chestnut Street Grill

2231 Chestnut Street (at Scott); 922-5558. Full bar. Monday-Thursday 11 a.m. to 11 p.m., Friday 11 a.m. to midnight, Saturday 10 a.m. to midnight, Sunday 10 a.m. to 10 p.m. MC/VISA. Score 13; price $8.50.

Popular both as a saloon and as a café, Chestnut also earned a spot as one of the Ten Best neighborhood pubs in Chapter 14. Walls are decorated with framed alumni photos of regulars who've patronized the place through the years, and we can assume that some come for the rather good hamburgers.

Our entry was properly cooked, although not seared, and offered with a choice of Swiss, American, cheddar, or provolone, on a toasted french roll. Fries were thick cut, skins off, and quite good. Among the condiments, served on the side, were a tomato slice, white onion, limp lettuce, green chilies, and dill pickle chips. The wine was thin, barely ordinary. The ambiance is what you'd expect for a comfortable San Francisco neighborhood pub—vaguely Victorian with wooden floors and high ceilings, decorated mostly with camaraderie.

9 Bill's Place

2315 Clement Street (at Twenty-fourth Avenue); 221-5262. Wine and beer. Sunday-Thursday 10 a.m. to 10 p.m., Friday-Saturday 10 a.m. to 11 p.m. No credit cards. Score 12.5; price $6.80.

Bill's is something of a Richmond District institution, dating back to 1959. Our seared cheddar cheeseburger was installed on a toasted sesame bun, made soggy by fried onions and a dollop of mayo. Lettuce and tomato slices resided to one side, and the fries were skins-on shoestrings—not awesome, but not bad. The wine had a hint of sweetness, although passable for a burger lunch.

Bill's offers some interesting specialty burgers, named for San Francisco personalities. No, we haven't had our name attached to a beef, avocado, and alfalfa sprout creation. The café's decor is simple, consisting mostly of souvenir wall plaques of American presidents and examples of White House china lining the main dining area. There's a landscaped garden out back, for those rare days when the outer Richmond fog permits the sun to shine.

10 What's Your Beef?

759 Columbus Avenue (at Greenwich); 989-1852. Wine and beer. Monday-Saturday 11 a.m. to 5 p.m. No credit cards. Score 12; price $6.35.

This tiny walk-up burger stand with a tinier dining room is one of only three hamburger joints to make the cut. Our "contemporary gourmet burger" was properly broiled, arriving fully assembled on a soft bun with a choice of *brie,* cheddar, Swiss, *bleu,* or *feta* cheese. (Feta on a hamburger? I think not.) Fries were skinny shoestrings, served hot and crisp; they were excellent. As an interesting alternative, try the "heremade" potato chips, deep-fried on the premises and quite tasty. Condiments were the conventional ketchup, mustard, and mayo, and the wine was a good buy, a fair-sized glass of rather light burgundy for $1.95.

This is the least expensive of our burger lunch winners, and you can trim the cost even more by opting for a smaller portion of fries. If your budget's really bent, you can get a cheeseburger–fries–soft drink special for $4.95.

The Ten Best Sun-Lunch Places

We've always loved alfresco dining, enjoying a meal and a glass of wine under the sun, watching the passing parade of people. Outdoor cafés have been popular for centuries in European cities, despite unpredictable weather. We're pleased that they're becoming more prevalent in San Francisco, despite its unpredictable weather.

1 Embarcadero Center

Off the Embarcadero, near the foot of Market (between Clay and Sacramento); 772-0500.

Our clear winner isn't an outdoor café; it's a huge collection of outdoor cafés. The Embarcadero Center is a complex of four sky-rise office buildings with ground-floor and podium-level (whatever that means) shopping areas. Many of its restaurants—including the Holding Company, Scott's Seafood, and Chevy's—have tables both outdoors and in. The shopping plazas are generously sprinkled with tables, chairs, and benches for the brown-bag set.

Nearly a dozen take out cafés and food stalls are clustered around the base of Embarcadero Four, near the Hyatt Regency. Dozens of tables and chairs are a few steps away, bolted to the concrete deck of spacious Justin Herman Plaza. The assorted takeouts offer hot dogs, sushi, deli items, pizza, ice cream, fruit salads, and designer cookies.

2 Ale Garden Café

The Cannery Courtyard (2801 Leavenworth, at Columbus); 928-4340. Italian and German; wine and beer. Weekdays 11 a.m. to 5 p.m., and weekends 11 a.m. to 6 p.m. MC/VISA, AMEX.

Occupying one end of the Cannery Courtyard, this modestly priced café with red-checked tablecloths serves a mix of Italian pastas and pizzas and German sausages. Diners can choose between a sunny patio and a glass-roofed dining room. German and other international beers are featured.

The Courtyard was a railroad siding for the old Del Monte cannery before it was fashioned into a patio for the Cannery shopping complex in the 1960s. Its benches invite alfresco brown bagging, and a couple of takeouts provide quick luncheon fare. The Courtyard stage sometimes offers free entertainment, or you can step indoors—for a fee—and chuckle at the adjacent Cobb's Comedy Club.

3 City Picnic

384 Hayes Street (at Franklin); 431-8814. Wine and beer. Open 8 a.m. to 4 p.m. Monday-Friday, 10 a.m. to 2:30 p.m. Saturday. No credit cards.

The pleasant little City Picnic deli-café lures the Civic Center lunch bunch with an out-back garden patio that has a few tables, benches, and risers. It's a quiet spot, sheltered from street noise by surrounding buildings.

The Picnic specializes in generously sized sandwiches on Italian *focaccia* bread; it also features assorted salads and sandwiches on conventional breads. Should you wonder, focaccia is a tasty, seasoned bread that looks like it started out to be a pizza, then changed its mind.

4 Compadres Mexican Bar & Grill

Ghirardelli Square (at North Point and Polk); 885-2266. Mexican-American; full bar. Open 10 a.m. to 10 p.m. Sunday, 11 a.m. to 10 p.m. Monday-Thursday, and 11 a.m. to 11 p.m. Friday-Saturday. Reservations advised on weekends; major credit cards.

This brightly decorated Mexican-American restaurant spills its camaraderie onto terraces and along the outdoor walkway of the 1899 Mustard Building in Ghirardelli Square.

From its second-floor vantage, it offers a visual sweep of Aquatic Park, Hyde Street Pier, Alcatraz, and sailboats at play on the bay. Mexican handicrafts, tropical plants, and a couple of macaws named Syd and Cesar give the place a proper Latin atmosphere. On Fridays it jumps with *pan hana,* a Mexican happy hour featuring live music.

Also at Ghirardelli, Vicolo Pizzeria has a few outdoor tables, and the square itself offers several places to perch.

5 Enrico's

504 Broadway (near Columbus and Grant); 397-3011. Continental; full bar. Daily 11 a.m. to 2 a.m. MC/VISA, AMEX.

After several years' absence, this legendary sidewalk café has returned, dressed in a new European look. For decades, Enrico Banducci held court here, surrounded not by today's tawdry topless joints but by legitimate night spots such as the Purple Onion and hungry i. Phyllis Diller, the Kingston Trio, and other luminaries found fame in these Broadway clubs and likely stopped by Enrico's for a late-night cappuccino. Banducci survived the arrival of Carol Doda and her topless dance at the nearby Condor. Enrico's was the city's premier people-watching place as assorted night owls, punk rockers, conventioneers, and other wide-eyed tourists paraded among and between Broadway's topless clubs. Then as Broadway declined, the club closed and Banducci moved on.

Reopened in 1992, the new version is spiffier than the original, with a light Continental café look. The menu is contemporary, with offerings such as seafood pizza and grilled chicken in green peppercorn sauce. Liquid offerings include an extensive wine list and a good array of *cappuccinos, lattes,* and the like.

6 La Trattoria

1507 Polk Street (at California); 771-6363. Italian; full bar. Open 11:30 a.m. to 11:30 p.m. Monday-Saturday; 11:30 a.m. to 10:30 p.m. Sunday. MC/VISA, AMEX.

Although it's roofed over, La Trattoria's "outdoor" dining area is open to the street; thus, it qualifies as an alfresco café. Heat lamps keep things cozy in winter. This has been a favorite lunch spot for years, serving inexpensive lasagna, tortellini, and other Italian-American fare. Traffic noise sometimes intrudes into conversation, but that isn't La Trattoria's fault. In a civilized European city, Polk Street would have been converted into a pedestrian *shoppingstrasse* by now. If you find the growl of the 19-Polk buses too distracting, you can retreat to an inside table.

7 Mission Rock Resort

817 China Basin (at Mariposa); 621-5538. American; full bar. Open 8 a.m. to 3 p.m. Monday-Friday; 8 a.m. to 4 p.m. Saturday-Sunday; the bar and a snack bar keep longer hours. MC/VISA.

The first trick is to find this place, and don't look for a mission, a resort, or a rock. Mission Rock is a funky, weathered café and bar at the waterfront on China Basin Way, just north of the foot of Mariposa Street.

On a windless day with a high blue sky, herds of white-collar types from the Financial District crowd onto the Rock's rustic outdoor dining area on an elevated dock. They prop their elbows on weathered wooden tables, eat hearty hamburgers and assorted fish fare, and absorb views of the waterfront at work. At a large drydock nearby, you may watch a fancy cruise ship or rusting freighter being overhauled. In addition to lunch, owners Robert and Norma Wahl whip up great breakfasts, including a hefty eggs Benedict Sunday brunch that'll sink your schooner.

8 Nosheria

Maiden Lane (at Grant); 398-3557. Deli; wine and beer. Open 7 a.m. to 5 p.m. Monday-Saturday. No credit cards.

Six days a week, the folks at the Nosheria pull a few gold and blue umbrella tables into the middle of traffic-free Maiden Lane. Hungry downtowners quickly start lining up for some of the thickest pastrami and corned beef sandwiches in the city.

The Nosh also serves an assortment of salads and quiches. The sandwiches are so large that you may wind up brown bagging from these outdoor tables.

9 Olive Oil's Bar & Grill

295 China Basin Way (at Pier 50); 495-3099. American; full bar. Monday-Friday 11 a.m. to 3 p.m., weekend brunch 10 a.m. to 3 p.m. No credit cards.

This is another South of Market waterfront place with indoor-outdoor dining. Like Mission Rock, it's popular with the North of Market lunch crowd, as well as waterfront workers. Fresh-air diners sit around old wooden cable spools on a deck just above water level, with a view of downtown Oakland across the way.

If the weather's chilly, you can adjourn to glossy bartop tables inside and admire pinups of Popeye's girlfriend. There's also a pool table to help pass the time. The lunch crowd can choose from hamburgers, grilled sandwiches, and fish and chips.

10 Suisse Italia Café

101 California Plaza (California at Drumm); 362-4454. Lunch deli; wine and beer. Open 5:30 a.m. to 6 p.m. Monday-Friday. No credit cards.

This large contemporary deli serves an amazing assortment of lunchtime goodies from the ground floor of the 101 California highrise. Sandwiches, quiches, salads, and cold pastas are dispensed efficiently, then carried by hungry Financial District folks to outside tables on the spacious plaza. It's a handsome wedge of open space with potted plants, a spillover fountain, and multilevel granite risers that can be used for additional seating.

Chapter 10

BITING THE BUDGET BULLET

The Ten Best Places to Dine Inexpensively

*The most remarkable thing about my mother is that for thirty years she
served the family nothing but leftovers. The original meal has never
been found.*

—*Calvin Trillin*

There will be times when you don't want your mother's leftovers, but you're
between paydays and you'd like to avoid the price of a restaurant meal. Fortunately, the city brims with inexpensive, informal cafés serving hearty meals for
about the price of a Stouffer's Lean Cuisine and deli salad: around $7.50. We aren't
talking about fast-food places that are proliferating around San Francisco.

Hundreds of Asian cafés can offer a bowl of something-over-rice or a stir-fried
whatever for a few dollars. But that's not necessarily a complete meal. To qualify
for our list, the restaurants must offer a tasty, filling meal with a main course, and
a side dish or veggie for $7.50 or less. And they must be open for both lunch and
dinner—at least until 8 p.m.

You won't need much money at these places, but take along a little; many
don't accept credit cards. Not surprisingly, many of our winners are ethnic restaurants. The Chinese, Japanese, Vietnamese, Italians, Thais, and others who have
enriched us with their bounty have done so at remarkably little cost. That's part
of the adventure of San Francisco budget dining. You can eat cheaply and send
your tummy on an around-the-world excursion.

1 May Sun Restaurant

*1740 Fillmore Street (at Post); 567-7789. Mandarin-teriyaki; wine and beer.
Open 11:30 a.m. to 9:30 p.m. Monday-Saturday. MC/VISA, AMEX.*

May Sun is not just our favorite inexpensive café in San Francisco; it's one of
our favorite restaurants at any price. Not only are prices remarkably reasonable,
but the food is consistently excellent, and it's served in a pleasant atmosphere.
This definitely is a cut above the typical ethnic Formica food stall. And it offers
intriguing variety, since it serves both Japanese teriyaki and Chinese dishes.

We don't know how Jim Lam Ngo and his family hold the prices down, but
you can buy a full teriyaki dinner with beef, pork, or chicken with fried wonton,
green salad, rice, and a fortune cookie for $6.95. Early bird dinners, served from
3 p.m. to 6 p.m., are only $5.25, with a choice of thirteen different entrées, plus
rice, soup, and egg roll. He also does the best *kung pao* prawns in the city, as part
of a complete lunch for under $5. It's rich with succulent and tender prawns, bam-
boo shoots, bell pepper wedges, and crunchy peanuts, accompanied with rice, a

Japanese-style broth, and fruit. In fact, he has twenty different lunches under $5! The lunch and dinner menu is surprisingly varied for such a small place, with a mix of spicy Mandarin and more subtly flavored Cantonese dishes, plus the featured Japanese teriyaki dinner.

May Sun is a prim little café with white-clothed tables on a burgundy carpet. A seascape painting fills one wall; coolers of chilled wines, beers, and soft drinks occupy another. Jim provides his patrons with a rack of newspapers—an implied invitation to enjoy an unhurried meal, then relax over tea. The restaurant is in the newly gentrified area of Fillmore Street, tucked under the bay window of an attractive Victorian.

2 Anthony's Seafood and Pasta

1701 Powell Street (at Union); 391-4488. Italian-American; wine and beer. Lunch 11:30 a.m. to 3 p.m. weekdays, dinner 5 p.m. to 10 p.m. Sunday-Thursday and 5 p.m. to 11 p.m. Friday-Saturday. MC/VISA, DISC.

Although this attractive new place goes an entire forty-five cents over our budget, we must bend the rules to include it. Somehow, it manages to offer live Maine lobster dinners with corn on the cob, roasted potatoes, and garlic popovers for $7.95. It also offers several other economically priced seafood dishes, plus some filling pasta dinners for under $7.50.

3 The Bagel Deli and Restaurant

1300 Polk Street (at Bush); 441-2212. Jewish-American deli-café; wine and beer. Open from 8:30 a.m. to 11 p.m. daily. No credit cards.

This place is easy to spot; just look for the huge AGEL painted on the Bush Street side of the building; the B is on Polk. The Bagel is strong on hearty kosher dishes, and it offers a good selection of basic meat-veggie-rice entrées, dished up from an old-fashioned serving bar. It's popular with Polk Gulch and Russian Hill regulars and neighborhood beat cops.

Some under-budget examples: hot dish of the day (meat or fowl with veggies or rice and roll), $4.75; Hungarian goulash, $6.35; stuffed cabbage sweet and sour, $5.80; and a complete turkey dinner, $6.40.

4 Cordon Bleu

1574 California Street (at Polk); 673-5637. Vietnamese; wine and beer. Lunch 11:30 a.m. to 2:30 p.m. Tuesday-Saturday; dinner 5 p.m. to 10 p.m. Tuesday-Thursday, 5 p.m. to 11 p.m. Friday-Saturday, 4 p.m. to 10 p.m. Sunday. No credit cards.

Cordon Bleu is one of the city's first Vietnamese restaurants, dating from 1972. Since the day it opened, critics have been raving about its delicious, low-cost food.

The little café, tucked under the marquee of the Lumiere Theatre, specializes in succulent five-spice chicken. A couple of low-budget examples: five-spice chicken with country salad and meat sauce over rice for $5.50; or how about chicken shish kabob, imperial roll, country salad, and rice for $6.25?

5 Il Pollaio

555 Columbus Avenue (at Union); 362-7727. Italian; wine and beer.
Open 11:30 a.m. to 9 p.m. Monday-Saturday. No credit cards.

This tiny wedge of a place just off Washington Square will put half a flame-broiled chicken with salad and fries before you for $6.25. Several other chicken dinners with salad or fries and Italian sausage dinners with salad also are well under our budget.

Il Pollaio means "chicken coop," but it's much better than that. The place is neat as a pin and rather brightly decorated for a budget restaurant.

6 Little Henry's

955 Larkin Street (corner of Post); 776-1757. Italian; wine and beer. Open from
11 a.m. to 10 p.m. daily. No credit cards.

Is it Henry Martinelli or Sorrento, perhaps? Nope. Henry Heng. Although the place is Italian, Henry and his prices are very Chinese. And you can get much more than a few raviolis here for under $7.50. A few suggestions: chicken cacciatore or chicken scaloppine for $6.75, breaded pork chops for $6.50, or stuffed bell pepper for $5.50. These dinners include a vegetable, plus spaghetti or rigatoni.

Henry's is a simple-but-cute little corner café, with simulated wood-grain wainscoting and red-and-white-checkered tablecloths.

7 Nippon Sushi

314 Church Street (at Fifteenth Street); no phone. Japanese; no alcohol. Open noon
to 10 p.m. Monday-Saturday. No credit cards.

Nippon Sushi is a tiny restaurant jammed with tables and chairs a block and a half off Market; it has no identifying sign out front and no listed phone, so you can't even call and ask how to get there. Just look for a nondescript storefront filled with people eagerly eating sushi. It's on your right as you walk down Church Street from Market.

What makes this place special is its amazingly cheap prices. Sushi-lovers can get a complete meal within our $7.50 range, and the food is quite good. The joint is rather basic, with a few hard seats and an oriental artifact or two. But at these prices, hungry diners aren't sitting around admiring the decor.

8 Siam Café

807 Geary Street (at Hyde); 775-5821. Thai; wine and beer. Open 11 a.m.
to 9 p.m. Monday-Saturday. MC/VISA.

If you order one of our favorites here—shrimp, bamboo shoots, onions, and red peppers—order a glass of water as well. This dish is so hot you'll be eating the onions to cool it down. All the entrées in this tiny Thai restaurant aren't firebrands, however. The menu offers an assortment of items mildly touched with lemon grass, peanut sauce, and other gentle Thai flavorings.

What all dishes do have in common is a low price: curry of the day for $3.75; roast duck, $4.25; ginger chicken with onions and fungus mushrooms, $4. At these prices, you get a generous dollop of rice, and there's room within your budget for a couple of egg rolls for a dollar each, or fried wonton for $2.50.

9 Vietnam

622 Broadway (at Grant); 788-7034. Vietnamese; wine and beer. Open 8 a.m. to 3 a.m. daily. No credit cards.

This wee place, not much wider than a hallway, serves excellent Vietnamese fare at remarkably low prices. Customers crowd around a few small tables and perch at a narrow counter; some are served at a shelflike window table, perhaps so passersby can see them enjoying themselves. And they should be happy. They're getting five-spice barbecued chicken over rice for $3.50 and noodle soup with tomato broth for $3, which in combination is well under our budget. Several other meat and soup or veggie pairings are available for less than $7.50.

10 Village Café

1426 Polk Street (near Pine); 771-9598. American; no alcohol. Monday-Saturday 7 a.m. to 9 p.m., Sunday 7 a.m. to 4 p.m. No credit cards.

This Chinese-owned café is strictly American in its simple diner decor and its remarkably inexpensive menu. Perch on a counter stool or pull up to a Formica table and order red snapper for $6.50 or Swiss steak for $5.95. These and other complete dinners include veggies, potato, and soup or salad.

We have thus dined well—and stretched our budget to next payday. The check, please.

Chapter 11

RUN AND EAT

The Ten Best Takeouts

> *Timid roach, why be so shy?*
> *We are brothers, thou and I.*
> *In the midnight, like thyself,*
> *I explore the pantry shelf.*

> —Christopher Morley

But suppose there is nothing on that pantry shelf but a can of tuna, a bottle of soy sauce, and one forlorn cockroach, who looks as hungry as you feel? It's 6 p.m. and you're not in a mood to cook, or you're stuck in a hotel room and weary of eating out. A TV rerun of the closing episode of "Cheers" starts in half an hour, and you have some sort of moral objection to fast-food places. What to do?

Fortunately, San Francisco brims with delicatessens and other intriguing takeouts. You never need be bored by their offerings, since they come in assorted nationalities. You can dine on anything from *piroshki* to quiche.

(If you want a serious meal without venturing out, call one of two restaurant delivery services in the city. Dial Waiters on Wheels at 252-1470 or Dine-One-One at 771-DINE. They deliver meals from fifty or more restaurants. They'll also send you a menu catalog, or your hotel's concierge may have one.)

What follows is a list of our ten favorite ethnic delis and other takeouts.

1 Vivande Porta Via

2125 Fillmore Street (at California); 346-4430. Italian. Open 10 a.m. to 7 p.m. Monday-Friday, 10 a.m. to 6 p.m. Saturday, and 10 a.m. to 5 p.m. Sunday; hot food served daily from 11:30 a.m. to 4 p.m.

An Italian cornucopia of cuisine, Vivande is the most beautifully appointed delicatessen-café in the city. It features brimming cheese and deli cases, a large wine and gourmet cookbook section, and a trim little restaurant with white-clothed tables. It is indeed more than a deli; it's also a *trattoria* and *pasticceria* (pastry shop).

Vivande offers a startling variety of pâtés, cold meats, cheeses, salads, and Italian bakery goods. A specialty of the house are mesquite-smoked chicken and trout, fresh-smoked without preservatives. Vivande also has fully prepared hot dishes to take home, such as cannelloni and lasagna. If you choose to dine here, you can watch busy chefs and bakers preparing pleasing pastas and pastries in the sleek stainless-steel open kitchen.

2 David's Delicatessen Restaurant

474 Geary Street (at Taylor); 771-1600. Jewish. Open 7 a.m. to midnight Monday-
Friday, and 8 a.m. to midnight Saturday-Sunday.

David's has been the ultimate Jewish deli and late-night dining haven for after-theater crowds and other night owls since 1952. It's across the street from the Geary and Curran theaters, and its walls are trimmed with framed photos of performers past and present.

The takeout section offers a large variety of kosher foods with a Chicago accent. Featured items include cheese blintzes, corned beef, pastrami, beef tongue, and, of course, *matzo* ball soup. Desserts are a specialty, and David's napoleons and rum balls are legendary.

3 House of Piroshki Delicatessen Café

1231 Ninth Avenue (at Lincoln); 661-1696. Russian-Mideastern, specializing in
piroshkis. Open 11 a.m. to 6 p.m. Tuesday-Friday, and 10 a.m. to 6 p.m. Saturday.

This place offers a curious mix for a deli. Stepping inside, you see a small candy case featuring truffles and pastries, several soft drink coolers, and a rather sparsely furnished deli case. But the heart of this "house" is a vertical stainless-steel heat cabinet behind the counter, from which emerges the best piroshkis in San Francisco. This Russian-Mideastern specialty comes in half a dozen varieties, with spicy fillings of cheese, beef, chicken, cabbage, and various combinations thereof. Do your *piroshki* shopping early; they're made fresh daily, and by midafternoon, many varieties are gone.

4 La Victoria Mexican Bakery and Grocery

2937 Twenty-fourth Street (at Alabama); 550-9292. Mexican. Open 11 a.m.
to 10 p.m. daily.

Several Mexican delis and markets are clustered along Twenty-fourth Street between Mission and Alabama, and La Victoria is the most versatile. It's a combined bakery, grocery, deli, and restaurant. The spartan little café is in the rear, reached by a mazelike corridor from the main store (or via an entrance on Alabama). Just about everything on its menu can go home with you: tasty homemade tamales, burritos, chile rellenos, and enchiladas. And don't forget a bag of homemade tortillas and tortilla chips.

On your way out, pass through the large bakery to pick up tasty pastries such as *cocadas* (macaroons) and *churros* (long and slender sugar-dusted Mexican doughnuts).

5 Lucca Delicatessen

2120 Chestnut Street (at Steiner); 921-7873. Italian. Open Monday 10 a.m. to 6:30
p.m., Tuesday-Friday 9 a.m. to 6:30 p.m., and Saturday-Sunday 9 a.m. to 6 p.m.

For more than sixty years, this tiny family-owned *rosticceria* and deli has dispensed its famous herb-flavored, vegetable-stuffed roast chicken to the Marina

District faithful and other fans lured from the city's farthest reaches. Another specialty—rare in these days of food-processing machines—is ravioli made by hand. Roast beef and turkey also are featured, plus *frittatas,* salads, and a fair assortment of cheeses, spiced meats, sausages, and wines.

The place has that special cluttered look of a good Italian deli, with overflowing food cases and counters, and fat sausages dangling from the ceiling. Lucca modestly calls itself The Tastiest Little Deli in the World. That may sound a bit brash, but withhold judgment until you savor the roast chicken.

6 Molinari Delicatessen

373 Columbus Avenue (at Vallejo); 421-2337. Italian. Open 8:30 a.m. to 5:30 p.m. Monday-Saturday.

In business since 1896, this cluttered North Beach deli is jammed to the rafters with sacks, cans, bags, bottles, and bins of just about everything that's edible, drinkable, and Italian. Large cans of olive oil are stacked on the floor, sausage ropes and garlic strings dangle from the ceiling, specialty foods fill floor-to-ceiling shelves, wine bottles crowd display racks, windows overflow with packages of pasta. Every thinkable type of spiced meat, fresh-cooked pasta, and pasta salad is stuffed into the deli case. Molinari is the unabridged Italian deli.

7 Neiman-Marcus Epicure

150 Stockton Street (at Geary); 362-3900. American-Continental. Monday, Thursday, and Friday 10 a.m. to 8 p.m.; Tuesday, Wednesday, and Saturday 10 a.m. to 6 p.m., and Sunday noon to 6 p.m.

It follows that San Francisco's most stylish department store would shelter the city's most elegant specialty foods shop. The fourth-floor Epicure offers a rich and expensive trove of upscale wines, candies, and gourmet specialty foods.

Browse amongst the carefully assembled displays of foie gras, salmon fumé, caviar, international cheeses, designer mineral waters, Australian dessert apricots, Godiva chocolates, cranberry-orange rum cake, truffles, assorted pâtés, and—perhaps inspired by the store's Texas roots—cowboy caviar.

Should the need for a sophisticated picnic suddenly arise, you can select from an assortment of hampers. The crystal wine goblets and sterling flatware aren't far away.

8 Pier One Deli

Pier 1, on the Embarcadero (just north of the Ferry Building); 982-3686. International. Daily 6 a.m. to 4 p.m.

This versatile delicatessen-café covers the international gamut from pizza to *piroshki* and salads to hot and cold sandwiches, including rather good hamburgers. There's even a low-cal plate, in case you've sampled too many San Francisco restaurants.

If you need a break from waterfront exploration, this is a handy place for the construction of an alfresco lunch. You'll find inviting picnic places at the adjacent

Ferry Plaza and the Embarcadero Promenade south of the Ferry Building, and across the Embarcadero at Justin Herman Plaza and the grassy parklands of the Golden Gateway residential complex.

9 Sunrise Deli and Café

2115 Irving Street (at Twenty-second Avenue); 664-8210. Mideastern. Open 9 a.m. to 8 p.m. Monday-Saturday, and 10 a.m. to 6 p.m. Sunday.

This modestly decorated, cheerful little café serves *shawarma,* tasty thin-sliced marinated lamb roasted on a vertical spit—a treat that's rare outside the Middle East. Also available to eat here or take for a walk are pita sandwiches and Mideastern specialities such as *falafel, dolmas* (stuffed grape leaves), *baba ghanoush* (pureed eggplant), *tabouleh* (a minced salad made of bulgur wheat, mint, parsley, and tomato), and *hummus* (pureed chick-peas).

10 Yuen's Garden Restaurant

1131 Grant Avenue (at Pacific); 391-1131. Chinese. Open 7 a.m. to 6 p.m. daily.

Tucked under a large burgundy awning, Yuen's is the most versatile of Chinatown's many takeouts, with a complete deli, a large bakery, and a small sit-down restaurant. The deli offers assorted Asian items such as sweet and sour pork, glazed ducks, spicy Chinese sausage, soy sauce chicken, chicken wings, and an extensive selection of stir-fried and braised dishes. The bakery has both Chinese and American confections and pastries.

Typical of Asian takeouts, it is devoid of decor and almost always crowded. Be prepared to hold your own in line on a busy morning. The chaos slows in the afternoon, but some items may be depleted by then.

Chapter 12

GOODIES

The Hit Parade of San Francisco Delicacies

Part of the secret to success in life is to eat what you want and let the food fight it out inside.

—Mark Twain

It's no surprise, as we've established thus far, that San Franciscans love to eat. So it's hardly startling that many specialty foods are either produced here or featured in the city's stores and restaurants.

San Francisco-style sourdough bread is legendary, and to a lesser degree, so is the salami produced in the Bay Area. With significant culinary influences from large Chinese, Italian, and Mexican ethnic groups, products such as pork buns, pizza, and tamales are popular. Further, residents will pay outrageous prices for a single scoop of ice cream, so long as it's considered *gourmet,* and they get into serious cocktail party discussions about which bakery produces the flakiest croissant and most wholesome bran muffins.

The San Francisco Seven and their palates were assembled in a corner of Scott's Seafood at Three Embarcadero Center one Sunday afternoon to conduct a serious series of tests. (Incidentally, we want to thank Malcolm Stroud's staff at Scott's for being very helpful hosts for this event.) Several examples of specialty foods were subjected to our panel's unforgiving taste buds, then scored and tallied on our Aurora Big Number Dual-Power calculator. It was a true blind tasting, with no labels showing.

Here are our results, listed in the order served. (Item No. 11 was Bromo-Seltzer.)

1 THE BEST SAN FRANCISCO-BAKED CROISSANT
La Petite Boulangerie

Several San Francisco outlets; check under "bakers—retail" in the Yellow Pages.

Owned by Debbie Fields of Mrs. Fields Cookies fame, La Petite took the field over four other serious contenders. Its flaky, soft *croissants* edged out Bakers of Paris, which placed second this time, after winning the taste-off in the two earlier editions of this book.

2 THE BEST SAN FRANCISCO-STYLE SOURDOUGH BREAD
Boudin

Several outlets, call 882-1849 for locations.

Isidore Boudin started making sourdough bread here in 1849, and his descendants obviously have learned their lessons well. The bread's properly crisp crust and soft, slightly sharp interior shamed four other competitors. According to the company, the bakery uses the same starter or "mother dough" that Isidore used when he came West, not seeking gold, but the proper recipe for a golden crust.

3 THE BEST CHINESE STEAMED PORK BUNS
Sweet Fragrance Café

631 Broadway (between Stockton and Grant); 986-2028. Open 6 a.m. to 11 p.m.; no credit cards.

A Chinatown specialty, pork buns are large, doughy creations filled with a mixture of pork, onion, egg, and a sweet sauce. They're prepared either steamed or baked; we chose the steamed version (*cha shu bao*), since it's more traditional. The rich filling of the appropriately named Sweet Fragrance pork buns was excellent. This small café on Broadway was a surprise winner, edging out some of the long-established *dim sum* bakeries.

4 THE BEST BAY AREA SALAMI
Molinari

Molinari Deli is at 373 Columbus Avenue; 421-2337. Open 8:30 a.m. to 5:30 p.m. Monday-Saturday; MC/VISA. For other retail outlets, call 822-5555.

It's said that the San Francisco Bay Area's cool, damp climate nurtures natural mold on salami casings, which assists in proper aging. Whatever the reason, Bay Area salami is rated among the best in the country. And the best of the best, according to our panel, was Molinari's—rich, spicy, and not too greasy. Founded by Italian immigrants, the firm has been stuffing good things into casings since 1896.

5 THE BEST SAN FRANCISCO-MADE TAMALES
Roosevelt Tamale Parlor

2817 Twenty-fourth Street (at Bryant); 550-9213. Open 9 a.m. to 10:30 p.m. Tuesday-Saturday, and 9 a.m. to 9:30 p.m. Sunday. MC/VISA.

Several establishments in San Francisco's Mexican community make their own cornhusk-wrapped tamales, encased in masa, a Mexican cornmeal dough. Most are along Twenty-fourth Street between Folsom and Potrero, a region of Mexican shops, produce stores, small restaurants, and delis. A repeat winner was the huge, meat-filled creations of Roosevelt Tamale Parlor, a restaurant that does a busy take-out service. A nice feature of Roosevelt's take-out tamale is that it comes with a small container of zesty chili sauce, which can be heated and poured over once you get home.

6 THE BEST PIZZA-BY-THE-SLICE
Golden Boy Pizza

542 Green Street (at Columbus); 982-9738. American-Italian; wine and beer. Open noon to 11:30 p.m. Monday-Thursday, noon to midnight Friday-Saturday, noon to 8 p.m. Sunday. No credit cards.

We've already elected Uno as the city's best place for pizza, in Chapter 8. In addition to sit-down pizza restaurants, the city is busy with pizza-by-the-slice parlors, handy for folks on the run—individuals seeking a portable lunch.

After sampling too many, we've awarded Golden Boy the literary brass ring for its huge, generously laden pizza squares. Unlike the skimpy wedges offered by some establishments, these squares are sufficient for a quick lunch, and they'll even make a serious dent in dinner. The pesto and meat version is the best of several that are created in this small slot of a café in North Beach. The pizzas aren't mass-produced, but carefully crafted by hand, even as you watch and salivate.

7 THE BEST NORTHERN CALIFORNIA JUG WINES
Fetzer

Face it, kids. We regular wine drinkers can't always uncork a bottle of Robert Mondavi Opus One or Mayacamus 1974 cabernet sauvignon for dinner. We thus seek a good, sturdy, and drinkable jug wine to go with our daily bread and beans. For our panel's unmerciful palates, we selected five northern California wineries that issue one-and-a-half-liter bottles of chardonnay and cabernet sauvignon.

The surprise came when we ripped away the brown bags and discovered that Fetzer, a southern Mendocino County winery, had won both tastings. Although not widely known, Fetzer has long been respected in serious wine circles. The chardonnay was lush, betraying a hint of the nutty flavor normally found only in higher-priced versions. The cabernet exhibited strong varietal character despite its youth, with rich fruit flavors and that proper whisper of chili peppers.

8 THE BEST WHOLE EARTH MUFFINS
La Petite Boulangerie

Several San Francisco outlets; check under "bakers—retail" in the
Yellow Pages.

Whole-grain muffins have challenged chocolate chip cookies as the city's snack of choice in recent years. And, guess what: Mrs. Fields, who invented the upscale chocolate chip cookie, was a double winner; her Boulangerie bakery won our competition for both muffins and *croissants.* Her muffins brimmed with rich, whole-grain flavor. For consistency, we used only bran muffins for our tasting, although these designer muffins now come in a startling assortment of flavors.

9 THE BEST DESIGNER CHOCOLATE CHIP COOKIE
Tom's Cookies

In Macy's department store, O'Farrell Street at Stockton; 397-3333
or 989-TOMS. Daily 10 a.m. to 8 p.m. MC/VISA, AMEX, and Macy's
credit card.

Large, tasty, and somewhat expensive chocolate chip cookies came into vogue in San Francisco and elsewhere several years ago. Although this walk-away munchie is losing some of its impetus in the wake of health-conscious snacking, the city still has a few stands, and local bakeries like to specialize in the product. In our latest cookie trials, Tom Roach's small cookie outlet beat out some tasty competition, including Mrs. Fields, to emerge as the new winner. Roach started in a storefront on Kearny Street, then moved his operation into Macy's, with outlets in the cellar and on the Fourth Floor. Tom's cookies are thick, chewy, and brimming with chocolate chips. If you read the news, Tom's was selected to provide cookies for President Bill Clinton's inaugural. It wasn't chocolate chip, however, but a peanut butter-banana cookie that graced the presidential taste buds. They're on sale at his outlets and we found them to be—well—curiously tasty.

10 THE BEST GOURMET ICE CREAM
Ben & Jerry's

1480 Haight Street (at Ashbury); 249-4685; also at Pier 41 near Fisherman's Wharf (in a small stand, just to the right of the Red and White Fleet ticket office), and in some supermarkets.

What? An upstart import from New England defeated local powerhouses such as Bud's, Double Rainbow, and Dreyer's Grand? It's enough to melt your vanilla! Indeed, the ice cream from this Vermont-based firm won our taste-off with its silky, smooth texture and rich flavor. We'd chosen Ben & Jerry's as one of our candidates because the firm has a couple of ice-cream stands in the city, and the rather pricey pints are available at most better grocers. Little did we know that this Eastern brand would seduce our judges' palates. For consistency, incidentally, we chose vanilla for our tasters.

Chapter 13

NIGHTS ON THE TOWN

Lists of the Ten Best Ways to Enjoy an Evening Out

They talk of the dignity of work. Bosh. The dignity is in leisure.

—*Herman Melville*

We've dined, wined, and even stocked the refrigerator. Now it's time to get out on the town. Anyone who can't find entertainment in this city just isn't paying attention to the pink section in the Sunday *Chronicle,* which, incidentally, is the best available guide to what's happening here and in the greater Bay Area.

As the only West Coast city with a major symphony, ballet, and opera company, along with several resident theater groups, San Francisco is the leading performing arts center west of the Rockies. (Los Angeles may have its Music Center, but that city often borrows our ballet and opera.)

> *Getting ticketed:* BASS is the major Bay Area ticket agency for arts and sporting events, with outlets at the Wherehouse and Tower Records stores. Call (510) 762-BASS for information and charge-by-phone tickets. The Downtown Center Boxoffice in the Downtown Center Garage at 325 Mason Street (between Geary and O'Farrell) is a good ticket source, along with the City Box Office at 141 Kearny Street (392-4400). STBS, tucked into an alcove on the Stockton Street side of Union Square, offers discounts on unsold day-of-performance tickets. It's also a regular full-service ticket agency; call 433-STBS.

Onstage: The Ten Best Performing Arts Groups

1 San Francisco Symphony

Davies Symphony Hall, Van Ness at Grove. Call 864-6000 between 9 a.m. and 5 p.m. weekdays for season ticket information or 431-5400 for individual tickets. For a list of upcoming performances, write: San Francisco Symphony, Davies Symphony Hall, San Francisco, CA 94102.

"Music is a constantly developing form," San Francisco Symphony Director Herbert Blomstedt once commented. "We discover something new every day, not only in the new music, but also in the old."

This best sums up the success story of the San Francisco Symphony, rated as one of the top civic orchestras in America. With each season, it wins new audiences in northern California and around the world. And it wins accolades and awards both for its classic works and for innovation.

The symphony was established in 1911, the descendant of small ensembles that had been performing in the city since the gold rush. Based in the Louise M. Davies Symphony Hall, it offers a rich and varied September-through-July schedule of more than two hundred programs, performing classics, pops, and youth concerts. It features guest performers the likes of Michael Tilson Thomas and Isaac Stern. Blomstedt's group also has taken several world tours, most recently to Europe, and it records under exclusive contract with London/Decca records.

You will understand why we placed the symphony atop our list if you witness a performance in the elegantly coiffed Davies Hall, with its eight-thousand-pipe Ruffatti organ. That is a sight to hear!

2 American Conservatory Theatre

Box office at the Geary Theater, 415 Geary Street; productions at the Stage Door Theater, 420 Mason Street (at Geary) and sometimes at the Marines' Memorial Theatre, 609 Sutter Street (at Mason), and the Orpheum, 1192 Market Street (at Hyde). For show information, dial 749-2ACT, or write: ACT Subscriptions Office, 30 Grant Avenue, Sixth Floor, San Francisco, CA 94108-5800.

Under the direction of Carey Perloff, the company performs a season of eight classic and contemporary plays, often exhibiting the works of new writers. Both season subscriptions and individual performance tickets are available. The group's home theater, the historic Geary, was damaged by the Loma Prieta earthquake and is to reopen in 1994. In the meantime, ACT performs at the Orpheum, Stage Door, and Marines' Memorial theaters.

Founded in Pittsburgh by William Ball, the company was brought to San Francisco lock, stock, and backdrop in 1967. It has since established itself as the Bay Area's leading resident theater group; it won a Tony Award for excellence in repertory theater and actor training in 1979. ACT is the only non-university affiliated theater in the country accredited to award a Master of Fine Arts degree.

3 Curran, Golden Gate, and Orpheum Theatre Series

For schedule and ticket information, call 776-1999 for the Curran Theatre (445 Geary Street), Golden Gate Theatre (One Taylor at Market), and Orpheum Theatre (1192 Market). Individual performance tickets on sale at the three box offices.

Three venerable San Francisco theaters have fallen under the wing of Carole Shorenstein Hays and James M. Nederlander, who present an ongoing series of comedies, dramas, musicals, dance revues, and individual performers. Stars such as Rex Harrison, the late Richard Burton, and Claudette Colbert have trod the boards in these old playhouses. Although most of their productions are prepackaged, Ms. Hays has produced her own shows, such as *Fences,* which won a Pulitzer Prize on Broadway.

4 Eureka Theatre

340 Townsend Street (between Fourth and Fifth streets); phone 243-9898 for ticket information.

This resident professional drama group, operating out of a new state-of-the-art complex south of Market, presents a season of innovative theater, ranging from serious drama to slapstick comedy. Founded in 1972, it moved to permanent quarters in 1985 after a fire destroyed its temporary home on Market Street. It has earned national recognition for fostering young writers and for premiering new plays that focus on contemporary social issues.

5 Lorraine Hansberry Theater

620 Sutter Street (in the Sheehan Hotel, near Mason); phone 474-8800 for show schedules and ticket information.

This award-winning African-American drama group found a permanent home in a theater off the lobby of the Sheehan Hotel in 1988. Its focus is contemporary drama, special adaptations from African-American literature, and musical revues featuring the works of musicians such as Duke Ellington.

In addition to functioning in its three-hundred-seat theater, it sometimes joins forces with the American Conservatory Theatre for special projects.

6 The Magic Theatre

Fort Mason Center, Building D; call 441-8822 for tickets and show information.

This highly acclaimed resident company seeks out and produces works of contemporary American playwrights, both established and emerging. It has premiered notable works such as Sam Shepard's Pulitzer Prize-winning *Buried Child*. The Magic has earned both drama awards and critical praise and was described by critic John Roszak as "the most adventuresome company in the West."

7 Marines' Memorial Theatre

In the Marines' Memorial Association building, 609 Sutter Street (at Mason). For ticket information, call 771-6900.

Charles H. Duggan presents an assortment of shows, usually prepackaged, that range from Broadway musicals to one-man specialty acts and dance recitals. Some examples are George Peppard in a one-man Hemingway show and Phyllis Diller in a farce called *Nunsense*. (The shows have nothing to do with the USMC; the theater and Duggan's offices just happen to be in a building owned by an association of former leathernecks.)

8 San Francisco Ballet

Performances at the War Memorial Opera House, 301 Van Ness Avenue (at Grove); offices at 455 Franklin Street (at Fulton). For schedule and ticket information, call the box office at 703-9400.

One of America's three largest ballet companies and certainly one of its best, the San Francisco Ballet schedules an ambitious season of classical and contemporary dance at the Opera House.

Established in 1933 to provide dancers for the San Francisco Opera, it became an independent company in 1942. During its half century of excellence, the ballet has gained international acclaim. It was the first American ballet troupe to tour the Orient (in 1957), and it has won two Emmies for TV performances.

Currently, the company begins its season with a fall tour of major American cities. It then opens at home in mid-December with its annual presentation of the *Nutcracker*, which has become as much a part of the city's Christmas as the lighted trees in Union Square. The company also operates a highly respected ballet school out of its elegant $13.8 million permanent home on Franklin Street.

9 San Francisco Opera

For schedule and ticket information, call 864-3330 or stop by the box office, or write: San Francisco Opera, War Memorial Opera House, Van Ness Avenue at Grove Street, San Francisco, CA 94102. Tickets go very quickly, so inquire as early as possible.

For decades, one of America's most honored opera companies has dazzled local audiences with its lavish and splendidly staged productions at the historic Opera House. It won national plaudits for its ambitious *Ring of the Nibelung* in 1985.

Operas generally are presented in two seasons: from May to June, and from early September to mid-December, although the spring season is sometimes dropped to permit a more ambitious fall schedule. The opera's fall opening is perhaps the leading social event of the San Francisco cultural calendar. The company also operates a nationally recognized training program for young singers.

Established in 1923, it has presented more than one hundred fifty major operas, including twenty-one American premieres. Unafraid of innovation, the company provides supertitles for its foreign-language operas. They're convenient for patrons who want to hear the operas in their original language instead of a stilted English translation, but who still want to understand what the soprano is shrieking.

10 Theatre on the Square

450 Post Street (in the Kensington Park Hotel, near Powell); call 433-9500 for schedules and ticket information.

This second-floor theater in the refurbished Kensington Park Hotel is the city's off-Broadway showplace, hosting comedies, dramas, and musicals particularly suited to small houses. The structure is an intriguing 1924 Mediterranean-Gothic hall, remodeled for live theater.

The Ten Best Clubs and Pubs with Live Amusements

San Francisco's list of night spots offering live entertainment is longer than a Sunday morning hangover, and with the South of Market dance clubs, it's getting longer. We're not big fans of the glitzy SOMA discos, where rock music is blasted over speakers the size of minivans, but we do like the flash and excitement of some of the new nightclubs opening in that area.

What follows is a Ten Best mix of some of the cabarets, clubs, and cocktail lounges offering live and hopefully lively entertainment.

1 The Great American Music Hall

859 O'Farrell Street (at Polk); 885-0750. Supper club; cover. Tickets at BASS agencies. Call for a schedule of performers or write: c/o 859 O'Farrell, San Francisco, CA 94109.

This classy little hall earns our number one spot for its selection of consistently good entertainers and its appealing old music hall decor. The city's most charming small supper club, it features a family-oriented mix of old favorites and rising new stars.

The Hall's eclectic blend ranges through folk, light rock, comedy, and jazz. Through the years, we've enjoyed everything from a revival of the Limelighters to a Zasu Pitts Memorial Orchestra concert-dance. The acoustics are excellent, the baroque gold leaf, red velvet trim is pleasing, food and drink prices are reasonable, and kids over six are allowed.

2 Beach Blanket Babylon Series

Club Fugazi, 678 Green Street (at Columbus); cabaret theater. Call 421-4222 for show times and tickets, or write the club at 678 Green Street, San Francisco, CA 94133.

This zany musical review has been makin' whoopee at Club Fugazi for more than two decades. A wildly paced blend of comedy, song and dance routines, and character impersonations, it's the longest running musical revue in the nation. Glittering props and rafter-reaching hats are trademarks of these imaginative productions by Steve Silver. They're changed periodically to bring in more contemporary material. One local critic called the show "a delightful 90-minute giggle."

3 Comedy Clubs

Cobb's, in the Cannery, at 2801 Leavenworth Street (at Columbus), 928-4320; Holy City Zoo, 408 Clement Street (at Fifth Avenue), 386-4242; The Improv, 401 Mason Street (at Geary), 441-7787; The Punch Line, 444 Battery Street (at Washington), 397-7573.

Feel the need to chuckle your cares away? San Francisco offers these four major comedy clubs and twenty or so minor ones. Considered the stand-up comic capital of the world, it launched the likes of Phyllis Diller, the Smothers Brothers, and Pat Paulson. Today's future stars are featured on a weekly cable TV show, and the city hosts an international comedy competition every fall. Stand-up comics tend to rotate among the major clubs, so call to find out who's dropping one-liners where. Some of the country's top new comics currently work here, including

Rita Rudner and *Police Academy's* Bob Goldthwait. Robin Williams finished second in the city's comedy competition and went on to major stardom; nobody remembers who finished first.

Clubs charge a modest cover, generally under $10. Most shows start at 9 p.m., with a second one at 11 p.m. on Friday and Saturday. Of the "majors," the Punch Line is the largest, rated best in the city by the *Bay Guardian* newspaper. Cobbs, also highly rated, draws heavily from tourist traffic around Fisherman's Wharf. The Improv is a mecca for improvisational comedy; you'll likely witness "An Evening at the Improv" taping by the Arts & Entertainment cable TV network. The Holy City Zoo is the father of them all, dating back over a decade.

4 Fairmont Hotel

950 Mason Street (at California); 772-5000. Live music in several lounges; modest cover in New Orleans Room.

The New Orleans Room is a lively jazz venue featuring international stars and Louisiana-style food. Shows begin at 8:30 p.m. Sunday through Thursday and 9 p.m. Friday and Saturday; there's a modest cover charge. In the BellaVoce Ristorante, the BellaVoce Singers serve up popular show tunes and bits from operas and operettas while the waitstaff serves seafood, pasta, and pizza; serenading begins at 6:30 nightly. Brightened but unchanged is the Tonga Room with its wonderful Polynesian excess; patrons can dance nightly in this jungle haven to a live band and to the periodic rumble of tropical storms.

5 Kimball's

300 Grove Street (at Franklin); 861-5555. Restaurant-jazz club; modest cover and food or drink minimum.

This cheerful, airy restaurant with light woods and old brick has become one of the city's leading jazz clubs, where the likes of Ahmad Jamal, the Hi-Lo's, and Buddy Collette perform. Live music is featured Friday, Saturday, and sometimes Sunday nights, with shows generally at 9 p.m. and 1 a.m. Located near Davies Symphony Hall, the Opera, and Civic Auditorium, it's a popular pre-theater restaurant, so dinner reservations are essential.

6 The Paragon

3251 Scott Street (between Lombard and Chestnut); 922-2456. Jazz club-bar-restaurant. Music Sunday-Wednesday starting around 9 p.m.; no cover or minimum.

For years, the home of Paul's bluegrass and country and western saloon, this space has been converted into a modern jazz club. Dark earth-colored walls are brightened by abstract art and cubist murals, with the surviving fireplace from Paul's as a cozy focal point. This modern grotto provides a pleasing setting for good jazz and other contemporary sounds. Local critics have had nice things to say about the *nouveau* American cuisine with Italian and Southwestern accents.

7 Pier 23 Café

On the Embarcadero at Pier 23, 362-5125. Jazz club-bar-restaurant; modest cover.

This comfortable waterfront club with a kind of 1930s funk decor offers a pleasant setting for a mix of jazz, soul, salsa, reggae, and Dixieland music. Different groups perform Tuesday through Saturday starting around 9 to 10 p.m.; there's also a Sunday brunch, plus afternoon music from 4 to 8 p.m.

Pier 23 is a fine, moderately priced restaurant featuring light lunches and dinners. An outdoor patio with bay views is popular when the weather cooperates.

8 The Plush Room

In the York Hotel, 940 Sutter Street (at Hyde); 885-2800. Cabaret; cover charge.

Beautifully refurbished a few years ago, this cozy 150-seat show club features lounge acts ranging from impressionists to Margaret Whiting to small musical revues. With its art deco elegance, the room has been described by local critics as the most inviting small show lounge in the city.

9 Slim's

333 Eleventh Street (at Folsom); 621-3330. Nightclub-restaurant; tickets through major ticket outlets or at the door an hour before show time.

Co-owned by Boz Scaggs, Slim's is one of the classiest of the South of Market clubs. The facade is old New Orleans, with plantation porch columns, chandeliers, and wrought iron, behind which lurk state-of-the-art sound and lighting systems. Opened in late 1988, Slim's offers a mix of American-roots musical groups, ranging from jazz to rhythm and blues to alternative music, including guest appearances by the Boz himself (in the guise of Presidio Slim).

The place also has a dance floor, and it features a full-service restaurant specializing in California and American regional cuisine.

10 The Warfield

982 Market Street (near Taylor and Golden Gate); 775-7722. Theater-nightclub; cover charge.

Refurbished in late 1988 by the late rock impresario Bill Graham, the old Warfield on Market Street was reborn as a glitzy Manhattan-style showplace with table and chair seating on the main floor and balcony theater seating upstairs. It books a variety of shows, ranging from national touring acts to stand-up comics to rock, jazz, and blues.

The Ten Best Places to Dance Your Sox Off

The warehouse area south of Market Street has been experiencing a gradual renaissance in recent years, with the appearance of housing developments, a few restaurants, and most notably, a crop of new discos and other night spots.

Don't expect SOMA to be a wall-to-wall glitter of night life, like the original Soho in London. The area is still mostly warehouses and dimly lit alleys where you might hesitate to venture unaccompanied. The clubs are widely spaced, and some are poorly marked, as if challenging you to find them. Others are lit up by obvious marquees.

Dancing—dirty and otherwise—experienced a major comeback a decade ago after John Travolta tried to dislocate his left hip in *Saturday Night Fever.* The fad has faded a bit, and some dance clubs, particularly those South of Market, have closed. However, you'll still find a sufficiency of places around the city where you can shake your sox. The listings are alphabetical, since we don't have a favorite venue for pelvic dislocation.

1 Alta Vista del Mar Floating Nightclub

Pier 3 (off the Embarcadero); 346-7783.

Translated, the name means "upper view of the ocean." In reality, it's a water-level view of the bay, since it's the lower car deck of the restored ferryboat *Santa Rosa* that becomes a dance hall on Friday and Saturday nights. The music, appropriate to the Spanish name, was salsa when we last checked.

2 Avenue Ballroom

603 Taraval Street (at Sixteenth Avenue); 681-2882.

You say you feel a little silly wriggling your hips with the hip kids at Club Oz? We mature citizens may relate better to this attractive ballroom out in the Sunset District. On different nights, you can dance to country, swing, big band, and jitterbug music.

3 Bahia Tropical

1600 Market Street (near Twelfth Street); 861-8657.

If you like to wiggle to a Latin beat, this club vibrates to the salsa, samba, and other South American dances Tuesday through Saturday. If you don't know a salsa from a cha-cha, lessons are offered several nights a week.

4 Club Oz

At the Westin St. Francis, 335 Powell Street (at Geary); 956-7777.

The city's only skyroom dance club, Club Oz occupies the thirty-second floor of the St. Francis. Despite its lofty perch, the focus is inward—to the dazzling, modern disco decor. It's the venue for Top 40 disco dancing—a kind of upscale setting for *Saturday Night Fever,* with a deejay spinning American and international platters (CDs, actually). Dancing is nightly except Sunday, and there's a cover charge.

5 DNA Lounge

375 Eleventh Street (at Harrison); 626-1409.

Live groups alternate with a disco deejay in this SOMA cabaret lounge. The music is basic numbing rock, and the clientele extends into the Baby Boomer generation.

6 DV8

540 Howard Street (at First Street); 777-1419.

The largest nightclub on the West Coast, this four-floor, forty-five-thousand-square-foot place is a Travolta-style survivor of the seventies, with music to match. The age limit is twenty-one, and the crowd doesn't go much beyond that.

7 The Palladium

1031 Kearny Street (at Broadway); 434-1308.

One of the city's largest disco dance venues, the Palladium echoes with rock and other Top 40 sounds from three dance floors. The latest from MTV emerges from a huge video screen. This is a late-night retreat, with dancing Thursday through Sunday from 9 p.m. until 6 a.m.

8 Sheraton Palace Garden Court

639 Market Street (at New Montgomery); 392-8600.

This splendid space beneath a glittering glass dome, popular for its Sunday brunches, becomes the city's most attractive dance pavilion on Friday and Saturday evenings. Appropriate to its grand yesterday look, with Ionic columns and crystal chandeliers, the music of choice is ballroom style, played by a live band.

9 Southside

1190 Folsom Street (at Seventh Street); 431-3332.

Trendy and slick, with an accompanying restaurant, Southside draws an upwardly mobile crowd. Live rock is featured on Wednesdays, with recorded music Thursday through Saturday.

10 The Starlight Roof

Atop the Sir Francis Drake Hotel, Powell at Sutter; 392-7755.

High atop the Drake, the Starlight Roof recaptures the era of grand hotel ballrooms. A live orchestra plays big band sounds nightly in this attractive, recently renovated skyroom. While fox-trotting and swinging with your partner, you can enjoy panoramic city vistas from this twenty-first-floor perch.

The Ten Best Places to Catch a Movie

Instead of shaking your sox, perhaps you'd prefer a quiet movie. Sadly, many of the city's grand old art deco theaters have been redeveloped out of existence or have taken on new roles; one is a glitzy nightclub, another a Korean church. But many survive, along with some newer showcases.

1 Northpoint

2290 Powell Street (at Bay); 989-6060.

The Northpoint is our favorite movie palace, offering the largest screen and one of the most sophisticated Dolby sound systems in the city. Built in the early 1970s, this modern film house features major first-run movies. It's one of the few big houses that hasn't been chopped up into minitheaters with small screens in narrow halls.

2 Balboa

3634 Balboa Street (at Thirty-eighth Avenue); 221-8184.

A venerable movie house with art deco trim, the Balboa has been showing first-run films in the Richmond District since 1926; it's still operated by the Levins, the family who built it. It offers a double bill of first-run features on each of two screens. We love its rocking-chair loges.

3 Castro

429 Castro Street (at Market); 621-6120.

The Castro theater is another grand old film palace that has escaped the redeveloper's wrecking ball. The big screen in this large theater shows oldies and goodies—a wide range of foreign and American classics. It features film star retrospectives and movies with common themes, and it hosts occasional film festivals. Between shows, patrons can listen to the sonorous notes of the theater's huge Wurlitzer pipe organ.

4 Clay

2261 Fillmore Street (at Clay); 346-1123.

The oldest continuously operating movie theater in the city, the Clay opened in 1913. Preceding the art deco period, it has a turn-of-the-century neoclassic look. The relatively small four-hundred-seat auditorium is filled with Ultra-stereo, a new state-of-the-art system. The theater shows first-run foreign films.

5 Coronet

3575 Geary Boulevard (at Arguello); 752-4400.

Built in 1949, the Coronet is another San Francisco movie house that still retains its big screen. One of the city's largest and most comfortable theaters, it offers high-backed seating and an excellent new THX sound system developed by Lucasfilms.

6 Galaxy

1285 Sutter Street (at Van Ness); 474-8700.

We make fun of the startling glass box architecture of this new-wave multiscreen theater in Chapter 20. But what do we know? It won a *Time* magazine architectural design award when it opened in 1984. The slick lobby is certainly worth a look, and the theater's four viewing rooms—two large and two small—are comfortable. The Galaxy features first-run films, and it hosted the world premiere of the Oscar-winning *Amadeus.*

7 Gateway

215 Jackson Street (at Battery); 421-3353.

Since its completion in 1967, this theater in the Golden Gateway Center has been the San Francisco art film center. When not hosting a premiere, benefit, or film festival, it shows major foreign and art movies.

8 Landmark's Lumiere

1572 California Street (at Polk); 885-3200.

Intimate and comfortable, the Lumiere is one of the city's more appealing art film theaters. With three small screens, it offers an ongoing mix of leading foreign movies, some of the more innovative American releases, plus film classics. Appropriately, its lobby is decorated with classic movie posters.

9 The Red Vic

1727 Haight Street (at Cole); 668-3994.

This cozy theater, owned and operated by its staff, shows current American and foreign classics, plus occasional cult films and some local independent productions. The theater is known for its funky, comfortable atmosphere; many of its seats are couches and love seats. The Red Vic even exhibits a culinary concern for its patrons, selling popcorn with nutritional yeast, served in wooden bowls, and home-baked goods from its spice bar. Not a Milk Dud in sight.

10 Vogue

3290 Sacramento Street (at Presidio); 221-8183.

The focus here is on classic foreign and domestic art films; the theater sometimes screens an important movie for several months. Built in 1913 (the same year as the Clay), this pre-art deco house originally was called La Petite, certainly appropriate, since it seats only 316. It's noted for its friendly, sometimes amusing staff, and it's a stopover for stars such as Cloris Leachman, Robin Williams, Elizabeth Ashley, and Carol Channing when they're in town.

Chapter 14

CRAWLING AMONG THE BEST OF PUBS

Lists of the Ten Best Places to Sit and Sip

A man's got to believe in something. I believe I'll have another drink.
　　　　　　　　　　　　　　　　　　　　　　—*W. C. Fields*

No, we didn't try to sample all 2,100 bars in San Francisco, or we would have been in no condition to complete this guide. Through the decades, however, we've paused in many of the city's popular pubs. And in doing this second revision of *The Best of San Francisco*, we've again focused on its cocktail lounges and saloons, visiting old favorites and discovering some new ones.

Bars and the men and women who built them, drank in them, wrote books and poetry in their dark corners, and made love in their upper rooms are the fabric of San Francisco history. Researchers say a *cantina* may have been the city's first business establishment, predating the 1849 gold rush by five years.

If your idea of a night out is to loaf in a grimy pool hall that smells of stale cigarette smoke and yesterday's spilled beer, you may disagree with many of our selections. We prefer brighter, livelier bars that appeal to couples. While we're certainly fond of comfortable old saloons with their mahogany planks and dusty moose heads, we're also drawn to some of the cheerful new watering holes, where drinking is more of a social exchange than a melancholy ritual.

The Ten Best Watering Holes

The ultimate pub must fill several needs for those seeking solace or social contact. It should be a gathering place where people come not merely to drink, but to meet and mingle. It also should provide quiet corners for those wishing private conversation. Although the pub can be part of a restaurant, it must be a saloon in its own right, and not merely a corner bar counter where you wait to be called to dinner.

Above all, the ultimate drinking establishment must be a place of good cheer.

1 Starlight Roof

Atop the Sir Francis Drake Hotel, Powell at Sutter; 392-7755.

What? A skyroom as the best bar in San Francisco? We've picked a tourist haunt as the city's answer to "Cheers"? Certainly. The Starlight Roof has all the elements of a fine cocktail lounge. It's roomy and airy, with comfortable upholstered seating and a few intimate corners, reasonably priced drinks (particularly for a skyroom), elaborate happy hour *hors d'oeuvres,* and quiet music that doesn't interrupt earnest conversation. Add to that a 180-degree view of the city and bay, and we have an unqualified winner.

The Starlight Roof occupies the twenty-fourth floor of the recently renovated Sir Francis Drake, one of the city's fine old hotels. It's a handsome place, done in varying shades of burgundy, with soft lighting from finned chandeliers. An elaborate happy hour spread is laid out from 4:30 to 7 p.m. Later, one can dance to upbeat music that swings without rattling the rafters or your eardrums. Newer high-rises now tower above the Drake's skyroom, although its location in the heart of downtown still allows impressive vistas—particularly of the city's night lights.

2 Harpoon Louie's

55 Stevenson Street (off Third Street, just south of Market); 543-3540.

Designers have done a convincing job of casting this warm and comfortable brick-walled pub into antiquity. Opened just a few years ago, it seems a survivor of the city's earliest days, with plank floors, historic prints, and vintage maritime memorabilia. Like any good pub, it offers complimentary nibbles during happy hour, conducted from 4 to 7 p.m. It also functions as a popular lunch venue, and it was one of our hamburger competition winners (see Chapter 9).

This is, of course, a good and proper watering hole, and patrons are expected to conduct themselves accordingly. To quote from the bar menu:

> *Notice to all ruffians, roustabouts, hooligans, miscreants, nefarious types, interlopers, sidewinders, claim-jumpers, four-flushers, bushwhackers, polecats, card cheats, counterfeiters, jerks and double dealers: Impolite behavior and reckless gunplay will not be tolerated during normal business hours.*

What you do on your own time is your affair.

3 Harrington's

245 Front Street (at California); 392-7595.

It takes two large rooms, each with its own bar and a score or more tables, to hold a proper Irish drinking crowd. That's what Harrington's has provided for as long as anyone can remember. This roomy, cheerful place is a lively stopover for homeward-bound Financial District commuters and a late-hour refuge for city-dwelling night owls. Harrington's is more Irish in spirit and attitude than in decor; what little trim you see in this place is nautical, not Gaelic.

4 The House of Shields

39 New Montgomery Street (at Market); 392-7732.

Opened in 1910 by one Eddie Shields, the city's last stand-up saloon sat down in the fall of 1986. To the dismay of some purists, bar stools were placed along the brass rail. The management even removed a couple of spittoons to make room. Happily, on our most recent visit, we noticed that most of those infernal creations had been removed again, so a fellow (and his lady in this liberated age) can belly up to the bar without tripping over a goldarned stool.

If you must sit, you can sink into a comfortable curved booth across the way.

Across the street from the Sheraton Palace, Shields is elemental old San Francisco, with heavy squared columns, walnut paneling, and a handsome back bar with shields carved into the woodwork. Tulip-glass chandeliers dangle from the high coffered ceiling. An elk head stares moodily from one wall, and a Cape buffalo glares from another. The high-backed booths are filled with a Financial District lunch crowd on weekdays. Like any proper San Francisco pub, Shields serves bar nibbles and puts out the dice cups during the evening cocktail hour.

5 Iron Horse

19 Maiden Lane (just off Kearny); 362-8133.

This pleasant cellar bar in the heart of the city provides a quiet, dimly lit refuge. Like most of our other selections, it offers both lively companionship at the bar and booths and tables for gazing into the eyes of someone special. It serves some of the most elaborate *hors d'oeuvres* of any San Francisco pub. Stop by during happy hour for tasty meatballs and sausage links in spicy sauce, fresh-cut veggies with dip, even fresh fruit. Bottoms up and *bon appétit!*

6 Perry's

1944 Union Street (at Laguna); 922-9022.

Tucked under the bay window of an old Victorian, Perry Butler's place is vintage San Francisco with its big mirrored back bar, warm woods, and embossed tile ceiling. It's kind of funky yet upscale—a proper venue for Marina District regulars and Marin-bound commuters. Butler describes his place as akin to an "atmospheric New York Third Avenue pub."

Like the Washington Square Bar and Grill, it's something of a media hangout, where the likes of radio's Scott Beach and *Sports Illustrated's* Ron Fimrite play liars' dice and swap lies with the barkeeps. Also like the "Square," it has an excellent restaurant, serving honest, substantial, and often creative American fare.

7 Raffles'

In Fox Plaza at 1390 Market Street (at Polk); 621-8601.

Tourists and downtown crowds haven't discovered this friendly, roomy place with its South Seas decor, candlelit tables, reasonable prices, and tasty oriental *hors d'oeuvres.* However, it has a large following. The clientele is a mix of Civic Center bureaucrats, next-door Auto Club regulars, and crowds bound for nearby Davies Symphony Hall, the Opera House, and Civic Auditorium.

It's also a rather good, moderately priced Polynesian-oriental restaurant. The decor consists of the requisite fishnets, glass floats, and stuffed swordfish. The objects on the walls probably haven't been dusted in a decade, but fortunately, the lights are kept low.

8 Redwood Room

At the Four Seasons Clift Hotel, 495 Geary Street (at Taylor); 775-4700.

The unquestioned opulence of the Clift—it has earned five diamonds from the American Automobile Association—is clearly visible in its distinguished Redwood Room. The look is that of a refined men's club, evident yet understated, with redwood veneer walls, art deco sconces, and overstuffed leather chairs. Even the bar stools are high-backed and plush.

A grand piano occupies the center of this carpeted retreat, and soft music often accompanies your glass of tastefully overpriced wine. In keeping with this aura of refinement and gentility, jackets and ties are requested of the gentlemen. We weren't told what's requested of the ladies; presumably, to be ladylike.

9 Vesuvio's

255 Columbus Avenue (at Broadway); 362-3370.

Jack Kerouac and the restless, rebellious Beat Generation are gone, replaced by bottom lines, BMWs, and upward mobility. Vesuvio's survives to remind us of that era when pondering over our reason for being was more significant than fretting over tax shelters and runaway medical costs.

Vesuvio's sits on its narrow corner in a pleasant state of arrested decay. It's gaudy in a funky way, still displaying the works of North Beach artists, and still offering sanctuary and cheap wine to the writer, the disillusioned leftist, and the occasional curious tourist.

Incidentally, several small streets in North Beach and elsewhere in the city have been renamed in honor of San Francisco writers and artists, at the suggestion of the City Lights bookstore folks across the alley from Vesuvio's. Appropriately, the alley between them is now Jack Kerouac Street; nearby Adler Place, site of the neighboring Specs' 12 Adler Museum Café, has become William Saroyan Street. City Lights is, by the way, the ultimate bookstore; a sign out front identifies it as A Kind of Library Where Books Are Sold.

10 Washington Square Bar & Grill

1707 Powell Street (at Union); 982-8123.

WSB&G founders Ed amd Mary Etta Moose retreated across Washington Square to establish Moose's in 1992. However, they left their legendary pub and media hangout in good hands and in good spirits. "The Square," as the faithful call it, remains the pub by which other San Francisco saloons are measured. Housed in a sturdy old Victorian and decorated mostly by noisy camaraderie, it's a convivial gathering place of powerbrokers, stockbrokers, journalists, and others woven into the white collar fabric of this city.

Scores of simultaneous conversations—concerning Joe Montana's abdication, the fluttering stock market, or Herb Caen's latest revelation—reverberate around the narrow barroom, nearly drowning out the thump of dice cups. On frequent occasion, the voices are stilled by live music from the corner piano, or from a jazz combo. Across a pony wall, in one of the city's more durable restaurants, diners dig into hearty Italian-American fare.

Perhaps more than any other pub, "The Square" captures the after-hours essence of San Francisco.

The Ten Best View Bars

San Francisco is of course famous for its views. So why not enjoy a proper glass of zinfandel while absorbing the city's sundry vistas? Although our favorite occupies one of the West Coast's highest custom-built perches, not all of our selections are skyrooms.

1 The Carnelian Room

Top floor of the Bank of America building, 55 California Street (at Montgomery); 433-7500.

This is the highest cocktail lounge in the city, with predictably imposing views. In addition to offering great vistas, the Carnelian Room cocktail lounge is handsome within, dressed up with fine old European paneling, chandeliers, and art objects. Although prices in most skyroom bars increase with the elevation, the tariff here isn't unreasonable for such an elegant place.

Incidentally, it's the private Bankers' Club during the daytime, so the bar isn't open to the public until 3 p.m. on weekdays and 4 p.m. on weekends. The adjacent dining room, listed among our Ten Best view restaurants (see Chapter 8), starts serving at 6 p.m.

2 Fairmont Crown Room

Atop the Fairmont Hotel, 950 Mason Street (at California); 772-5131.

Since the Fairmont Crown sits atop Nob Hill, it's the city's second-highest skyroom although it's only twenty-four stories in the air. On this lofty perch, there's little to interrupt its nearly 360-degree sweep of the city, bay, ocean, and distant hills. The interior is eye-catching as well. With candlelit tables, comfortable seating, recessed lighting, and mirrored columns, this is a pleasing place for admiring the globe's most handsome city.

3 Gabbiano's Restaurant and Oyster Café

One Ferry Plaza (just south of the Ferry Building, off the Embarcadero); 391-8403.

Often, the city's best cocktail views are right on the ground. Gabbiano's is an impressive two-story structure built on a pier at the water's edge. The ground floor Oyster Café and cocktail lounge, a glittering study in brass and light woods beneath a greenhouse roof, offer impressive vistas of the Bay Bridge, the south bay front, and the East Bay. This stylish lounge also is a popular business lunch spot.

4 Holmes Esquire

Atop the Holiday Inn Union Square, 480 Sutter Street (at Powell); 398-8900.

This new skyroom, a product of the recent Holiday Inn renovation, is an appealing creation in burgundy and brass, with candelabra chandeliers. The look, according to the decorators, is upscale old English pub. Few pubs, however, offer such a view. A glimpse out the floor-to-ceiling windows will reveal a pleasing northern vista, taking in Telegraph Hill, Coit Tower, and the bay front toward Fisherman's Wharf. Free nibbles are proffered during the nightly happy hour.

5 Thirteen Views

In the Hyatt Regency, Five Embarcadero Center (foot of Market Street); 788-1234.

The Hyatt Regency's lobby bar earns a niche in this list because of its spectacular *interior* view. Order a slightly overpriced glass of wine and absorb vistas of the hotel's soaring sixteen-story atrium ceiling, a massive circular sculpture suspended above a spillover fountain, and the "Star Trek" elevators shooting up and down the inside walls. This spacious bar tempts you further with live music and *hors d'oeuvres* on week nights. The Regency and its lofty inner space underwent a $22 million renovation in 1993, so it will be even glossier by the time you arrive.

6 Phineas T. Barnacle

At the Cliff House, 1090 Point Lobos Avenue (on the ocean); 386-3330.

Seal Rocks and the Pacific are just outside your reach if you're fortunate enough to get a highly prized window table at this handsome old-style nautical pub. Even with a lesser seat, however, you'll have a pleasing Pacific panorama through the floor-to-ceiling picture windows. It is, as we suggested in Chapter 3, a great place to watch the sunset. Light fare is served in the Barnacle; two Cliff House restaurants—also offering imposing views—are adjacent.

There has been a Cliff House of some sort perched on these rocks since 1850, when the city's earliest arrivals must have glanced back over their shoulders and said: "Dang my britches, that's a nice view!"

7 Tarantino's

206 Jefferson Street (above the boat basin at Fisherman's Wharf); 775-5600.

Many Fisherman's Wharf bars and restaurants offer aquatic views, and Tarantino's has the best. The small yet open and roomy cocktail lounge is built on stilts right above the Jefferson Street boat basin. It's a great place for observing the passing parade of fishermen and tourists. The bar view is even superior to the vista from the dining room.

8 Top of the Mark

Atop the Mark Hopkins Inter-Continental, California and Mason streets; 392-3434.

The Top of the Mark has been synonymous with romantic vistas since 1939. The oldest of the city's skyrooms, this nineteenth-floor perch is still one of the best, sharing the Fairmont Crown's enviable post atop Nob Hill. Like the Crown, it has a view that's almost full circle. It's a comfortable haven for admiring city, hill, and bay—with high-backed chairs and mirrored columns. Recessed lights avoid reflective conflict with San Francisco's dazzling night light show.

9 Victor's

Atop the Westin St. Francis, 335 Powell Street (at Geary); 956-7777.

Most of this thirty-second-floor aerie is occupied by Victor's restaurant. However, a few tables are set aside for cocktails. They occupy curtained bay-window alcoves, providing both wide-angle panoramas and shelter from other eyes. The most inviting vista is straight down, to the geometric patterns of Union Square and the clustered rooftops of downtown. Lift your eyes, and study the sweep south and east, over the Bay Bridge to Oakland.

10 The View

San Francisco Marriott, 55 Fourth Street (between Market and Mission); 896-1600.

While the gaudy "jukebox Marriott" looks strange from outside, the view from the inside looking out is remarkable. The hotel's thirty-ninth-floor skyroom, simply called The View, is set off by giant spiderweb windows that look to be thirty feet tall (the cocktail waitress wasn't sure). The impressive glass-walled room resembles a surrealistic movie set for Batman's lair. The view from The View is east and south, over the Bay Bridge and down the East Bay, and north as far as Alcatraz and Angel Island.

The Ten Best Neighborhood Pubs

A proper neighborhood pub may differ somewhat from the ultimate watering hole. Comfort, familiarity, and intimacy are important. The atmosphere should encourage relaxation and lively companionship. One goes to the corner bar to unwind, and possibly to refuel. Most neighborhood pubs reflect the life-style of the district, so our selections differ from area to area. These are in no particular sequence, except alphabetically by neighborhood.

1 CHINATOWN
Li Po

916 Grant Avenue (at Washington); 982-0072.

We begin with an exception. Li Po doesn't reflect the life-style of busy, industrious Chinatown; it's a haven *from* it. Most Asians, explains my Chinese wife and coauthor, are too ambitious to waste time hanging around bars. Perhaps that's why Chinatown can support more than a hundred restaurants but only one real neighborhood pub.

Li Po has been a quiet retreat from the multicolored confusion of Chinatown for more than half a century. With its subdued lighting, the place has an almost grim look, except for a huge yellow-and-red lantern hanging from the ceiling.

A bronze gong and brass Buddha occupy dusty niches behind the cluttered bar. Sitting on a worn stool, sipping Tsing Tao beer, you expect Charlie Chan to brush through the beaded curtain. Or at least Sydney Greenstreet.

Except there isn't a beaded curtain.

2 GLEN PARK AND TWIN PEAKS
Glen Park Station

2816 Diamond Street (near Glen Park BART station); 333-4633.

This is the exemplary neighborhood pub: an honest working folks' saloon where denizens of Glen Park and the hills above gather to sip suds and swap shop-talk and sports statistics. Three TV sets beam the latest ball game from any angle, and Garth Brooks bawls from the jukebox. A much-used pool table occupies a back room, remote from the friendly commotion of the main bar, so players can concentrate on a serious game of eight ball.

3 HAIGHT-ASHBURY AND SUNSET
Achilles Heel

1601 Haight Street (at Clayton); 626-1800.

In recent years, gentrification has reared its capitalistic head in the old neighborhood of the Flower Children; Achilles Heel offers a suitable bridge between past and future. Its mix of Victorian chandeliers, ferns, old settees, and worn carpet speaks of earlier days, while the newcomers to the neighborhood can identify with its white wine list and the selection of reading material, like *CitySports* and *Focus* magazine, which invites lounging. The look is Victorian funk, but this is no punk rock hangout; the clientele is a blend of neighborhood white shirts and short skirts.

4 THE MARINA
Chestnut Street Grill

2231 Chestnut Street (at Scott); 922-5558.

The Marina District is second only to North Beach for its collection and selection of drinking establishments. What to choose here for the best neighborhood pub: the raucous Pierce Street Annex, upscale Perry's, the earthy Bus Stop, the trendy brass-and-glass Golden Gate Grill? We settled on the Chestnut Street Grill, which works at being a neighborhood pub. Regulars are honored by special sandwiches bearing their names; patrons sign up for group outings to ball games or gather to scream themselves hoarse during Monday night football. Indeed, this place is noisy, but it's gregarious noise.

5 THE MISSION
La Rondalla

903 Valencia Street (at Twentieth Street); 550-9002.

For nearly four decades, this convivial Mission District Mexican restaurant and bar has encouraged the accumulation of clutter and Christmas decorations in its three oversized rooms. Festive garlands and tinsel go up each year, added to those remaining from the season before. Neighbors and curious outsiders gather nightly to sing with a mariachi band or relax and sip Corona Extra and Dos Equis in the shadow of a stuffed antelope head wearing a red Christmas ball.

6 NORTH BEACH
Specs' 12 Adler Museum Café

12 Saroyan Street (off Columbus near Broadway); 421-4112.

Not a café but almost a museum, Specs' remains a haven for North Beach locals simply because most visitors can't find the place. It's tucked into a short alley across Columbus from Vesuvio's, with a small sign reluctantly confirming its presence. Those who do find it discover a funky blend of bar and museum filled with sundry artifacts from assorted global corners. The regulars quaffing their beer and swapping familiar tales politely ignore outsiders, who lean over them to study African and New Guinea relics in the wall-mounted display cases.

7 PACIFIC HEIGHTS AND FILLMORE
Harry's Saloon

2020 Fillmore Street (at Pine); 921-1000.

Harry's is an upscale watering hole decorated mostly by noisy ambiance. Offering friendly barkeeps, pretty waitresses, fair food, and honest drinks, it has found quick success on a site where several others have failed. Opened in the late 1980s, it is the watering hole for yuppies of Pacific Heights and the newly trendy upper Fillmore; it's currently in vogue as a singles bar.

Harry's is a stylish-looking place and kind of clubby, decorated with half a million dollars worth of mahogany, brass, and mirrored walls opposite a mirrored back bar. Light meals are served on an elevation just above the plank.

8 RICHMOND
Churchill's

455 Clement Street (at Sixth Avenue); 752-0580.

With its dusky decor of wood-paneled walls and weathered tables and chairs, Churchill's is beginning to look out of place on a street now dominated by Asian restaurants, markets, and shops. This comfortable old corner saloon, stuck under a curiously pink Victorian, offers peaceful sanctuary in a neighborhood now invigorated by the ambitious newcomers.

Although certainly open to all, the pub lures primarily middle-class whites. They seem more tempted than their Asian neighbors to place elbows on the well-worn bar, sip something cool, nibble from the snack bowls, and watch football on one of two telly screens.

9 SOUTH OF MARKET
The Paradise Lounge

1501 Folsom Street (at Eleventh Street); 861-6906.

Since we wrote the original version of this book, South of Market has become a major nightlife area of the city. Most of the new places are too contrived or dance-oriented to qualify as local pubs. However, the Paradise Lounge fits that role nicely. It's a properly funky corner bar with a main lounge, a cozy little back room offering live rock and jazz sessions, and even a smoky old pool room called Above Paradise among the rafters upstairs.

This place may seem a bit upbeat for a neighborhood pub, but then, SOMA is a rather upbeat area. Between shows and discos—listed on psychedelic posters outside—you can find quiet retreat at the back room tables. And yes, the main lounge does offer bar nibbles, an essential for a neighborly saloon.

10 UPPER MARKET AND CASTRO
Metro Bar and Restaurant

3600 Sixteenth Street (at Market); 431-1655.

This darkly contemporary lounge, done in purple and gray with touches of violet neon, is haven for both the gays and straights of upper Market and the Castro District. It's a handsome second-floor place, with window-walls looking over busy Market Street. A large oval bar dominates the room, and small tables line the walls. A restaurant is adjacent.

Unlike the intense heavy-leather aura of some Castro Street bars, the scene here is a bit more mellow. A straight couple would not feel ill at ease, unless he or she is bothered by loud music.

The Ten Best Bars of a Specific Sort

Like people, saloons often have distinct characteristics. What follows is the Ten Best bars with the most interesting personalities.

1 THE MOST ELEGANT BAR
The Ritz Carlton Lobby Bar

In the Ritz Carlton Hotel, 600 Stockton Street (near California, atop the Stockton Tunnel); 296-7465.

With its plush chairs, crystal chandeliers hanging from a high coffered ceiling, rich marbles and wood paneling, this is easily the most civilized cocktail lounge in the city—perhaps in the state.

Sink into a high-backed chair, watch the light-and-shadow dance of the fireplace, and listen to a tinkling piano or the soft voice of a soloist. Tables are set with bud vases, and the cocktail napkins are cloth, of course. A dessert cart resides beneath a huge flower-filled urn, tempting you with its tortes, truffles, and fresh strawberries. Drinks begin at a sensible $6, or you can sip a Remy Martin Louis XIII cognac at $95 a pour, accompanied by an ounce of beluga caviar for $70.

Elegance, indeed.

2 THE BEST SINGLES BAR
Pierce Street Annex

3138 Fillmore Street (at Greenwich); 567-1400.

We must point out that the Annex is not primarily a singles bar. It is the definitive drinking establishment, the ultimate pub for those seeking the noisy intimacy that only a good saloon can provide. A huge island bar dominates the barnlike interior, although regulars tend to wedge themselves around a smaller plank near the entrance, clutching sweating bottles of Beck's and Corona Extra. Live entertainment emanates from a small stage; several TV sets hang from the high ceiling to draw the sports crowd. Cartoon sketches of regulars—some dating back a couple of decades—fill one wall.

The singles scene is mellow but not subtle. A set of rules printed on a wall suggests the proper procedure for approaching someone, and the bar's matchbooks provide space for a name and phone number.

3 THE NOISIEST BAR
Cadillac Bar and Grill

One Holland Court (off Howard, between Fourth and Fifth streets); 543-8226.

Behind an innocent-looking red and green sign in an alley off Fourth Street lurks the Fourth of July, New Year's Eve, and Cinco de Mayo. The friendly chaos is jammed between four walls decorated with Mexican flags, other Latin trim, and cacti, both potted and painted.

Amazingly, an award-winning Mexican restaurant manages to function right beside the incredibly noisy bar, fenced off from the chaos but not from the roar of the crowd. The only way to carry on a conversation is to get within two inches of the listener's ear. We did notice, on our last visit, that a dance floor has been added, so you can pursue your conversation while in the grip of the light fantastic.

The management of the Cadillac is quite proud of its spirited clamor, incidentally. Its bimonthly publication is called *The Noise,* which may or may not have been inspired by our nomination.

4 THE QUIETEST BAR
Piazza Lounge

In the main lobby of the Parc 55 Hotel, 55 Cyril Magnin Street; 392-8000.

What a wonderful place to recover from Cadillac Bar burnout! Lean back in an overstuffed chair, admire the artwork around you, and listen to the pleasant tinkle of a grand piano. Sounds drift upward to be absorbed by crystal chandeliers hung from the four-story atrium ceiling of this spacious lobby bar. The bar service area is off to one side; even the slosh and tinkle of drink preparation are remote. Here, you lean toward your partner's ear only to whisper.

5 THE BEST SPORTS BAR
Pat O'Shea's Mad Hatter

3754 Geary Boulevard (at Third Avenue); 752-3148.

Any pub posting a sign proclaiming *We Cheat Drunks and Tourists* is all right in our book. The Mad Hatter is a favorite Richmond District hangout that serves good food along with good cheer. It's also the consummate sports bar, with half a dozen TV sets posted around the walls and a blackboard listing upcoming jock telecasts.

Satellites provide O'Shea's with all the sports action. On a given autumn Sunday, one can watch two or more football games concurrently. Heads swivel left to cheer the 49ers, then swing right to boo the Rams. And of course, the decor includes a scatter of sports regalia.

6 THE BEST TOURIST BAR
The Buena Vista Café

2765 Hyde Street (at Beach); 474-5044.

The term *tourist bar* is not intended here as an insult. The weathered old Buena Vista, housed in a landmark Victorian near Fisherman's Wharf, has been a haven for locals and a magnet for visitors for decades. It is not a tourist *trap*, but an honest pub where visitors often get their first sample of San Francisco togetherness: the oversized tables beneath the high windows are expected to be shared. Incidentally, the place also functions as a fine little café, particularly noted for its hearty breakfasts.

Of course, the Buena Vista is famous for its Irish coffee, introduced here in 1952 by the late Stan Delaplane. Read all about it in Chapter 2.

7 THE BEST LOBBY BAR
The Compass Rose

In the Westin St. Francis Hotel, Powell at Geary; 774-0167.

Amidst the splendor of fluted Greek columns and scalloped drapes in this exquisite bar off the St. Francis Hotel lobby, you can settle into a plushly upholstered chair and watch the parade of human passage. Sip your drink slowly while listening to the delicate strains of a cello and piano duet during evening cocktail hour. Or go for lunch or midafternoon high tea.

8 THE BEST WINE BAR
London Wine Bar

415 Sansome Street (at Sacramento); 788-4811.

It was San Francisco's first, opened in 1974, and it's still the best bar for wine aficionados. You can choose from as many as thirty table wines by the glass and another dozen aperitifs and dessert wines. Sippers have a choice of a long bar, tables, or cozy booths. Wine, wine, everywhere and every drop to drink. The essence of the grape lines the back bar, decorates high shelves around the wall (empty bottles, actually), and boxes of wine are stacked near the entrance. If you descend to the little basement café, where these civilized folk forbid smoking, you'll find—what else?—a wine cellar.

9 THE BEST BAR FOR INTELLECTUAL CONVERSATION
Caffé Trieste

601 Vallejo Street (at Grant); 392-6739.

In this survivor of the Beat Generation, you can sit in the same seats warmed by Jack Kerouac and Allen Ginsberg and ponder the state of society with an understanding friend. Like other coffeehouse survivors of the sixties, it serves no hard liquor but offers espresso and cappuccino, wine, beer, and sundry aperitifs.

Although the service bar looks suspiciously like a deli, Caffè Trieste is still a pub of sorts. It offers sanctuary for seekers of quiet conversation beneath walls cluttered with scenes of old North Beach, intermixed with glossies of opera stars, film stars, and snapshots of Trieste regulars and irregulars, past and present. Little changed for decades (except for a recent exterior face-lift), it is terminally crowded. Yet, no matter when you arrive, there seems inevitably to be one or two available seats.

10 THE MOST HISTORIC BAR
The Saloon

1232 Grant Avenue (at Fresno Alley); 989-7666.

This cranky old man of a bar stands stubbornly on upper Grant Avenue, where it has stood for well over a century. Housed in a rust-colored Victorian (or is that just rust?), it may be the oldest drinking establishment still active in San Francisco. The Saloon was constructed in 1861 as the Fresno Hotel Bar, and it has survived a tempestuous life as a whorehouse and Prohibition speakeasy. It even survived the great 1906 earthquake and fire. Sailors helping fight the blaze, perhaps recalling fond memories of a night with one of the upstairs ladies, rushed with fire hoses to drench the tough old bar, saving it from approaching flames.

The place has achieved a measure of respectability of late as a blues bar, but it's a raucous respectability that the ghosts of the old saloon probably enjoy. Every Monday through Saturday evening (and sometimes Sunday), the ancient pub rattles to the sounds of a blues band that keeps slipping into hard rock, stopping just short of heavy metal. Herds of celebrants crowd into a small space before the band to dance and stomp up a storm. The ancient floorboards shudder and sway; you can't help thinking that the ghosts are dancing, too.

It seems appropriate to end our bar chapter in the old Fresno Hotel saloon, raising a little hell with the spirits of the San Francisco that was, and sometimes, still is.

Chapter 15

FOR MATURE ADULTS ONLY

The Ten Naughtiest Things to Do in San Francisco

The most romantic thing any woman ever said to me in bed was:
"Are you sure you're not a cop?"

—Larry Brown

Perhaps grown weary of the erotic overkill of the 1960s and 1970s, San Francisco is no longer America's sexual freedom center. Many of the topless-bottomless shows along Broadway have been called on account of disinterest; even the Condor Club, shrine of the topless movement, has been converted to a café. Out along Castro Street, fear of AIDS has muted the gay community; throughout the Bay Area, swingers' clubs are going out of fashion.

But permissiveness still survives in this indulgent city that introduced topless and bottomless dancing to America. Here are ten harmless ways to pursue naughtiness in San Francisco. They are listed in no particular order.

1 Watch Them Take It Off on Broadway

Most topless bars are concentrated along Broadway, immediately east of its junction with Columbus and Grant avenues.

Business was slow at the Condor Club on the opening night of the Republican National Convention in 1964. It got brisk when a waitress-turned-dancer named Carol Doda donned a topless bathing suit and stepped onstage. The DA's staff thumbed nervously through the law books, and it took the police several days to bust (pardon the expression) Ms. Doda. Then the courts ruled that nudity of itself was not pornographic, and the topless revolution was in—uh—full swing. Carol has retired her silicone assets, and the Condor is now a café. However, other more-or less-endowed women dance and prance at a few surviving nude parlors along Broadway.

When I last strolled this boulevard of bosoms, a lady in leather shorts tried to lure me into the hungry i at 546 Broadway while the next-door Roaring Twenties promised Sensational Live Nude Girls. Across the street at 529 Broadway, Adam and Eve calls itself San Francisco's Garden of Eden, and the nearby Casbah promises Naked Harem Dancers and Wall-to-Wall Sex. Mostly what you get in these places is overpriced drinks and a parade of unremarkable women, most of whom seem to be fighting boredom as they wriggle and squirm to recorded rock.

If you're fascinated by history, examine the outside wall of the Condor and you'll discover this plaque, cleverly disguised as a California historical landmark:

The Condor, where it all began. The birthplace of the world's first topless and bottomless entertainment. Topless, June 19, 1964; bottomless, September 3, 1969, starring Ms. Carol Doda. San Francisco, California.

Inside the Condor restaurant, you'll find photos of those bawdy old days along Broadway and a portion of the club's famous blinking-nipple marquee—still winking at you.

2 Shop for—Uh—Good Vibes

Good Vibrations, 1210 Valencia Street (at Twenty-third Street); 974-8980.
Daily 11 a.m. to 7 p.m.

Several years ago, sex therapist Joani Blank decided it was time to bring adult turn-ons out of the closet, so she opened a wholesome sex shop on Valencia Street. Unlike those seamy places along Broadway and in the Tenderloin, usually tended by a scruffy character wearing yesterday's shirt and a three-day beard, Good Vibrations is an attractive, well-lighted place. It might be a typical corner market or gift shop, except that the shelves are lined with massage lotions, designer condoms, naughty books and movie videos, and what the brochure describes as an "unbeatable array of sex toys."

The shop's name is a great double entendre, but don't tell your grandmother. The store also features what may be the world's only museum of antique vibrators.

3 Take A Peek at a Naughty Movie

Mitchell Brothers' O'Farrell Theater, 895 O'Farrell Street (at Polk); 776-6686.
Open from 11:30 a.m. Monday-Saturday and from 5 p.m. Sunday (giving patrons sufficient time to attend church); varied closing hours.

While Carol Doda was shaking things up at the Condor, the Mitchell Brothers pursued pornographic breakthroughs in the naughty film business. A shocking family murder ended the brothers' partnership a few years ago, although the Mitchell Brothers' O'Farrell Theater continues to thrive.

"This place sort of runs itself," the lady at the box office said laconically.

Two or more reels of raunch are screening on any given day in this showroom of sex. The place also features live-and-onstage topless dancers, the Ultra Room where naked ladies cavort behind glass, and the Copenhagen Lounge, offering close encounters of the—well—close kind.

All of this happens behind a handsome facade; a jungle mural covers the building's outer walls. (Longtime customers will recall that it originally was an aquatic scene but, like the ladies inside, it began peeling.)

4 Skinny-Dip with Someone Special

Baker Beach, off Lincoln Boulevard in the Presidio.

Rangers of the Golden Gate National Recreation Area are faced with a curious dilemma. While the National Park Service does not encourage skinny-dipping, much of the city's beachfront is part of the GGNRA and there's nothing in federal law specifically prohibiting nudity.

"If we hauled a nude sunbather before a federal magistrate, we'd be laughed out of court," a ranger told us. "So we ask them to limit themselves to particular areas."

Essentially, those areas consist of the northern end of Baker Beach and several small rock-sheltered coves between there and the Golden Gate Bridge. Most of the skinny-dippers are slender young men, but I've noticed some remarkable exceptions.

5 Buy a Naughty Netsuke

Look for them in window displays at Tangerine Accents, 733 Grant Avenue (near Sacramento), 982-6033; and in the window and a downstairs display case at America souvenir and video shop, 500 Bush Street (Grant Avenue at the Chinatown gate), 397-0140.

Netsuke are tiny ivory Japanese figurines, used in ancient times by Samurai warriors to close the drawstrings of their pouches. Most depict animals, people, or assorted symbols, while some portray consenting adults in *very* compromising positions. Now rather expensive collector's items, netsuke—ranging from innocent to indecent—are available in many Chinatown shops.

6 Read All About It in a Very Adult Newspaper

Available in news racks or by subscription: The Pleasure Guide, P.O. Box 410411, San Francisco, CA 94141.

Have you ever wondered what was inside the pages of those provocative-looking one-dollar tabloids in the sidewalk news racks? Most are published in Los Angeles, but at least one, *The Pleasure Guide,* is a local product.

The inside pages are full of what's left of the sexual revolution: classified ads for swing parties, escort service, phone sex, outcall massage, and lots of bosomy photos. It also features some badly written porn stories, and articles discuss your erogenous zones. Actually, the entire publication is an erogenous zone. If you're too embarrassed to pull one of these tawdry tabloids from a news rack in public, you can get a subscription; the fine print says you're supposed to be at least eighteen years old.

Incidentally, it's illegal to pretend you're someone else when you communicate with this tawdry tabloid. (Apparently, some people place classified ads in friends' names as a practical joke.) The paper quotes from the California Penal Code, Section 480:

Every person who signs any letter addressed to a newspaper with the name of a person other than himself and sends such letter to the newspaper, with intent to lead the newspaper to believe that such letter was written by the person whose name is signed thereto, is guilty of a misdemeanor.

Say what?

7 Get Rubbed—Sometimes the Wrong Way— at a Massage Parlor

Look in the yellow pages under Massage.

There are two kinds of masseuses in San Francisco: those who do *shiatsu* massage and those who can't even pronounce it. You can get massaged by the second variety, but mostly in the wallet. Police no longer license massage parlors, but they keep careful tabs on them to discourage prostitution. The odds are that when you pay for a massage in this town, that's all you'll get.

Of course, many legitimate places are in business to give you a skilled, professional rubdown. The tone of their ads will reveal if a particular outfit is more serious about rubbing your body than your pocketbook.

During a special—uh—investigative trip to one of the bawdier parlors, I was rubbed every way imaginable for $50, then the masseuse offered to "fulfill all my fantasies" for a mere $200 more. She clicked a hand-held imprinter expertly across my VISA card, then led me into a "special room." But the only thing special there, other than a red-tasseled canopy over the massage table, was the price. I did get rubbed with palm oil, but for $200 I could have bought my own palm tree.

8 Nibble a Little Sin

The Cake Gallery, 290 Ninth Street (at Folsom); 861-CAKE. Mee Mee Bakery, 1328 Stockton Street (at Broadway); 362-3204.

Put down the phone, lady, we're talking about *food*. The Cake Gallery will bake you an X-rated cake or other naughty nibbles for special occasions. They can be as anatomically complete as you wish. The firm also is a regular bakery with a full line of G-, PG-, and R-rated pastries, and it delivers.

Mee Mee Bakery sells X-rated fortune cookies, although they're not really very naughty. Fortunately, they're good fortune cookies.

9 Giggle with the Gentlemen of the Chorus at Finocchio's

506 Broadway (at Kearny); 982-9388. Show times vary with the seasons; the minimum age is twenty-one.

After more than half a century, the Finocchio Club has become San Francisco's institution of harmless naughtiness. Its small, lively cast of female impersonators prances and dances about convincingly, to the applause of the tour bus crowd, conventioneers, and every Bay Area resident's midwestern cousin who ever visited this city.

In these jaded times, the show is no longer shocking, and only barely naughty. It's a harmless satire of a striptease that is neither bawdy nor off-color; a film version probably would get no worse than a PG rating. We think it's kind of cute.

10 Spend a Little for Even Less at Midsummer Nights Lingerie

Pier 39, second level (off the Embarcadero); 788-0992. Open 10:30 a.m. to 8:30 p.m. daily. Major credit cards.

This Pier 39 lingerie store offers enticing little bits of sensual fluff and other provocative gifts for m'lady. It's a refined place; you'll find none of the tawdry peek-a-boo attire featured in the Frederick's-of-Hollywood-type shops. The selection ranges from filmy nighties to Kama Sutra Oil of Love. So if you're a sensuous lady seeking something silky, or a gentleman seeking to impress such a lady, this place is quite nice. The naughty comes later.

Chapter 16

A CITY CELEBRATES

The Ten Best Festivals

Make the coming hour o'erflow with joy
And pleasure drown the brim.

—Shakespeare, All's Well That Ends Well

San Franciscans not only like to party individually and with consenting friends, they also enjoy it with organized groups. Any excuse is a good reason for a celebration in this city, and its rich ethnic legacy adds cultural spice to the festivities. The San Francisco Visitor Information Center in Hallidie Plaza at Market and Powell has specifics on the city's many celebrations, or call 391-2000. Our Ten Best San Francisco festivals are listed in chronological order.

1 Chinese New Year's Celebration

February to March in Chinatown and downtown San Francisco; Chinese Chamber of Commerce, 730 Sacramento Street, San Francisco, CA 94108; 982-3000.

Don't even try to figure out the day on which Chinese New Year falls; it has something to do with moon phases. Just check the local papers or call the Chinese Chamber of Commerce or the San Francisco Visitor Information Center (391-2000). New Year's Day itself is celebrated quietly in Chinese homes. The holiday goes public a few days later with a Miss Chinatown USA pageant, the explosions of thousands of ear-jarring little red firecrackers, lion dancers, folk dancing, martial arts demonstrations, crafts exhibits, and such.

The grand finale is a parade, one of the city's largest. The star of the procession is the block-long *gum lung,* the glittering golden dragon that snakes and snorts along the parade route, held aloft by dozens of dragon-bearers.

2 Cherry Blossom Festival

Middle to late April in Japantown and Japan Center, Post and Webster; 922-6776.

In Japan, where space is precious, thousands of acres are given over to a cherry tree that bears no fruit, only blossoms. The Japanese honor the brief two-week spring bloom with a celebration called *Sakura Matsuri.* The tradition has come to *Nihonmachi,* the Japanese community in the Western Addition.

Activities include classic theater, folk dances, flower arranging, bonsai demonstrations, and other things Japanese. Most events occur in and about Japan Center and the adjacent Buchanan Street Mall. In the festival's climactic parade, sweating youths carry portable shrines through the streets while *taiko* drummers pound out their thunder.

3 Opening Day of the Yachting Season

The last Saturday in April on San Francisco Bay.

You don't have to own a yacht or even a dinghy to enjoy this aquatic spectacle. Virtually every sailboat in the greater Bay Area takes to the waters, filling the bay with glittering white triangles and brilliant billows of spinnakers. The best viewing points are Fisherman's Wharf, the Golden Gate Promenade between Fort Mason and the Golden Gate Bridge, the bridge itself, Fort Point, and Marin Headlands above the bridge. Pray for sunshine and take your camera.

4 Latin Festivals

Cinco de Mayo and Carnival, both during May in the Mission District; 826-1401.

Cinco de Mayo is celebrated during the week including May 5 with folk dancing, art exhibits, guided tours past the neighborhood's two hundred murals, special food shows, and the like. There's a parade, of course, usually scheduled on the Sunday closest to May 5.

In case you wondered, *Cinco de Mayo* does not celebrate the fact that José Cinco of Guadalajara invented mayonnaise. It marks the Battle of Puebla on May 5, 1862, when a greatly outnumbered Mexican force defeated the invading armies of Napoleon III.

Carnival is the Latin community's version of Mardi Gras, held the last weekend of May instead of the pre-Lenten period. Festivities represent the cultures of Mexico, Central and South America, and the Caribbean. Activities include costumed dancing, street parties, live bands, arts, crafts, international foods, a parade, and the world's longest conga line, which—in a good year—stretches for more than several blocks. For information, call the Mission Economic and Cultural Association at 826-1401.

5 Black and White Ball

Late May in the Civic Center; call 552-8000 for ticket information.

Can a formal ball really be worth more than $100 per ticket? Only in San Francisco, and only if it involves a dozen orchestras playing everything from waltz to rock in five major Civic Center buildings, while dozens of merchants and wineries offer free food and drink.

Possibly the world's largest ball, the Black and White is the annual fundraiser for the San Francisco Symphony. In a good year, more than seven thousand attend. They trip the light fantastic—and sometimes over one another—in the Davies Symphony Hall, Opera House, Veterans Memorial, City Hall, and Civic Auditorium. Outside, streets are blocked off, and a giant rotating mirror ball dangling from a crane casts a fantasy of moving light throughout the Civic Center.

The idea here is to focus your attire on various combinations of black and white. The gents usually are stuck with the tux, but the ladies have a ball conjuring original and unusual ball gowns. It's a day at Ascot turned into night and multiplied a hundredfold. Even if you can't spare the price of admission, pause a few moments on the sidelines to watch the spectacle of thousands of Ascot-theme celebrants moving around the Civic Center, bathed in a twinkle of revolving lights.

6 Festivals of the Feet

Bay to Breakers, third Sunday in May, call the San Francisco Examiner Promotions Department at 777-7770; **San Francisco Marathon,** *mid-July, 391-2123;* **San Francisco Hill Stride,** *mid-September, 626-1600.*

A fitness-oriented city, San Francisco sponsors three major foot races every year, and you can win one of them in a walk.

The famous Bay to Breakers, attracting tens of thousands of runners, dashes from the edge of the bay at the Ferry Building to the ocean on the Great Highway, about 7.5 miles away. Fewer but more serious runners show up for the San Francisco Marathon, a grueling, gasping, and groaning 26.2 miles through the streets of the city.

The newest foot festival, begun here in 1985 and now spread to several other cities, is called the Hill Stride, a walking race that rivals the Bay to Breakers in attendance. Sponsored by *CitySports* magazine as the country's first major walking race, it takes power striders over some of the city's steepest hills.

7 Fourth of July

July 4 at Crissy Field, sponsored by the San Francisco Chronicle; 777-7120.

The small landing field along the Presidio waterfront is San Francisco's Fourth of July focal point. All-day festivities include a fifty-cannon salute to the states, comedy shows, bluegrass music, kids' games, band concerts, and other folksy stuff to keep the crowd amused until fireworks light up the sky, starting at 9 p.m. The rockets' red glare, glimmering off the Golden Gate Bridge and reflecting colored ripples in the bay, is a sight to see.

The idea is to get there early; and walk—don't drive. The pre- and post-fireworks traffic jams are awesome.

8 The San Francisco Fair

Civic Center in early September; call 703-2729 for specifics.

There isn't a cantaloupe patch in sight, but San Francisco's county fair is one of the city's most popular celebrations. This is an urban-style county fair, with popular restaurants setting up food booths, wineries offering tastings, and more than six hundred performers, from jugglers to stand-up comics to operatic divas. The street artists are in full form, carving their sculptures, weaving their macramé, and potting their pots. This delightfully San Franciscanized version of a county fair offers events such as a fog-calling contest, landlord-tenant tug-of-war, and the Impossible Parking Space Race.

9 San Francisco Blues Festival

Mid-September on the Great Meadow at Fort Mason and at Justin Herman Plaza opposite the Ferry Building; 826-6837. Tickets at major ticket agencies.

The San Francisco Blues Festival is a huge outdoor concert series held over a weekend in September, from 11:30 a.m. to 6 p.m. each day. Dozens of local and national blues artists perform. Look for folks like Elvin Bishop, C. J. Chenier and his Red Hot Louisiana Band, Johnny Copeland, and something called the SuperHarps. One magazine called this *"the* blues event of the year on the West Coast."

10 Columbus Day Festivities

The week including Columbus's birthday (October 12); 673-3782 or 391-2000.

Old Chris never got this far. However, thousands of other Italians have settled here, and they celebrate his discovery of America with festivities from late September through his birthday. It begins quietly with the blessing of the fleet at Fisherman's Wharf. Later, Chris finally arrives in California with a reenactment of his landing, at Aquatic Park.

Festa Italiana, centered around the wharf and North Beach, is a three-day revel with ethnic food fairs, street dances, live entertainment, a bocce ball tournament, and nightly fireworks. The Columbus Day Parade proceeds from the foot of Market up—where else?—Columbus Avenue.

Chapter 17

THE CULTURAL AND THE CURIOUS

Lists of Museums and Galleries

The Devil whispered behind the leaves, "It's pretty, but is it art?"

—Rudyard Kipling

We counted fifty museums in the San Francisco Yellow Pages, celebrating everything from Turkish art to tattoos. Some are world class, others virtually unknown. We offer herewith our lists of the Ten Best museums, first large and then small. We conclude with the city's Ten Best galleries, where you can buy something from the art world for your very own.

You'll note that nominees in the first two lists aren't all art museums; they fit the broader classification of places that preserve for future generations the things of the past. (Some other specialized museums are listed under attractions in Chapter 2.) Admission charges are modest, and some museums are free; those that do charge often have free days, so call ahead if you're short on cash.

The Ten Best Major Museums

1 M.H. de Young Memorial Museum

Golden Gate Park, just off John F. Kennedy Drive; 863-3330 or 750-3600. Open 10 a.m. to 4:45 p.m. Wednesday-Sunday; closed Monday and Tuesday. Admission $5 for adults, $3 for seniors, and $2 for juniors twelve to seventeen, younger kids free. Ticket is good the same day for the Asian Art Museum in the same building and the Palace of the Legion of Honor Museum in Lincoln Park (see following listings). Free all day the first Wednesday of each month and from 10 a.m. to noon the first Saturday of each month.

Our favorite San Francisco museum is the oldest, largest, and one of the most honored municipal museums in the West. It traces the cultural development of Western people from the pharaohs to America's greatest artists. Among its outstanding displays are American sculptures and paintings, tribal and folk arts of Asia and the Americas, and an outstanding collection of textiles. It also hosts world-caliber traveling exhibits, ranging from tomb relics of Tutankhamen and art nouveau dress to the Dead Sea scrolls and Tiffany glass.

2 Ansel Adams Center for Photography

250 Fourth Street (between Howard and Folsom); 495-7000. Tuesday-Sunday 11 a.m. to 5 p.m. (first Thursday of each month until 8 p.m.); adults $4, students and seniors $3, and kids $2.

Ansel Adams, who turned black-and-white photography into a highly advanced art form, is honored at this large photo museum south of Market Street, operated by the Friends of Photography. Several galleries feature changing exhibits ranging from early-day art photos to contemporary work. You won't find many scenics here, except in the Adams gallery, where his legendary photos of Yosemite and other areas are often on display. The Optics Art Gallery upstairs displays creativity and whimsy in artistic constructions done with neon, mirrors, video, and assorted kinetics. A downstairs shop offers an extensive selection of photo books.

3 Asian Art Museum

Golden Gate Park, sharing a building with the de Young Memorial Museum; 668-8921. Open 10 a.m. to 5 p.m. Wednesday-Sunday (to 8:45 p.m. the first Wednesday of each month); free days are the same as at the de Young. Admission is $5 for adults, $3 for seniors, and $2 for juniors twelve to seventeen, younger kids free. Ticket is good the same day for the de Young and the Palace of the Legion of Honor.

Although it shares the de Young building, the Asian Art Museum is a separate entity. It exhibits the priceless Avery Brundage collection of ten thousand oriental *objets d'art,* plus other sculptures, paintings, jades, bronzes, and ceramics from forty Asian countries. It hosts traveling exhibitions and offers periodic thematic exhibits from its permanent collections.

4 California Palace of the Legion of Honor

In Lincoln Park; 750-3600. Open 10 a.m. to 4:45 p.m. Wednesday-Sunday. Admission $5 for adults, $3 for seniors, and $2 for juniors twelve to seventeen, younger kids free. Ticket is good the same day for the Asian Art Museum and de Young museums in Golden Gate Park (see previous listings). Saturdays (except during special shows) and the first Wednesday of the month are free days.

This splendid building, fashioned after the original in Paris, was undergoing a major renovation at this writing, to be completed by mid-decade. If the above number doesn't work, call the de Young at 750-3600 to ensure that it's reopened. Exhibits focus on European art, including a major Rodin sculpture collection, paintings, tapestries, furniture, prints, drawings, and porcelains. Light nibbles are available at the museum's Café Chanticleer.

5 Mexican Museum

Fort Mason Center, Building D, 441-0404. Open noon to 5 p.m. Wednesday-Sunday. Adults $3, students and seniors $2, kids under ten free; First Wednesday of each month free from noon to 8 p.m.

Permanent and changing exhibits focus on Mexican art and culture, ranging from pre-Hispanic and colonial to contemporary Chicano art. La Tienda, the museum shop, sells carvings, tinware, books, and other art from Mexico and Latin America.

6 Museum of the City of San Francisco

In the Cannery at 2801 Leavenworth Street (near the foot of Columbus); 928-0289.
Wednesday-Sunday 11 a.m. to 4 p.m. Free; donations appreciated.

Opened in the summer of 1991, this new archive is a scrapbook of San Francisco's past, "weaving a simple story of this unique patchwork of humanity and topography." The two major earthquakes—1906 and 1989—are focal points, with extensive photo exhibits. You'll also find such intrigues as hand-tinted photos of old Chinatown and a 1913 coin-fed player piano that a docent will activate on request. Look up, and you'll see an elaborately carved coffered ceiling, spirited from a thirteenth-century Spanish monastery by agents of newspaper baron William Randolph Hearst.

7 Old U.S. Mint Museum

88 Fifth Street (at Mission); 744-6830. Open 10 a.m. to 4 p.m. Monday-Friday; free.

Have you ever stared at a million dollars in gold bars and coins? You can do so in this imposing cut-stone building, which functioned as the San Francisco Mint from 1874 until 1937. Restored to its original nineteenth-century appearance, this is an intriguing museum of coinage and mining equipment, with hourly tours.

Among its displays are relics from the California gold rush, Western art, gold medals and coins, assaying equipment, and coin minting machinery. Some of the displays are housed in the original thick-walled vaults in the basement.

8 Presidio Army Museum

Lincoln Boulevard (at Funston) in the Presidio, 561-4115; for guided tours, call
921-8193. Open 10 a.m. to 4 p.m. Tuesday-Sunday; free.

The facility focuses on the military history of San Francisco, going back more than a century, when the Presidio housed the Spanish garrison that accompanied the first padres to this area. Exhibits range from old military uniforms to photos and artifacts from the 1906 earthquake. (*Note:* Although the Presidio will be deactivated to become part of the Golden Gate National Recreation Area in mid-decade, it's likely that the museum will continue to function.)

9 San Francisco Museum of Modern Art

Veterans Memorial, Van Ness Avenue at McAllister, 252-4000. Open 10 a.m.
to 5 p.m. Tuesday-Friday (until 9 p.m. Thursday); 11 a.m. to 5 p.m. on weekends.
Adults $4, seniors, and kids $2; free on the first Tuesday of the month and half-price
Thursday from 5 p.m. to 9 p.m.

San Francisco's fascinating contemporary museum challenges your perception of art. It's one of the country's leading exponents of the leading edge of the modern art movement.

Is some of this stuff art? Is it even pretty? Go decide for yourself. The museum also has a fine little café and an excellent art bookstore. A privately endowed facility, it is scheduled to move to larger quarters on Third Street between Mission and Howard in 1995.

10 Treasure Island Museum

Just inside the Treasure Island gate; park outside and walk in; 395-5067. Open 10 a.m. to 3:30 p.m. daily except Thanksgiving, Christmas, and New Year's Day; free.

The TI museum is concerned with our sea services—Navy, Marine Corps, and Coast Guard—with exhibits relating to their worldwide exploits. It also tells the story of Treasure Island's 1939-40 Golden Gate International Exposition, the Bay Bridge, and the China Clipper seaplanes that flew from here between 1939 and 1946. As we've mentioned earlier, views of the city and the Golden Gate are awesome from this area.

The Ten Best Small Museums

We haven't picked a favorite here because each of these facilities is different in character and subject; they're listed alphabetically.

1 American Indian Contemporary Art Gallery

685 Market Street, Suite 250 (in the Monadnock Building between Third Street and New Montgomery); 496-7600. Tuesday-Saturday 10:30 a.m. to 5 p.m. (until 6 p.m. in November and December); free; donations accepted.

Both a gallery and a museum, this often overlooked showplace offers a fine collection of contemporary American Indian arts, some for sale, others to admire. Sales shop items include silver, beadwork, turquoise jewelry, classic Santa Rosa pottery, Zuni fetishes, and Navajo blankets. Gallery art ranges from surrealistic to whimsical, displaying the skills and imaginations of today's Indian artists. We particularly liked a clever transitional piece called *Road Warrior,* a Cadillac hubcap festooned in the manner of a traditional war shield.

2 Cartoon Art Museum

665 Third Street (between Brannan and Townsend); 546-9481. Open 11 a.m. to 5 p.m. Wednesday-Friday, 10 a.m. to 5 p.m. Saturday, and 1 p.m. to 5 p.m Sunday; $3 for adults, $2 for teens and seniors, and $1 for preteens.

Located on the fifth floor of the Northern California Print Center, this little-known facility features art, books, and figures from the world of cartooning. Exhibits range from original comic strip panels to self-portraits of noted cartoonists; displays change every three to four months. An exhibit concerning the history of printing is in the foyer outside the museum.

3 Craft and Folk Art Museum of San Francisco

Fort Mason Center, Building A; 775-0990. Open 11 a.m. to 5 p.m. Tuesday-Sunday, 10 a.m. to 5 p.m. Saturday; adults $1, seniors and youths 50 cents, kids under twelve and groups free. First Wednesday of each month free from noon to 8 p.m.

Displays range from elegant to witty in this museum featuring American folk art, contemporary jewelry, and ethnic arts from the United States and other countries. Exhibits change frequently.

4 Jewish Community Museum

121 Steuart Street (at Mission); 543-8880. Sunday-Wednesday 11 a.m. to 5 p.m., Thursday 11 a.m. to 7 p.m., closed Friday-Saturday and on some national and Jewish holidays; adults $3, seniors and students $1.50, kids under twelve free.

San Francisco's only Jewish museum offers a fresh perspective on contemporary and traditional Jewish art and artifacts. Changing exhibits focus on art, culture, history, and contemporary issues. Museum-sponsored activities include art education, performing arts, lectures, holiday celebrations, workshops, and special events directed toward young adults.

5 Museo Italo Americano

Building C, Fort Mason Center; 673-2200. Open noon to 5 p.m. Wednesday-Sunday; adults $2, seniors and students $1. First Wednesday of each month free from noon to 8 p.m.

The museum features exhibitions of works by Italian and Italian-American artists. It also sponsors programs concerning Italian language, history, literature, music, and art.

6 The Octagon House

2645 Gough Street (at Union); 441-7512. Open noon to 3 p.m. on the second Sunday, and second and fourth Thursdays of the month (closed during January); free, donations accepted.

The Octagon House displays furniture, silver, lacquer ware, and pewter from America's colonial and federal periods, plus documents of those eras. If you can't catch the exhibits because of the facility's limited hours, the building itself is worth a look. It's a curious octagonal structure with a cupola on top, resembling a fortress or perhaps a lighthouse.

7 San Francisco Fire Department Museum

655 Presidio Avenue (at Bush); 861-8000, extension 0365. Open 1 p.m. to 5 p.m. Thursday-Sunday; free.

In a city frequently tormented by fires and earthquakes, the fire department obviously has a rather colorful and exciting history. Nearly a century and a half of fire-fighting memories are preserved in this pioneer memorial museum. Displays include one of the city's first fire engines, historic photos, and old fire-fighting regalia.

8 The San Francisco Room

Third floor of the main library, Larkin at McAllister (in the Civic Center); 557-4567. Open Tuesday, Wednesday, and Friday from 1 p.m. to 6 p.m., and Thursday and Saturday from 10 a.m. to noon and 1 p.m. to 6 p.m.; free.

This little-known mini-museum is housed in the archive room of the San Francisco Public Library. It features early-day memorabilia such as old keys to the city, artifacts unearthed from the 1906 earthquake and fire, and a silver shovel used by Mayor "Sunny Jim" Rolf in Civic Center ground-breaking ceremonies in 1913. It also has an extensive collection of books on San Francisco, the Bay Area, and the West. It's a great hangout for serious scholars and historians.

9 Tattoo Art Museum

841 Columbus Avenue (near Mason); 775-4991. Open noon to 6 p.m. daily; free.

The world's only museum devoted to tattoo art, started by the legendary Lyle Tuttle, moved to North Beach after his Seventh Street shop was ruined by the 1989 earthquake. Lyle has retired, although his museum and tattoo parlor remain active. Exhibits include photos of tattooed folks, sheets of old tattoo designs, and a "hall of fame" of famous tattooists. And of course, you can still get needled with a decoration of your choice.

10 Wells Fargo History Museum

420 Montgomery Street (at California); 396-2619. Open banking days from 9 a.m. to 5 p.m.; free.

An original Concord stagecoach, gold rush memorabilia, and a large collection of Western postage stamps and franks are featured in this attractive bank museum. Visitors can take an imaginary ride in the "Stagecoach Under Construction" exhibit on the mezzanine.

The Ten Best Art Galleries

What follows are the Ten Best places in the city in which to go art shopping or browsing. Gallery prowlers will find the largest concentration along Sutter Street, particularly in the 200 to 600 blocks (including several at 250 Sutter), and at Ghirardelli Square. *San Francisco Gallery Guide,* produced by the William Sawyer Gallery, 3045 Clay Street (921-1600), offers names, addresses, and hours of dozens of local art shops. It's issued bimonthly, listing the latest exhibits and shows. The West Coast edition of the monthly *Art Now Gallery Guide* covers San Francisco galleries, plus those in other cities from San Diego to Vancouver, B.C.; call (908) 638-5255. Both guides are available at many hotels and galleries.

Our good friend "Von" Von Schlafke, retired from the San Francisco Museum of Modern Art and much a part of the contemporary art scene, guided us in our gallery selections. They are listed alphabetically.

1 Braunstein/Quay Gallery

250 Sutter Street, third floor (near Kearny); 392-5532. Open 10:30 a.m. to 5:30 p.m. Tuesday-Friday, and 11 a.m. to 5 p.m. Saturday.

"'Tis pretty, but is it art?" This contemporary gallery features sculptures, assemblages, and paintings representing the leading edge of modern art. The focus is on Bay Area artists, although the gallery also draws some of its engrossing works from afar.

If you'd like a ceramic milk carton, a glass cube with a brass ring handle or some such other curiosity, this is your place. Among its featured artists are Peter Voulkos and Nancy Keinholz.

2 Campbell-Thiebaud Gallery

645 Chestnut Street (at Columbus); 441-8680. Open 11 a.m. to 5:30 p.m. Tuesday-Friday, from noon to 4 p.m. Saturday.

The gallery displays works of contemporary artists from the Bay Area and around the world. Eclectic exhibits range from American Indian and pre-Colombian art and Indian miniature paintings to the works of gallery co-owner Wayne Thiebaud, Manuel Neri, Christopher Brown, and others.

3 Circle Gallery

Ghirardelli Square at 900 North Point, 776-2370; and 140 Maiden Lane (near Grant), 989-2100. Weekdays 11 a.m. to 7 p.m., weekends 10 a.m. to 9 p.m.

These galleries feature extensive collections of contemporary art, ranging from paintings to art prints. Should you want Donald Duck, Fred Flintstone, or Wile E. Coyote on your wall, the Ghirardelli branch specializes in cels and hand-painted reproductions of works by noted cartoonists. (Cels are individual frames used in movie animation.)

Architectural historians will be intrigued to learn that the Maiden Lane gallery was designed in 1949 by Frank Lloyd Wright. Its fan-shaped brick facade, barrel-arched entry, circular interior ramp, and ceiling with circles-on-circles are exemplary Wright.

4 Conacher Galleries

134 Maiden Lane (off Kearny); 392-5447. Open 9:30 a.m. to 5:30 p.m. Monday-Saturday.

In business for more than three decades, Don Conacher's comfortable showplace makes art affordable by featuring lithographs, serigraphs, and other fine art prints. Among its famous artists—mostly contemporary—are Leroy Neiman, Dong Kingman, John Weidenhamer, Alan Maley, and Eyvind Earle.

5 Harcourts Gallery

460 Bush Street (between Kearny and Grant); 421-3428. Open 10 a.m. to 5:30 p.m. Tuesday-Saturday.

Paintings, sculptures, and graphics by major nineteenth- and twentieth-century artists are exhibited; included are works by Picasso, Chagall, Matisse, and Renoir. Also shown are contemporary American works by artists such as Theophilus Brown, Nancy Genn, and Roland Petersen.

6 San Francisco Art Exchange

458 Geary Street (at Taylor); 441-8840. Open at 9 a.m. daily; various closing hours.

Paintings and prints of the "perfect women" from the estate of Alberto Vargas are available here. Also on sale are works by Roger Dean, noted for his album covers for rock groups Yes and Asia, artworks by Rolling Stones guitarist Ron Wood, and by other contemporary artists.

7 San Francisco Art Institute Galleries

800 Chestnut Street (at Jones); 771-7020. Open 8 a.m. to 5 p.m. Monday-Saturday (until 8 p.m. Thursday).

The Art Institute, housed in an old Spanish-style structure, has two public galleries. The most famous is the Diego Rivera Gallery with an original Rivera mural. Contemporary works are exhibited in the Walter/McBean Gallery. Student artwork, which is for sale, is displayed in the Rivera Gallery and the courtyard.

8 Vorpal Gallery

393 Grove Street (at Gough); 397-9200. Open 11 a.m. to 6 p.m. Tuesday-Saturday.

The Vorpal Gallery features contemporary painting, sculpture, and graphics. Its two floors offer a survey of recent works by California and international artists. It also has a large collection of graphic arts, including works by M. C. Escher, Jesse Allen, and Yozo Hamaguchi.

9 William Sawyer Gallery

3045 Clay Street (at Broderick); 921-1600. Open 11 a.m. to 6 p.m. Tuesday-Saturday.

Sawyer's long-established gallery specializes in original sculptures and paintings by emerging and established contemporary American artists. The emphasis is on landscape and realism, with a number of abstract artists also represented.

10 Xanadu Gallery

Ghirardelli Square (North Point at Polk); 441-5211. Open 10 a.m. to 6 p.m. Monday-Thursday, 10 a.m. to 9 p.m. Friday-Saturday, and 11 a.m. to 6 p.m. Sunday.

Is it an art gallery or an import shop? It's an interesting balance of both. Xanadu features tribal art and artifacts from assorted Asian, African, and South Pacific island tribes. Included in the collection are tribal objects from Papua New Guinea and fine Asian textiles.

Chapter 18

BROWSING AND BUYING

A Shopper's Ten Best

Whoever said money can't buy happiness didn't know where to shop.

—Author unknown

In addition to its many other attributes, San Francisco is the premier shopping center for northern California. Its shopping complexes, department stores, and upscale boutiques offer everything except enough chairs for weary, package-toting husbands.

The Ten Best Places to Shop 'Til You Drop

1 THE BEST SHOPPING COMPLEX
Embarcadero Center

At the foot of Market Street (at Drumm).

Nearly two hundred shops and restaurants occupy four open-air plazas at the base of the high-rise Embarcadero Center complex. With its open breezeways, monumental works of art, outdoor cafés, and sunny patios, this upscale center offers a wide range of stores, from trendy boutiques to affordable clothiers to specialty shops. Concerts and seasonal activities add to the interest here.

2 THE BEST THEME SHOPPING CENTER
Ghirardelli Square

900 North Point.

The first is still the best. William Matson Roth saved this collection of fine old brick buildings from redevelopers and opened the city's first theme shopping center in 1962. Originally housing a chocolate factory, woolen mill, and other light industries, the fine brickwork now shelters eighty shops and restaurants, focused around plazas and a wonderful Ruth Asawa fountain. Ghirardelli avoids the gimmickry to which many tourist-oriented shopping complexes fall victim.

3 THE MOST ATTRACTIVE SHOPPING CENTER
San Francisco Shopping Center

865 Market Street (at Powell and Fifth Street).

The impressive San Francisco Shopping Centre offers eye appeal and downtown convenience. Dozens of upscale shops line mezzanine floors of a dramatic eight-story atrium. The tiered center is served by a fascinating architectural lacework of curving escalators—the only such devices on the continent.

The major player in this architectural drama is Nordstrom, filling the four top floors beneath a bold oval dome. In addition to the usual departments, Nordstrom

has a spa, a pub, five restaurants, and a concierge. Independent shops and boutiques occupy several floors below the big department store, and the Emporium—a
longtime Market Street fixture—is dovetailed into the new complex. When you've
finished shopping, return to the patio level and call for your car, because, of course,
San Francisco Shopping Centre offers valet parking.

Of course.

4 THE BEST SHOPPING DISTRICT
Union Square

A couple of decades ago, as veteran downtown stores began closing, we feared
that the shopping focus would shift to parking lot suburbs, a fate undeserved by
a cosmopolitan city. Then the stores began returning, and new ones arrived,
including such prestigious retailers as Neiman-Marcus, Nordstrom, and Saks Fifth
Avenue. The opening of San Francisco Shopping Centre just across Market in late
1988 was a major stimulus for downtown. Now more than ever, this area—
including the nearby Crocker Galleria at Post and Montgomery—offers the most
complete shopping facilities in northern California.

5 THE BEST SHOPPING STREET
Union Street

*Three blocks south and parallel to Lombard's "motel row"; most shops are
between Franklin and Scott streets.*

This handsome street in the Marina District has come a long way from its
Cow Hollow days, when the area was the site of several dairies. It's now lined
with trendy shops, boutiques, galleries, and restaurants, many of them in fine old
Victorians. It's the proper promenade for crystal, upscale clothing, artwork,
antiques, and home decorator items. You can find everything along Union Street
except a place to park.

6 THE BEST ETHNIC SHOPPING AREA
Richmond District

Outer Geary Boulevard and Clement Street.

The Richmond has become an ethnic restaurant row in the past couple of
decades. Clement Street and Geary Boulevard are lined with small cafés—mostly
of Asian roots. The district also offers a fine international mix of shops, specialty
stores, and foreign grocers. You can find Chinese, Vietnamese, Russian, and other
ethnic stores and cafés along Clement Street, and several Korean shops stand along
nearby Balboa Street. Japanese crafts, artwork, foods, and souvenirs spill from
Japan Center at Geary Boulevard and Buchanan Street, in the Western Addition,
just outside the Richmond District (see Chapter 1).

7 THE BEST DEPARTMENT STORE
Macy's

Stockton Street at O'Farrell, 397-3333.

The largest department store in San Francisco has gotten even larger, with
the addition of the former Liberty House across the street. Although the newer

Nordstrom got a lot of attention when the San Francisco Shopping Centre opened a few years ago, Macy's is still *the* place to shop in the city.

As you push through one of its many doors onto the huge main floor, you're offered a perfume sample; down in Macy's Cellar, someone in a chef's hat demonstrates cookware by stirring up something that smells wonderful; up in the toy department, a clerk is toying with a new electronic game. The maze of aisles brim with the tempting products of our consumer society. With its Easter floral extravaganza and elaborate Christmas window displays, Macy's has been woven into the fabric of San Francisco. What a wonderful place in which to mistreat your credit card!

8 THE BEST IMPORT STORE
Cost Plus

2552 Taylor Street (at Bay); 928-6200.

Want a Tijuana taxi horn, Moroccan goat bells, a batik shirt, Mexican paper flowers, a pound of Kona coffee, or a teak coffee table? Cost Plus isn't an import store; it's an import empire scattered over thousands of square feet in several buildings. If you can't find a particular import item here, no one anywhere has made it yet.

9 THE BEST DISCOUNT STORE
Whole Earth Access

401 Bayshore Boulevard (at Courtland; take Army Street exit from Bayshore Freeway—U.S. 101—and go east); 285-5244.

Despite the funky name, Whole Earth Access isn't a Haight-Ashbury health food store; it's a discount chain that stacks merchandise to the rafters. These are stark barnlike places devoid of all decor, but they offer a wide range of merchandise, and we like the price tags. When we shopped recently for new kitchen appliances, Whole Earth's prices were lowest, and the follow-up service was surprisingly responsive for a discount place. (Like everything else in our book, this is an unsolicited testimonial.)

10 THE BEST SUPERMARKET
Plaza Foods

Fulton Street at Masonic (formerly Petrini Plaza); 567-0976 for grocery department; other departments listed in the Yellow Pages in the "grocers— retail" section, under Plaza Foods.

Why can't all supermarkets be like this? Plaza Foods resembles a friendly corner market that multiplied. It's actually a collection of individually owned shops gathered under a single roof. It has a large grocery department, a huge meat department, an equally large fish and deli section, tangy-smelling take-home things cooking in roasters, a flower stand, and a bakery.

It was Petrini's when I lived in a shabby Victorian flat across the street more than three decades ago. The store was always crowded, noisy, busy with the smelling and selling of good things to eat. Other than the name, it hasn't changed a bit. Fortunately.

The Ten Best Stores of a Specific Sort

Where do you go when you need a pound of Kona-Moroccan coffee, a star map, or the tastiest truffles this side of a weight-loss clinic? We'll tell you where.

1 THE BEST BAKERY
Fantasia Confections

3465 California Street (at Laurel, in Laurel Village); 752-0825.

The Weil family's Fantasia bakery has been luring people away from diets since 1948, offering a savory array of cakes, pies, cookies, and other sweets. A specialty is European cookies and pastries; Fantasia makes the best *Linzertorte* west of Vienna, plus a tasty assortment of *stollens* and *petits fours*. A few small tables occupy one corner, and you can order coffee, tea, or chocolate with your goodies, in case you can't wait to get them home.

2 THE BEST CAMERA STORE
Adolph Gasser

181 Second Street (at Howard), 495-3852; 750 Bryant Street (at Fifth Street), 543-3888; and 5733 Geary Boulevard (at Twenty-second Avenue), 751-0145.

Gasser is the camera store for professionals and serious amateurs. Adolph's crew invariably has that hard-to-find piece of equipment as well as examples of virtually every photographic brand on the market. Gasser also rents camera and video equipment for pros and people who want to take home images of their San Francisco visit.

3 THE BEST COFFEE STOP
Spinelli Coffee Company

2455 Fillmore Street (at Jackson), 929-8808; 3966 Twenty-fourth Street (at Sanchez), 550-7416; 2255 Polk Street (at Green), 928-7793; and 1257 Folsom Street (at Eighth Street), 862-2272.

That's right, coffee *stop*, not coffee shop. Spinelli's offers one of the largest selections of gourmet coffees in the city. Shoppers can step up to gleaming coffee grinders to create their own special blends from whole beans. Fresh-brewed coffee is sold by the cup, and seats in many of the outlets invite patrons to linger a while.

4 THE BEST LIFE SCIENCES STORE
The Nature Company

Four Embarcadero Center, 956-4911; Ghirardelli Square, 776-0724.

Intrigued by lofty stars or lowly bugs? The Nature Company specializes in the natural world around us. Offerings include telescopes, star maps, sundials, wildlife guides, and other nature books, wall prints, nature toys, and such. For those on your Christmas list who have everything, how about sending a cassette recording of whale sounds? (*That* should get them off your list.)

5 THE BEST ORGANIC FOOD STORE
Harvest Ranch Market

2285 Market Street (at Noe); 626-0805. Daily 9 a.m. to 11 p.m.

This upper Market whole earth haven is the ultimate natural foods shop and deli. Selections include "athletic foods" for the superactive, organic gourmet foods, and sundry fruits, vegetables, and meats produced without additives. Browse among displays of millet rice, granola, oat bran, whole-grain breads, scones, herbal teas, and trail mixes. A drink case contains the latest in trendy health sippers, and you can build the basis for a take-out lunch or a picnic at a soup and salad bar.

6 THE BEST RECORD STORE
Tower Records & Video

2525 Jones Street (at Columbus and Bay); 885-0500.

Listen, you want the latest on the charts? Some funky oldies, classics, elevator music? Tower Records probably has the largest selection in the city. Busy, narrow corridors are filled with records, cassettes, videocassettes, compact disks, noise, and finger-snapping teenagers; it's the way a record shop should be.

7 THE BEST SWEET SHOP
Joseph Schmidt Confections

3489 Sixteenth Street (at Sanchez); 861-8682.

Joe does some of the best truffles and chocolate sculptures in town. The expression "sinfully rich" comes to mind when we browse his shop, eyeing elegant little creations that rival the finest crafted chocolates from Switzerland. What a way to ruin a diet.

8 THE BEST TOY STORE
F A O Schwarz Fifth Avenue

48 Stockton Street (at O'Farrell); 394-8700.

In this huge children's paradise with its chugging choo-choos, windup toys that are always wound up, and cute things dangling from the ceiling, *everyone's* still a kid. Recently relocated from smaller Post Street quarters, Schwarz's new home is even more delightfully cluttered with children's dreams.

9 THE BEST WINE SHOP
The Jug Shop

1567 Pacific Street (near Polk); 885-2922.

With its fine selection of California and European wines and knowledgeable staff, the Jug Shop has been a favorite stop for wine aficionados for more than three decades. Should you wish to sample before you buy, a few interesting bottles are open for sips at a corner tasting bar, for a small fee.

Its shelves also brim with a variety of varietal jug wines and most major liquor brands. Staff members, all serious about wine, will discuss what goes with what you're having for dinner. They'll even help you set up or revamp your wine cellar.

10 THE BEST SELECTION OF RIDICULOUSLY SPECIALIZED SHOPS
Pier 39

Off the Embarcadero; most shops open daily 10:30 a.m. until 8:30 p.m., some later in summer.

You say you're having trouble finding that perfect refrigerator magnet to match the new tile trim around the sink? Look no further than Magnet P.I. And if you've always wanted a Mountain Dew coin bank, the Trademark Shop has them. Wound About sells only key-wind and battery-operated toys including—unfortunately—Moonies that drop their drawers at the flip of a switch. The list continues at the city's ultimate tourist trinket shopping center: Ready Teddy for stuffed animals, Kites of the World for just that, Cartoon Junction for cartoon character merchandise, and—only in San Francisco—the Cable Car Store.

Chapter 19

PILLOW TALK

Lists of Special Places to Rest Your Head

> *A great hotel is like a duck swimming—composed and serene above the water, but paddling like hell underneath.*
>
> —*Hotel executive Tim Carlson*

Finding a place to stay in San Francisco is no clever trick—unless there's a major convention in town. The city brims with world-class hotels, and Van Ness Avenue and Lombard Street are rimmed with motels. But suppose you're tired of look-alike motels, and you want something more intriguing than a $150-a-night hotel room with a view of the adjacent hotel?

In recent years, many venerable Victorians, scruffy small hotels, and even tired old apartment houses have been converted into bed and breakfast inns or smart new midsized hotels. This book isn't intended as a budget guide, but we will point out that, in most cases, these smaller places are considerably less expensive than the major hotels. For preservationists such as ourselves, the nicest thing about this trend is that it redeems many older buildings that otherwise would have been reduced to parking lots.

The rates were current at the time we compiled this guide but, of course, they're subject to change, invariably upward. All rates listed are for two persons per room.

The Ten Best Bed and Breakfast Inns

When California's bed and breakfast movement began in the 1970s, San Francisco—with its hundreds of Victorians—was a natural growth area. A visit to a B&B is a journey back to a kinder and gentler time, be it Victorian San Francisco, rural England, or provincial France. Or perhaps a visit to Grandmother's house, assuming the old lady was loaded and could afford her own interior decorator.

1 Château Tivoli

1057 Steiner Street (at Golden Gate); 776-5462 or (800) 228-1647. Doubles $80 to $125, suites $125 to $200; MC/VISA, AMEX. Eight units; some private, some shared baths; all have room phones, two have fireplaces. Expanded Continental breakfast.

This 1892 French Renaissance château is one of San Francisco's most striking examples of nineteenth-century architectural filigree. It is certainly the city's most attractive and opulently furnished bed and breakfast.

The château is a fairy castle conglomeration of turrets, towers, decorative friezes, and gingerbread trim. Rooms are an interior designer's vision, with stained glass, frescoed ceilings, canopy beds, marble baths, and color-coordinated decor. The museum-quality furnishings include pieces from the estates of Cornelius Vanderbilt, Charles de Gaulle, and J. Paul Getty. They are a mix of Victorian and French antiques, accented with rare artwork. (Château Tivoli also is listed under *The Ten Most Handsome Victorians* in Chapter 20.)

2   The Bed & Breakfast Inn

Four Charlton Court (off Union, between Laguna and Buchanan); 921-9784. Doubles $68 to $184; no credit cards. Ten rooms, six with private baths; TV and phones in most rooms. Large Continental breakfast; street parking, public garages nearby.

The first bed and breakfast in the city, the Bed & Breakfast Inn remains one of the most charming. The look is cheery colonial English, with grass cloth, bamboo, louvered window shutters, and ceiling fans. The rooms are bright, airy, and comfortable, with none of the somberness of some Victorian inns.

The location is excellent: within a few steps of the Union Street shopping area and a short drive from downtown. Tucked into the end of a short street, it's a surprisingly quiet refuge within the busy city.

3   Dolores Park Inn

3641 Seventeenth Street (at Dolores); 621-0482. Doubles $60 to $150; MC/VISA. Six rooms, two with private baths; TV in rooms, some fireplaces. Full breakfast; off-street parking.

This 1874 Italianate Victorian inn, with a garden, patio, and spa, offers quiet sanctuary from the busy city. The rooms are handsomely appointed, with antiques, ceiling fans, and ceramic fireplaces. Considering the high quality of accommodation, it's one of the city's best B&B bargains.

The inn is located in the upper Market Street area, less than a block from Mission Dolores and a few minutes from downtown.

4   Hermitage House

2224 Sacramento Street (at Buchanan); 921-5515. Doubles $80 to $120; MC/VISA, AMEX. Six rooms, all with private baths, TV, and room phones, some fireplaces. Full breakfast; off-street parking.

A turn-of-the-century manor house with a bold curving two-story bay window, the Hermitage is one of the city's most impeccably furnished inns. It's a pleasant mix of antique and modern, accented by leaded glass, crystal chandeliers, and redwood wainscoting. The rooms are bright and cheery, even with the use of dark woods and antiques.

A sunny sitting room and a formal English garden offer quiet retreats from the city. The inn is located in Pacific Heights, handy to Fillmore Street restaurants and Union Street shops.

5 Inn San Francisco

943 South Van Ness Avenue (at Twentieth Street); 641-0188. Doubles $75 to $175; MC/VISA, AMEX. Twenty-two rooms with TV, refrigerators, and room phones; seventeen with private baths. Full buffet breakfast; some off-street parking.

This handsomely restored 1870s Italianate, once the home of a city commissioner, is tucked into a row of old mansions in a little-known Victorian area of South Van Ness. Room decor is true to the period, with oriental carpets, fainting couches, decorative borders on print wallpaper, and big poofy bedspreads. Deluxe rooms feature spa tubs and feather beds; some have fireplaces.

A garden, sun deck, and hot tubs make this a particularly appealing haven. For total privacy, you can rent a garden cottage with a separate sitting room.

6 Jackson Court

2198 Jackson Street (at Buchanan); 929-7670. From $108 to $150; MC/VISA, AMEX. Ten rooms with private baths, TV, and phones, some fireplaces. Continental breakfast; street parking.

A square-shouldered brick mansion with a mansard roof, Jackson Court has more the look of a New England town house than a Victorian. The opulent interior is a tasteful blend of modern and antique. Dark woods accent a bright, rather cheerful decor of textured wallpaper, lace, and brass. One room has its own patio garden.

The Court is situated in Pacific Heights, handy to Fillmore and Union street restaurant and shopping areas.

7 Petite Auberge and White Swan

863 and 845 Bush Street (at Mason); 928-6000 (Auberge) and 775-1755 (Swan). From $110 to $250; MC/VISA, AMEX. Each has twenty-six rooms with private baths, TV, and phones; most have fireplaces. Full breakfast; valet parking.

We've grouped these together because they're practically next door and owned by the same family; services and amenities are similar.

Beautifully fashioned from two old bay-windowed row-house hotels, the two inns have a pleasing European country look, with print wallpaper, armoires, and fireplaces. Petite Auberge is done in French country fashion; the Swan is described as "English garden style." Both have exceptionally pretty breakfast rooms. We like their location: within a short walk of Union Square and all that is happening in downtown San Francisco.

8 The Spencer House

1080 Haight Street (at Baker); 626-9205. From $95 to $155; MC/VISA. Six rooms with private baths. Full breakfast; street parking.

One of the most charming attractions of this elegant Victorian is hostess Barbara Chambers; she'll greet you with a warm smile—and possibly in her bare feet—then invite you into the kitchen to chat while she prepares a teatime snack.

The house is an 1877 Queen Anne; the rooms are spacious and beautifully furnished with antiques, feather mattresses, poufed coverlets, and hand-carved armoires. Padded fabric wall covering and thick theatrical curtains complete the feel of opulence. The Spencer House is in a neighborhood of Victorian mansions in the Haight-Ashbury, across from Buena Vista Park.

9 Union Street Inn

2229 Union Street (at Fillmore); 346-0424. From $125 to $225; MC/VISA, AMEX. Six rooms, all with private baths, TVs, and room phones. Continental breakfast; limited street parking; public garages nearby.

It's a pleasant surprise to step off busy Union Street and into the large, beautifully landscaped garden that frames this 1902 Edwardian home. The interior look is nineteenth-century European-American, with hand-woven rugs and wood paneling. The furnishings are a mix of antique and contemporary. The inn is located in the heart of the Union Street shopping district.

10 Victorian Inn on the Park

301 Lyon Street (at Fell); 931-1830 or (800) 435-1967. From $94 to $154; major credit cards. Twelve rooms, all with private baths, TVs, and phones; some fireplaces. Large Continental breakfast; ample street parking.

One of the most impeccably restored inns we visited, this 1897 Victorian is a study in European splendor, with coffered ceilings, carved wood paneling, velvet drapes, and bordered print wallpaper. The large rooms have antique furnishings, armoires, and queen-size beds. The third-floor rooms are charmingly cozy little retreats shaped by cupolas and gabled roofs.

The Victorian Inn sits across Fell Street from the Golden Gate Park panhandle, a short drive to the Civic Center and downtown.

The Ten Best Boutique Hotels

Concurrent with the growth of bed and breakfast inns has been the arrival of many boutique hotels. For lack of a better measure, we define boutiques as small inns with fewer than ninety rooms, generally done in an old-world style. Many on our list are reincarnations of older hotels, so again we applaud the new innkeepers as preservationists.

Although the line separating a B&B from a boutique hotel is sometimes fuzzy, the latter usually has more rooms and hotel-like amenities such as room phones and TV sets. A B&B always serves some sort of breakfast. Some of our boutique inns do; others do not. Many offer free limo service.

1 The Sherman House

2160 Green Street (between Fillmore and Webster); 563-3600 or (800) 424-5777. Rooms from $235 to $375, suites from $550 to $750; major credit cards. Eight

*rooms and six suites, many with fireplaces. Restaurant for guests, serving
breakfast and dinner, plus 24-hour "butler's menu." Parking available.*

Lush elegance is a proper description for San Francisco's finest boutique hotel.
Fashioned from a French-Italianate mansion built in 1876 by music magnate
Leander Sherman, it exudes opulence from its ornate lobby to its guest rooms
attired in European antiques. Fireplaces, canopied and draped beds, and bowls of
sweet-smelling potpourri add final touches of refinement to the rooms. Guests can
lounge in window seats piled high with pillows and absorb vistas of the Golden
Gate Bridge and San Francisco Bay. Music whispers from speakers hidden behind
fabric wall covering.

Despite its small size, the Sherman House is a full-function hotel, with 24-
hour room and food service, room TV and phones, concierge, airport pickup, and
limo service in vintage cars. Exquisite multi-course meals emerge from a busy little
kitchen, served in a handsomely coiffed dining room—which is available to guests
only, except by special arrangements.

Others agree that this is an outstanding hotel. Despite its vest pocket size,
it won fourth place among the top twenty-five hotels in America in the 1993
Zagat survey. It rated higher than two other San Francisco lodgings picked by
that survey—the Ritz-Carlton (number eleven) and the Mandarin (number
twenty-four).

2 The Archbishop's Mansion

*1000 Fulton Street (at Steiner); 563-7872 or (800) 543-5820. From $100 to $250;
MC/VISA, AMEX. Fifteen rooms, ten with fireplaces. Large Continental breakfast;
off-street parking.*

More than a decade ago, Jonathon Shannon and Jeffrey Ross purchased one
of San Francisco's landmark mansions and fashioned it into one of northern
California's most luxurious small hotels. The former residence of the archbishop
of San Francisco, this French Empire-style manor is regally costumed with canopied beds, carved armoires, embroidered linens, and valanced drapes. Crystal chandeliers grace coffered ceilings, tapestries adorn the walls, and a great oval
leaded-glass dome glitters above a three-story grand stairway.

Appropriately, the mansion is on the edge of Alamo Square, in the heart of
the city's finest collection of nineteenth-century homes. Not surprisingly, it has
been designated as a San Francisco historic landmark.

3 Golden Gate Hotel

*775 Bush Street (between Mason and Powell); 392-3702 or (800) 835-1118. From
$55 to $89; MC/VISA, AMEX, DIN. Twenty-three rooms with TV, some with
room phones. Continental breakfast and afternoon tea.*

Built in 1913, this venerable Edwardian inn was refurbished in 1986. The
owners preserved the classic bird cage elevator, bay windows, and antique claw
foot tubs. If not elegant, the hotel is prim and neat; one of the city's better room
buys. Rooms are individually decorated, with modern plumbing, queen or twin

beds, antiques, and original artwork. Some rooms have full baths; others have washstands with bath facilities down the hall. The Golden Gate is located near the downtown area, a short walk to Union Square and major shopping facilities.

4 Hyde Park Suites

2655 Hyde Street (at North Point); 771-0200 or (800) 227-3608. From $165 to $220; all major credit cards. Twenty-four rooms. Full kitchens, honor bars, and two TVs in each room. Continental breakfast; parking available.

An all suite hotel, Hyde Park offers a pleasant mix of old-world and modern decor, with terrazzo tile floors, pastel colors, and contemporary furnishings. Each unit has a separate living room and bedroom; some are two-bedroom suites.

Two particularly pleasing features are a landscaped atrium courtyard and a roof garden with a view of San Francisco Bay. Hyde Park Suites is on the edge of Fisherman's Wharf.

5 Inn at the Opera

333 Fulton Street (at Franklin); 863-8400 or (800) 325-2708. From $99 to $180; MC/VISA, AMEX. Forty-eight rooms. Wet bars, microwaves, and in-room honor bars. Continental breakfast. ACT IV lounge and restaurant; garage parking across the street.

Once a retreat for visiting opera stars, the Inn at the Opera has been transformed into a sophisticated little boutique hotel. The furnishings are a balance of European and contemporary American, set off by pastel colors, with coordinated drapes and spreads.

On the fringe of the Civic Center, a few steps from the Opera House, Davies Symphony Hall, and Civic Auditorium, the hotel attracts a theatrical crowd, both performers and patrons. Guests have included such luminaries as Placido Domingo and Mikhail Baryshnikov. Act IV is a popular and handsomely styled California-Continental restaurant.

6 The Majestic

1500 Sutter Street (at Gough); 441-1100 or (800) 252-1155 in California and (800) 824-0094 outside. From $89 to $200; major credit cards. Sixty rooms, with four-poster canopied beds, writing desks, fireplaces in most rooms, refrigerators in suites. Café Majestic and cocktail lounge off lobby; valet parking and street parking.

Restored "beyond its original elegance," the Majestic rivals the Sherman House and Archbishop's Mansion as one of the most lavishly attired boutique hotels in the city. Built in 1902 as a luxury hotel, the Majestic has retained its posh Edwardian look, with canopied beds and a mix of eighteenth- and nineteenth-century museum-quality antiques and artwork.

The lobby is an opulent study in gilt-edge mirrors, crystal chandeliers, and valanced drapes. **Café Majestic** continues this European elegance with bentwood chairs, wainscoting, and crisp white linens. Its menu is based on updated old San Francisco recipes; the adjoining bar has a stately men's club look. Sitting just off Van Ness Avenue, the Majestic is not far from the Civic Center and downtown.

7 The Mansions Hotel

2220 Sacramento Street (at Laguna); 929-9444. From $74 to $150; major credit cards. Twenty rooms. Billiard and game room; sculpture gardens. Restaurant; full breakfast; parking available nearby.

Who says elegance can't be fun? Certainly not Robert Pritikin, who fashioned an 1887 twin-turreted Queen Anne mansion into a plush hotel and furnished it with museum-worthy antiques and paintings. Then, to reinforce his sense of humor, he added a macaw (alive), a chirping monkey (stuffed), a Lawrence Welk bubble machine, and other bits of whimsy. A surrounding garden contains an awesome collection of Benny Bufano sculptures. A next-door Victorian has been refurbished to increase the room count.

Guests in the hotel's opulent Mansion Restaurant sit down to tasty international fare. Weekend dinners are preceded by madcap music and magic shows. They feature the irrepressible Pritikin, who serenades guests on his musical saw and performs such magic feats as the "incredible Peking snow duck double transfer." Weeknight concerts spotlight resident ghost Claudia Chambers, who plays invisibly at a very visible piano.

The guest list at the Pacific Heights hotel-restaurant has included Barbra Streisand, Joel Grey, George McGovern, Paul Simon, and Alan Funt, who must have thought he'd stumbled into a gag set for "Candid Camera."

8 Nob Hill Inn

1000 Pine Street (at Taylor); 673-6080. From $89 to $229; major credit cards. Twenty-one rooms, many with fireplaces, some kitchen units. Continental breakfast; garage parking available nearby.

The Nob Hill is an exquisite boutique hotel with a very European feel: floral wallpaper, brass beds, and elaborately carved armoires. A fascinating focal point in the nicely appointed lobby is a glassed-in European-style lift.

Located atop Nob Hill, it's handy to downtown and the Financial District. Guests are served afternoon tea and sherry.

9 Queen Anne Hotel

1590 Sutter Street (at Octavia); 441-2828 or (800) 262-2663 in California and (800) 227-3970 elsewhere. From $99 to $150 for rooms, and $175 to $275 for suites; major credit cards. Forty-nine rooms, some with fire places. Continental breakfast; off-street parking.

The Queen Anne began life in 1890 as Miss Mary Lake's School, a boarding school for proper young ladies of San Francisco's upper class. It's an attractive boutique hotel today, with a mix of European and American antiques in individually decorated rooms and suites.

The grand parlor is particularly impressive, with its thick red carpet, fluted columns, tulip chandeliers, and scalloped drapes. The Queen Anne is in Pacific Heights, at the opposite end of the block from the Majestic.

10 Warwick Regis Hotel

490 Geary Street (at Taylor); 928-7900 or (800) 827-3447. From $95 to $205; major credit cards. Eighty rooms, with honor bars, some fireplaces. La Scene Café and Bar adjacent; valet parking.

Warwick International Hotels recently purchased this stylish nineteenth-century inn. The rooms are furnished with Louis XVI French and English antiques, half-canopied beds, and scalloped drapes. The bathrooms are Italian marble with brass fixtures.

The Regis is in the downtown area, a short walk from theaters and restaurants, and a few minutes from the Financial District. The adjoining **La Scene Café and Bar** specializes in American cuisine.

The Ten Best Midsized Hotels

Candidates for this category are larger than the boutiques: up to 160 rooms, but substantially smaller than the major hostelries of Nob Hill and Union Square. Many offer amenities similar to those in the big houses and often at a lower price.

Our winner is not inexpensive, but it rivals—and perhaps excels—the city's largest hotels in ambiance and service.

1 The Mandarin Oriental

222 Sansome Street (at Pine); 885-0999 or (800) 622-0404. From $260 to $1250 (lower weekend rates); major credit cards. One hundred fifty rooms with city and bay views, mini-bar refrigerators, three phones, modem terminals, large desks. Silks Restaurant and Mandarin Bar; valet parking.

Opened in 1987 and managed by the prestigious Mandarin Oriental group of Hong Kong, this is a stylish creation built into the top eleven floors of the twin-towered First Interstate Center. It's the city's third tallest building, and every room offers striking aerial views. Glass catwalks connect the two hotel towers, providing more awesome vistas.

The circular ground-level lobby is done in glossy marble; oriental art objects and a huge beaded chandelier provide touches of elegance. The comfortable and quiet Mandarin cocktail lounge is off the lobby. A stairway leads to Silks, an exquisitely designed restaurant featuring creative California cuisine and some of the most sinfully delicious desserts we've ever tasted. The dining room decor is rich with warm reds, golds and burnt auburns that enhance the *faux bois* woodgrain walls and distinctive Chinese cracked ice window treatments.

The rooms are what you'd expect for $260 and up: bright, modern, and spacious, with an almost sinful opulence. They were redecorated recently with warm yellows, Asian chintz fabrics, and oriental-modern collages done by local artist Dennis Parlante. Room amenities range from remote-controlled entertainment centers to hair dryers, robes, and Thai-silk slippers. Guests can soak away their cares while absorbing the scenery; the tubs in the Italian marble bathrooms offer picture window views of the city.

2 Campton Place Hotel Kempinski

340 Stockton Street (at Post); 781-5555 or (800) 426-3135. From $180 to $250; major credit cards. One hundred twenty-six rooms with writing desks, dual phones for computer use; roof garden. **Campton Place Restaurant** *off lobby; valet parking.*

Campton Place rivals the larger world-class hotels in its guest-pampering service. Valets accompany patrons to their rooms, offering to unpack their luggage, then repack when they depart. An in-house laundry can have a bit of stray ketchup removed from your jacket before you've finished dinner.

All this coddling occurs in an atmosphere of cool elegance. Rooms are done in taupe and apricot, with English antique reproductions and contemporary artwork. The adjoining Campton Place Restaurant is one of the city's finest, featuring excellent contemporary American cuisine, including the city's most formidable power breakfast.

3 Hotel Diva

440 Geary Street (at Mason); 885-0200 or (800) 553-1900. From $99 to $275; major credit cards. One hundred eight rooms with mini-refrigerators and VCRs; use of IBM computers. Continental breakfast; valet parking; free limo service.

It looks like a set for an avant-garde Italian movie. The Diva is a sleek creation in stainless steel, chrome, and glass. Its colors are glossy black lacquer, burgundy, and gray. This art nouveau hotel won a Design of the Year award from Interior Magazine.

It's commodious as well as stylish, with down comforters and surprisingly pillowy furniture for a hotel moderne. Some describe the look as Euro-modern; others compare the rooms to upscale New York apartments. The Diva is in the city's main shopping area, a block from Union Square.

4 Donatello

501 Post Street (at Mason); 441-7100 or (800) 792-9837 in California, and (800) 227-3184 outside. From $155 to $200; major credit cards. Ninety-five rooms with minibars and tape decks. **Ristorante Donatello and cocktail lounge;** *valet parking.*

The Donatello is in a league with the Mandarin Oriental and Campton Place as the city's premier midsized hotels. It exudes quiet elegance with its Fortuny fabric wall covering, Carrara marble, and glittering lobby chandelier of Venetian glass. Room furnishings are elegantly modern, accented by European antiques and fine art.

The adjoining Ristorante Donatello, which we selected as the city's best restaurant (see Chapter 5) rivals the hotel in popularity; indeed the hotel's name was changed from Pacific Plaza to Donatello in 1986. The restaurant is coiffed in nineteenth-century fashion; the menu is contemporary regional Italian. Mr. Donatello—should you wonder—was an Italian Renaissance artist.

5 The Huntington Hotel

*1075 California Street (at Taylor); 474-5400 or (800) 652-1539 in California and (800) 227-4683 outside. From $165 to $645; major credit cards. One hundred forty rooms; some are suites with kitchens or wet bars; fitness club adjacent. **Big Four** restaurant; cocktail lounge; valet parking; limo service downtown.*

The Huntington is a world-class hotel in everything but size, offering all the amenities of its larger Nob Hill brothers. The rooms—all with city or bay views— are designer blends of contemporary and classic Europe, with comfortable furnishings and fine artwork. Each room has its own distinctive decor, part of an ongoing refurbishing program to create a "look of the 1990s," using warm colors with soft leathers, raw silks, and velvets.

Among the hotel's amenities are free limo service and use of a nearby fitness center. Guests can dine at one of the city's finest restaurants, the Big Four, named for California's railroad barons, featuring contemporary Continental fare (listed under *The Ten Best Restaurants* in Chapter 5). The hotel was constructed in 1922 as a luxury apartment building, the first steel and brick high-rise west of the Mississippi, then converted to a hotel shortly after World War II.

6 Hotel Juliana

*590 Bush Street (at Stockton); 392-2540 or (800) 328-3880. From $119 to $155; major credit cards. One hundred seven rooms with honor bars, two TVs in mini suites; nonsmoking rooms available. **Vinoteca Restaurant** adjacent; garage parking nearby.*

Fashioned like a high-style French pension, the Juliana sits atop the Stockton Street tunnel, a quick walk from Chinatown, Nob Hill, or downtown. The decor is cool European, with light woods, soft burgundies, and pastels; the term *restful elegance* comes to mind. The rooms feature floral color-coordinated drapes and spreads; some offer city views.

The small lobby, with its pale marble fireplace, coffee, and tea bar, and framed prints, is one of the most pleasing in the city. The Vinoteca Palm restaurant serves southern Italian cuisine.

7 Monticello Inn

*127 Ellis Street (near Cyril Magnin Street); 392-8800 or (800) 669-7777. From $120 to $180; major credit cards; ninety-one rooms with writing desks and mini-bar refrigerators; nonsmoking rooms available. Continental breakfast included; **Corona Bar and Grill** adjacent; valet parking, free limo service.*

The Monticello, fashioned from a 1906 hotel, offers a light, cheerful early American look, from its quiet lobby parlor with its rich colonial decor to the half-canopied beds and color-coordinated fabrics in the rooms. Visitors can end the day before a crackling fire in the library, sipping gratis wine, and admiring historic prints and other Thomas Jefferson memorabilia. Room furnishings are a mix of antique and contemporary, with full baths and oversized beds.

It's one of the best located of our midsized hotels, on the edge of the Union Square shopping district, a block off Market Street, and a quick walk to BART and the Powell Street cable car turntable. The adjoining Corona Bar and Grill is a popular upscale Mexican-Southwestern restaurant (listed in Chapter 7).

8 The Orchard

562 Sutter Street (at Powell); 433-4434 or (800) 433-4434 in California and (800) 433-4343 outside. From $93 to $180; major credit cards. Ninety-six rooms, some with minibar refrigerators. **Sutter Garden Restaurant***; lobby bar; parking available.*

Yet another old structure—this one dating from 1907—was rescued with the creation of the Orchard hotel. There's a feel of old Europe in the lobby, with its crystal chandeliers and damask couches and chairs.

The rooms are more contemporary, offering pastel colors offset by rather striking dark mahogany furniture. Sutter Garden Restaurant offers assorted American and Continental dishes.

9 The Raphael

386 Geary Street (at Mason); 986-2000 or (800) 821-5343. From $89 to $109, penthouse $195; major credit cards. One hundred fifty-two rooms; nonsmoking rooms available; FAX machine. **Mama's Restaurant** *adjacent; parking available.*

The Raphael was the first of the city's new midsized hotels, dating back to 1971. The rooms have since been redone, achieving a light Continental look: a mix of European and American contemporary. Paneled walls, a beadwork chandelier, and a print carpet give the lobby a pleasing turn-of-the-century European feel.

It's in a good location, in the heart of downtown. Mama's Restaurant serves Continental cuisine with an Italian tilt.

10 Hotel Vintage Court

650 Bush Street (at Powell); 392-4666 or (800) 654-1100. All rooms $119; major credit cards. One hundred six rooms with minibar refrigerators; nonsmoking rooms available. Complimentary French Continental breakfast; off-street parking available. **Masa's** *restaurant adjacent.*

Vintage Court is a real charmer. The furnishings are modern, with European accents, and the rooms are color coordinated. We particularly like the hotel's wine theme. Rooms are named for California wineries, wine prints grace the walls, and gratis glasses of the grape are served before the fireplace in the attractive lobby each evening.

The adjacent restaurant needs little introduction; Masa's is one of the most expensive in the city, and some call it one of the finest French restaurants in the country. Perhaps the hotel's relatively modest prices will make dining more affordable.

Chapter 20

ARCHITECTURAL DELIGHTS AND DISASTERS

Lists of the City's Greatest and Ghastliest Buildings

> *Of all the efflorescent, floriated bulbousness and flamboyant craziness*
> *that ever decorated a city, I think San Francisco may carry off the prize.*
>
> —New York Times, *1883*

That writer was talking about the new gingerbread Victorians. If he were here today, he'd probably prefer those efflorescent structures to some of the drab slabs built in recent decades. Frankly, we like those bulbous Victorians, and even some of the new high-rises that have stepped out of the Wheaties box mold to offer a little form and shape.

The city probably contains the greatest mix of building styles of any community in America. As we prowled about to research this book, wandering through the architectural museum called San Francisco, we began compiling lists of interesting buildings that caught our eye—both the awesome and the awful.

The Ten Most Handsome Victorians

1 Haas-Lilienthal House

2007 Franklin Street (at Jackson); 441-3000. Tours noon to 4 p.m.
Wednesday, and 11 a.m. to 4:30 p.m. Sunday. Adults $3, kids and
seniors $1.

Our premier Victorian is a delightful clutter of all the elements of that architectural period: gingerbread trim, turrets, cupolas, dormer windows, and more filigree than you'll find in great-grandmother's hankie. It's colored a somber gray, probably more appropriate to the Victorian era than many present-day restorations with their Technicolor paint jobs.

The Haas-Lilienthal House is a museum of period furnishings. Built in 1886, this Queen Anne classic is home to the Foundation for San Francisco's Heritage.

2 Château Tivoli

1057 Steiner Street (at Golden Gate).

This bed and breakfast inn is among the city's most elaborate gingerbready Victorians—a fun conglomeration of cupolas, witch's-hat towers, balconies, and gabled roofs. It's decorated with wrought iron, crests, friezes, leaded glass, and curlicues. The color scheme of this four-story mansion is busy as well: assorted shades of brown, burgundy, green, and turquoise. We list it in Chapter 19 as the city's best bed and breakfast inn.

3 Haight-Ashbury Victorian

500-502 Cole Street (at Page).

The former haven of the Flower Children offers another extensive collection of Victorians, and current gentrification of that neighborhood is leading to many restorations. Our favorite in this area is a gabled and turreted four-story mansion with curved glass bay windows and a cut-stone chimney; the colors are turquoise, gray, and beige.

4 Henry Ohlhoff House

601 Steiner Street (at Fell).

Another elaborate architectural mix of towers, cupolas, and bay windows, this house sports a distinctive multifaceted roof. The colors are rust and light gray. It's a Queen Anne–Romanesque mansion, now owned by the Episcopal Diocese of California.

5 Italianate-Style House

817 Grove Street (at Webster).

This private home wins our vote as one of the most attractive small Victorians in the city. The restrained and tasteful use of colors on the little false-front home—gray, blue, and white—is particularly eye-pleasing.

Italianate homes typically have straighter, less elaborate lines than the more complex Queen Annes of the later Victorian era; they were often built with false fronts to conceal the pitch of the roof. Our nominee here is one of three matching row houses.

6 Queen Anne-Style House

1701 Franklin Street (at California).

Built in 1895 and now housing law offices, this is a particularly noteworthy example of the Queen Anne look, with twin towers and a decorative frieze that circles the structure just under the roof line.

The Queen Anne style was in vogue at the close of the Victorian period, at the turn of the century. It's identified by rounded turrets and towers and curved bay windows. Queen Anne ruled before Victoria, but the more elaborate styles of that earlier period returned to popularity in England during the later years of Victoria's reign; they were then copied in California.

7 "Russian Consulate"

1198 Fulton Street (at Scott).

A large four-story Italianate mansion built in 1875 to house the consular corps of Imperial Russia, this structure is an elaborate version of the San Francisco Stick style. It is slender with many vertical lines, including a particularly striking square lookout tower. The building is privately owned.

8 Spreckels Mansion

737 Buena Vista West (off Haight).

Built in 1887 for sugar baron Adolph Spreckels, this great square-shouldered Victorian has several cupolas cut into the roof. Colonial columns at the entrance support an unusual half-moon portico. Once an opulent bed and breakfast inn, it's now a private home.

9 "Tower House"

573 South Van Ness Avenue (at Sixteenth Street).

Surrounded by a rather scruffy commercial neighborhood, this elaborate Victorian is a fine example of a "tower house," which has one or more towers as a predominate architectural feature. The ornate red and white frieze adds a touch of brightness to this carefully restored 1878 Queen Anne.

10 Victorian Duplex

2527–2531 Washington Street (at Fillmore).

Many Victorians survive in the Fillmore District on the edge of Pacific Heights, and this is one of the more curious examples. It's a perfectly symmetrical duplex, a fusing of two skinny garage-over San Francisco Stick Victorians, with scalloped columns supporting twin entries. The purple paint job is rather gaudy, but the distinctive vertical duplex design makes it worthy of our list.

The Ten Most Attractive Commercial or Public Buildings

1 The Audiffred Building

100 Embarcadero (at Mission).

This French Renaissance office building with its green inset columns, red brick, and filigreed mansard roof is indeed the most attractive commercial structure in the city. It was built in 1889 by Hippolite d'Audiffred, who started his fortune selling charcoal to Chinatown merchants. The building was saved from the 1906 earthquake and fire when the operator of a ground-floor saloon bribed the fire laddies with booze to keep them from blowing it up as a firebreak.

International Longshoremen's Union president Harry Bridges occupied upstairs offices during the 1934 waterfront strike, and it thus became the focal point of that violent period. The building now houses professional offices; you can step into the foyer during business hours and view a small historical exhibit.

2 Alcazar Theater

650 Geary Street (at Jones); 441-4042.

Sometimes whimsy can be handsome. Built in 1917 as an Arabian-style Islamic temple, the Alcazar offers just what architectural critics need: an outlet for their sense of humor. Picture if you will a Mideastern lace facade with filigreed arches and balconies above, topped off by a big coffee ice-cream scoop of a dome. The color scheme is blue, beige, and violet. Try it on visually; you'll love it!

Rescued from an inglorious occupation as a rental car office, it was carefully renovated in 1992 and now houses a theater presenting dramas, comedies, and revues.

3 Conservatory of Flowers

John F. Kennedy Drive, Golden Gate Park. Open daily from 9 a.m. to 5 p.m.; $1.50 for adults, 75 cents for seniors and kids.

A grand greenhouse in the old English manner, the senior structure in Golden Gate Park was fashioned after London's Kew Gardens Conservatory. Ordered as a gift to the city of San Jose by real estate magnate and philanthropist James Lick, it was built in Europe, taken apart, and shipped around Cape Horn. Then Lick had a falling-out with San Jose officials and, in a huff, left the thing in its crates, where it remained until his death.

In 1877, a group of San Francisco businessmen bought it from Lick's estate and had it assembled in Golden Gate Park. The big wedding cake of a conservatory contains thirty-three tons of glass, held together by three tons of putty. (I'll never complain about caulking the shower stall again.)

4 Levi's Plaza

Just off the Embarcadero, near Pier 23.

It isn't a building but a comely collection of structures, done up in smoked glass and brick with gently rounded corners. The circular brick columns in this upscale commercial center are a particularly striking feature. Terraces, patios, and a waterfall-fountain add an open-space feel to the attractive facility.

The plaza was built several years ago as corporate offices for Levi Strauss & Company, and this prompts us to offer a bit of historical trivia: Many folks think Levi Strauss made his fortune by selling denim pants to forty-niners. Actually, he made pants from gray tent canvas. The familiar blue denim wasn't added to the company line until the 1880s, with the development of indigo dyes. The word *denim* comes from *serge de Nimes,* the strong fabric that Levi imported from Nimes, France. Incidentally, Levi didn't develop the famous pocket rivets. They were invented by a Nevada tailor named Jacob Davis in 1873. Levi hired Davis and bought his patent.

5 101 California Plaza

101 California Street (at Davis).

The 101 California building offers a fine example of the proper use of space in a downtown high-rise. The most impressive feature here is the plaza, a huge wedge of open space with granite slab terraces, a spillover fountain, and plenty of potted plants. Although the high-rise portion is a lofty glass tower, its surface is broken by vertical terracing. The ground floor features a sloping glass roof sheltering a virtual jungle of potted trees and plants.

6 The Palace of Fine Arts

Baker Street near Marina Boulevard.

This great Romanesque colonnaded rotunda stands before a reflecting pool in the Marina District. It was built as a temporary showplace for the 1915 Panama-Pacific Exposition, then restored in 1962 for $4 million, ten times the original cost. If you live in the Bay Area, you likely know that it isn't an art gallery, despite the name. The rear portion houses the Exploratorium science museum (see Chapter 2). The reflecting pool is busy with ducks and geese, always looking for a handout.

7 Parc Fifty-five

55 Cyril Magnin Street.

One of the city's most striking hotels, the Parc Fifty-Five (formerly the Ramada Renaissance) features ranks of bay windows that pay homage to San Francisco's architectural trademark. Like 101 California, the structure's sides are terraced to avoid the ugly blockhouse look. The base is set with columns and arches, with scalloped awnings over the entrances.

8 Rincon Center

Mission Street between Spear and Steuart.

Not only did the builders of the new Rincon Center preserve a landmark, they improved it. The result is an effective fusion of the classic art deco Rincon Annex post office built in 1939 with a modern atrium shopping and business complex, completed in 1988. Both the facade and the lobby of the old post office have been preserved, along with the California history murals created by Russian artist Antone Refregier, perhaps the finest example of New Deal WPA artwork in America.

The old post office lobby remains intact, although boutiques now lurk behind the closed postal windows. Graphics describe the Refregier murals, and several display cases contain relics of early San Francisco. The new Rincon Center continues the art deco look, with square columns, angular planters, and a galleria roof. To complement the Refregier murals, a decorative frieze of modern San Francisco scenes enhances the new center's atrium lobby.

9 St. Mary's Cathedral

1111 Gough Street (at Geary). Open 9 a.m. to 5 p.m. daily; call 567-2020 for details.

St. Mary's is perhaps the most imposing example of modern church architecture in the West, with winglike rooflines that sweep up into a cross. The massive yet graceful structure occupies two city blocks and soars skyward two hundred feet, presumably toward heaven. Inside, the lofty concept continues as your eyes trace four brilliant strips of leaded glass up the walls to the top of the distinctive square-fluted dome.

10 Transamerica Building

Corner of Columbus, Washington, and Montgomery streets.

No, not the notorious Pyramid. We've nominated an intricately designed stone office building opposite the pointed high-rise. It's part of the Transamerica property and houses a branch of the Sanwa Bank. The off-white masonry, fluted inset columns, black and gold circular stairway, and elaborate stone walls are a visual treat. A slender wedge of a building, it's one of the city's nineteenth-century "flatiron" structures. These were built to conform to pie-shaped corners created by the city's many diagonal intersections.

The Ten Best Architectural Uglies

Since architectural beauty and the lack of it are in the eye of the beholder, we list these diplomatically in alphabetical order.

1 Bank of the West, North Beach Branch

Corner of Green, Columbus, and Stockton.

Here we have an example of a structure that's ugly primarily because it's in the wrong place. It's a curious creature with arched glass window-walls and a three-domed roof; it looks like a surrealistic beehive. And it's plopped right in the middle of North Beach, near some fine old bay-windowed Victorians. It would look better elsewhere.

In Utah, for instance.

2 Cala Foods

California and Hyde streets.

Who's responsible for this ungainly critter, anyhow? With its painted window panels and indented, upswept roofline, it looks like a psychedelic owl that crash-landed on a vacant lot. The recent addition of a marbled green paint job on the roof does not help.

3 Financial District-Chinatown Holiday Inn

750 Kearny Street (at Washington).

Most Holiday Inns are merely functional; this one is ugly. Its boxy tower juts skyward in gross disruption of the fine old Chinatown neighborhood that it invaded several years ago. Its base splays out in a curious spraddle-legged fashion. It looks like a man with one foot on the pier and the other in a boat. Or something worse.

4 Galaxy Theater

Van Ness Avenue and Sutter Street.

This is a quick lesson in how to construct a new-wave theater building. Find a giant child with poor eye-to-hand coordination, give him a set of huge glass building blocks, and turn him loose. See? He can't even get any symmetry in his stack. The silly thing's lopsided. (We were reminded by the management, however, that the structure won a *Time* magazine architectural design award when it was completed in 1984. So, what do we know?)

5 Hilton Hotel Tower

333 O'Farrell Street (at Taylor).

The rose-colored addition to the Hilton Hotel complex, with its glow-in-the-dark dome, is something of an improvement. But the original tower—an aluminum-colored square stump—still dominates the skyline. The windows are boring little squares with no trim. It's the quintessential architectural cube.

6 Hotel Ana

50 Third Street (between Market and Mission).

Although it's imposing within, and has earned a AAA Four Diamond rating, the Ana is an awkward thing from without (like this sentence). It's a skinny structure with mismatched slab siding and a knife-edge wedge of a corner facing southeast. The hotel originally was built as the Meridien, and the new occupants have done little to amend the ungainly exterior.

7 Imperial Bank/Coast Savings Building

460 Montgomery Street (at Sacramento).

This has to be the most abrupt and jarring fusion of architectural styles in the city. In an effort to preserve an old cut-stone colonial-style building with Greco-Roman columns, architects stuck a square, drab Wheaties-box high-rise right on top of it. The effect is like an elaborate wood carving sprouting a two-by-four.

8 King of China Restaurant

939 Clement Street (at Eleventh Avenue).

This shiny curiosity, with its silos of stainless-steel and gaudy expanses of glass, is a head-on collision between art deco and oriental excess. An oversized bulge of a bay window is the focal point of the futuristic two-story design, with an incongruous dragon crest above. Flanking the bay window are two glass and stainless steel columns that look like outside elevators with nowhere to go. But never mind all that if you're hungry. The place serves excellent food, and it's one of the best *dim sum* parlors in the city.

9 Nieman-Marcus Store

Geary Street at Stockton.

We have here another example of architectural fusion that leads to visual confusion. Attempting to preserve the rotunda of the old City of Paris (the store it replaced), Neiman-Marcus sports a curious glass silo that emerges from a flat-sided building. The effect is inelegant, like a well-dressed woman wearing gaudy glass beads. The alternating dark and light brown granite diamonds decorating the exterior walls would look better on a pack of playing cards.

10 San Francisco Marriott

Fourth and Mission streets.

Herb Caen calls it the jukebox Marriott, an apt description for this new high-rise hotel with curious glass accents. The mix of glass and granite might have been pleasing, but it's topped by irregular spires and glass facades that fan outward, offering the impression of a jeweled Egyptian death mask or the wizard's castle in Oz. Or perhaps a galleria stood on end. We do like its stylish skyroom cocktail lounge called The View, however (see Chapter 14).

Chapter 21

TAKE A HIKE OR PEDAL A BIKE

The Ten Best Pathways

> *I love this hilly city of yours. When you get tired of walking around,*
> *you can lean against it!*
>
> —*tourist quoted in* Herb Caen's San Francisco, *1957*

The hills haven't gotten any flatter since the city's pundit laureate wrote his affectionate guide to San Francisco more than thirty-five years ago. With its lumpy but compact terrain, it is a wonderful walking city and a cyclist's haven. So enough of this passive sightseeing, bar-hopping, and stuffing ourselves; it's exercise time!

To find the Ten Best routes, we hiked and biked San Francisco from bay to ocean and crossed the Golden Gate Bridge into Marin County. Where pathways get complicated, we offer maps to help you find your way. We recommend transferring our street directions or sketches to a more detailed city map, using one of those highlighter pens. (AAA's San Francisco map is best, but you have to be a member to get one.)

The Ten Best Hike Routes

Herewith, the Ten Best places to take a hike in San Francisco. We're serious walkers, so most of these outings are designed to give you a good aerobic workout. We've also included some moderate ones for those who just want to stroll around and enjoy some city scenery. They're listed in no particular order of preference, although the first is our favorite, offering a fine strolling sampler of the city.

1 The First San Francisco Hill Stride Route
Moderate to strenuous; 6.8 miles. (See Festivals of the Feet in Chapter 16 for details on the annual walking race.)

In the summer of 1985, *CitySports,* a magazine not intended for couch potatoes, sponsored the first San Francisco Hill Stride, with the focus on power walking instead of running. It has since grown to the City Stride, one of the world's largest walking events, held yearly in several cities.

Striding isn't strolling, incidentally; it's stepping out at a brisk four-mile-an-hour clip. Doctors and fitness gurus call it the ideal aerobic workout, without the spinal stress of running or the limitations of finding a place to swim.

The Hill Stride, held each September, has been expanded to more than seven miles, but we'll walk the original course, which is a bit less challenging for the

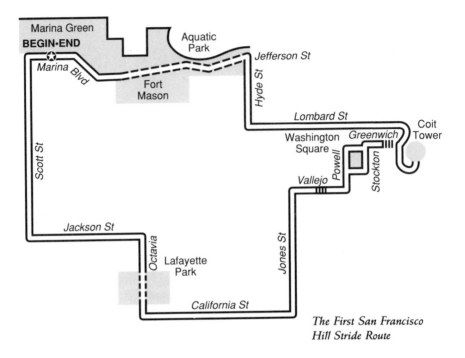

*The First San Francisco
Hill Stride Route*

novice power walker. It's an ambitious and complicated route beginning and ending at the Marina Green; it takes you over seven hills, with awesome vistas along the way. Some steep climbs are involved, but much of it is level or downhill, and you'll pass through some nice parks.

You'll note as you transfer this outline to a regular map that one stretch along Vallejo seems to go where there is no street; that's because it goes up a set of steps. That's right, up. We said it was a good workout. On the final leg, you descend Scott Street, with visions of the bay dancing before you. When you crawl back to your Marina Green starting point, you'll know you've done a day's work.

2 The Squiggly Lombard, Coit Tower, Embarcadero Walk

*Easy stroll to moderate climb; about a mile; a tough 2 miles if you do it
round-trip.*

The first part of this hike contains a section of the original Hill Stride. Begin at Hyde and Lombard by walking down the "crookedest street," and just keep tooling along Lombard until you hit a set of concrete steps, then follow a shady pathway leading up to Coit Tower. After enjoying the vistas, follow the Greenwich Steps down toward the waterfront. They begin at the point where the road enters the Coit Tower parking lot; look for a Greenwich sign.

You'll clump down several flights of steep steps past hillside homes and landscaped terraces. You have several choices because the steps wander all over the side of Telegraph Hill, but eventually you'll emerge on level land at the Embarcadero, probably near Levi's Plaza. If you want to retrace your route, bear in mind that the trek back up to Coit Tower involves 494 steps. See you at the top.

3 Wharf Ramble

Completely level; 2.5 miles.

This stroll along the Embarcadero is so obvious that we hesitate to include it, but it is a pleasant walk. It has been made even more pleasant by the removal, early in this decade, of that ugly Embarcadero Freeway.

Begin at the concrete promenade built by the San Francisco Port Commission just south of the Ferry Building. Then start strolling—leisurely or briskly, as you wish—north to Fisherman's Wharf. Places to pause along this ramble include Ferry Plaza, the historic Ferry Building, Justin Herman Plaza with its funny boxy fountain, handsome brick Levi's Plaza opposite Pier 23, tacky Pier 39, Fisherman's Wharf, and the historic ships of Hyde Street Pier.

4 Golden Gate Promenade

An extension of the Wharf Ramble; a breeze to walk and pretty as a picture; 3.5 miles.

When the Golden Gate National Recreation Area was created, officials designated a walking and running trail from Hyde Street Pier to Fort Point beneath the Golden Gate Bridge. You're never out of sight of the bay on the Golden Gate Promenade, and the views are wonderful. Although it can accommodate bikes, we prefer to follow it on foot because it's crowded and contains some sandy and gravelly stretches.

The route is easy: From Hyde Street Pier, walk toward the Golden Gate Bridge, past Aquatic Park, over a green Fort Mason hill, through the Marina Green, and along the Presidio shoreline. The path is marked here and there with gold, blue, and white signs. If you lose track of the route, just keep edging toward the bay. But stop short of getting your feet wet.

5 Mexican Mural Walk

Mostly level; about 3 miles.

More than two hundred murals are scattered through the city's Mission District. To see about fifty of the more interesting ones, follow the route we've outlined. You'll be trekking through a simple working folks' neighborhood and some of it's a bit scruffy, so don't expect a lot of fancy vistas. Murals range from strong political statements and slices of Latin life to simple whimsy; they're wonderful examples of Mexican-American folk art.

Begin by hopping a Daly City-bound BART train, and get off at Twenty-fourth Street. You'll see your first mural, just above the station, showing humanoid T-columns holding up BART tracks. (BART on the backs of the people?)

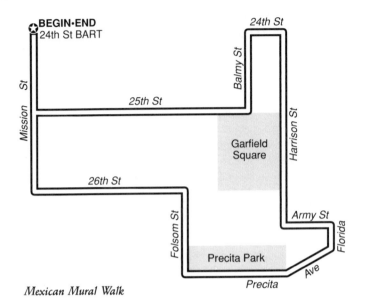

Mexican Mural Walk

As you walk and gawk about our mural route, note three areas in particular: Garfield Square park at Harrison and Twenty-sixth, with several murals on park buildings and a nearby housing project; the beautifully decorated Leonard R. Flynn Elementary School near Precita Park at Precita Avenue and Harrison; and Balmy Alley, with an astonishing thirty murals in a one-block stretch. Sadly, some murals have been defaced with senseless graffiti, but most are intact.

The Precita Eyes Mural Center at 348 Precita Avenue (285-2287), a nonprofit group dedicated to mural creation and preservation, conducts walks past the Mission District murals on the first and third Saturday of each month. They depart at 1:30 p.m., and the fee is $3 for adults, less for kids and seniors. Also, a $2 pamphlet from the Mexican Museum in Building D at Fort Mason Center (see Chapter 17) shows the location of many of these outdoor paintings.

6 Victoriana to the Haight Hike

Level to moderately steep; 3.4 miles.

On this walk, you'll get a look at some of San Francisco's finest Victorians and the Haight-Ashbury District, where Flower Children once reigned.

Begin beside Alamo Square, a Victorian historic district, where Pierce Street T-bones into Hayes. This is the best vista point for viewing the famous Painted Ladies, those six matching Victorians on Steiner Street that you often see on postcards. After following our route around the Alamo Square neighborhood, which brims with Victorians, take a long hike on Haight Street into Haight-Ashbury, with its funky shops, galleries, and bookstores. Then return along Page Street, where you'll see more Victorian beauties in their bright makeup.

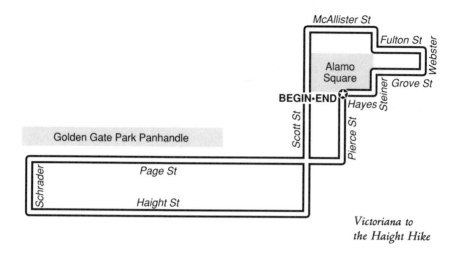

*Victoriana to
the Haight Hike*

7 Wilderness Coast in the City Hike

*Some climbing, but mostly level; 9.2 miles. The Golden Gate National Recreation
Area brochure, available at most GGNRA facilities, shows the two Coastal Trail
sections of this hike.*

The same folks who brought you the Golden Gate Promenade also carved out
the Coastal Trail that follows the cliffs above the Pacific on the northern and western edges of the city.

The trail begins at the Golden Gate Bridge viewpoint near the toll plaza and
ends at Fort Funston near Lake Merced. It isn't all signed, but when in doubt just
scuff along the beach or follow a city street until you can find another chunk of
this seacoast trail.

From the bridge viewpoint, follow the trail under the bridge anchorage, past
a maintenance yard, then travel along the edge of Lincoln Boulevard in the Presidio until the trail drops down to Baker Beach. There, you'll catch some great views
of the bridge over your right shoulder. The vistas become even more dramatic if
you backtrack up the beach a few hundred yards. On warm days, you'll also
encounter some views of sunbathing in the buff, so just keep staring at the bridge
if that sort of thing bothers you. Or pick a cold day to do your hike.

Continuing south on the trail from Baker Beach, you'll emerge at the swank
Sea Cliff residential community. Follow El Camino del Mar, then pick up the trail
again near the edge of Lincoln Park Golf Course. From here, it's up-and-down hiking through a beautifully craggy area of steep headlands with rocky, surf-pounded
beaches below. The bridge-and-sea views are tremendous. Eventually, you'll reach
the Cliff House; now follow Ocean Beach, which parallels the Great Highway,
to Fort Funston.

GGNRA rangers asked us to warn you not to climb over rocky outcroppings
above the surf or wander off the trail where it's notched into sea cliffs. The rocks

and off-trail areas are steep, slippery, and dangerous. Rangers must make several rescues a year, and some hikers have been killed.

8 Urban Wilderness Hike

Very steep in parts; various lengths.

Mount Sutro Forest, on the slopes below Twin Peaks near the University of California Medical Center, offers a virtual wilderness in the heart of the city. It has many trails and informal goat trails that take you into thick stands of evergreens and eucalyptus. It's intriguing to lunge through a primeval thicket, then top a ridge to be greeted by a panoramic cityscape.

We won't attempt to outline a formal route here; we instead suggest a rather random exploration of the slopes and ridges around the Med Center. A good starting point is Belgrave Avenue. To get there, drive up Market Street, take a half right onto Seventeenth Street (at Castro), and turn left onto Stanyan. Go up a steep grade to Belgrave, turn right, and you'll run out of street. Before you is an inviting trail into an urban wilderness.

You'll probably get misplaced wandering around here, emerging unexpectedly onto the Med Center grounds or into one of the hillside residential areas. Take along a detailed city map to help maintain your bearings.

At the other end of Belgrave Avenue, incidentally, is a trail that takes you up to Tank Hill, whose viewpoint we raved about in Chapter 3.

9 Chinatown Stroll

Easy walk; some hills; probably less than a mile.

It's both simple and complicated to outline a route through Chinatown. The simple part: Start at the Gate of Chinatown (Grant Avenue at Bush), follow Grant to Broadway, go up a block, double back on Stockton, and walk it to the Stockton Tunnel. The complex part: After doing that, prowl every cross street and alley of Chinatown to capture the real flavor of this place.

Some things to look for:

- The wonderfully cluttered gallery of Asian artifacts on the four floors of Canton Bazaar at 616 Grant, between California and Sacramento.
- The elaborate Bank of America "Chinese temple" at Grant and Sacramento, with dragon-entwined columns flanking the entrance.
- The "produce corner" sidewalk markets at Stockton and Broadway.
- The Great China Art Company herbal shop at 857 Washington (at Spofford Alley, between Grant and Stockton), where clerks still use hand-held balance scales.
- Golden Gate Fortune Cookies Company at 56 Ross Alley (off Jackson, between Grant and Stockton), where you'll finally discover how they get those little messages inside.
- A dragon hanging within the spiral staircase at China Trade Center, 838 Grant, between Clay and Washington.

For a more intimate look at Chinatown, sign up for one of Shirley Fong-Torres's Wok Wiz tours. These behind-the-scenes strolls range from $24 for three and a half hours ($33 with lunch) to $15 for an hour-and-a-half version. Call 355-9657.

10 Original Shoreline Hike

Flat and easy; about 2 miles.

As our map indicates, much of San Francisco's present downtown area was under water at the time of the gold rush. The shaded area indicates the original shoreline. Filling the bay began rather inelegantly; debris and sand were dumped onto the hulks of ships that had been abandoned by their crews, who had stampeded to the Sierra Nevada gold fields.

The heart of the Financial District extends about eight blocks into what was once shallow bay water and mud flats. If the original shoreline were intact, the Transamerica Pyramid would get its big buttresses wet, for that area was an inlet called Yerba Buena Cove.

It's interesting to zigzag along the original shoreline; the streets we've marked follow it rather closely. At the corner of Bush and Market, you'll find a bronze

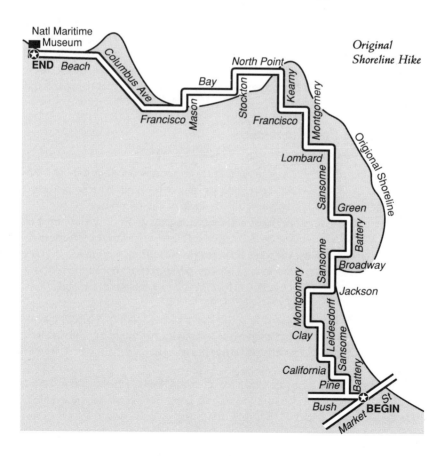

plaque detailing the pre-gold rush shore. As you wander through the area, watch for other plaques heralding anything from the inventor of the slot machine (Market at Battery) to the original office of the Pony Express (marked by several plaques on the California National Bank building at Clay, just up from Montgomery Street).

The Ten Best Bike Routes

We're assuming that you'll buckle your bike rack to your car and drive to starting points, so we've tried to select places where ample and unmetered parking is available. All of our routes are round-trip, so you can return to your Belchfire V-6. These routes can be negotiated quite easily with a standard three-speed or ten-speed street bike or with a mountain bike; some are even suitable for single-speed cycles. One of our routes takes us across the Golden Gate Bridge to Sausalito; two others explore next-door Marin County. If we had our way, we'd do all of our city biking early on a Sunday morning, the most traffic-free time of the week. The first is our favorite, and the rest appear in no specific order, except that in some cases, one route leads to another.

If you'd like to rent wheels, you'll find most bike rental places centered near Golden Gate Park, the city's most popular biking area. Contact Magic Skates and Bikes at 3038 Fulton Street (Sixth Avenue), 668-1117; Fog City Cycles at 3430 Geary Boulevard (near Stanyan), 221-3031; Park Cyclery at 1865 Haight Street (near Stanyan), 751-RENT; or Stow Lake Boat and Bike Rentals at the boathouse in Golden Gate Park, 752-0347.

1 Potrero to the Waterfront

Level, with moderate upgrade on return; 10 miles round-trip.

We love to pedal along the waterfront early on a sunny Sunday morning, passing tired old freighters dozing at dockside, pausing at the handsome Embarcadero Promenade, getting to Fisherman's Wharf ahead of the tour buses.

Our route is a simple one, filled with rewarding views. Begin at the corner of Mariposa and Missouri, in the city's Potrero Hill District. It's an area of Victorians and hilly streets, although the route down to the waterfront is a gradual decline. Pedal down Mariposa, noting views of the city skyline off to your left. Cross busy Third Street, keeping straight until you hit China Basin. Now turn left and follow the waterfront.

Your wharfside route blends into the Embarcadero, taking you past magnificent views of the bay, ships at anchor, the venerable Ferry Building, and the sleek Embarcadero Center. Ultimately, you arrive at Fisherman's Wharf, where aromas of crab cookers fill the air.

Three good suggestions for breakfast along the route: Mission Rock Resort (see Chapter 9), just after you turn onto China Basin, for outside bayview dining; Lou's Pier 47 (see Chapter 8), 300 Jefferson Street at Fisherman's Wharf; or the

Buena Vista Café (see Chapter 14), just up from the wharf at Hyde and Beach. Now, retrace your tracks back to your starting point.

Warning: Many railroad tracks crisscross the waterfront; they often cross streets at odd angles, and a track groove can cause a bad spill.

2 Cliff House to Lake Merced

Level except for one slight upgrade; 3.5 miles round-trip.

This is another simple route, with views of the restless Pacific instead of the bay. It's often windy out there, so take a wrap.

Begin just below the Cliff House on the Great Highway, where you'll find plenty of unmetered parking for your bike-toter. Ride south along the highway, catching glimpses of the sea between grassy dunes. You might like to pull over occasionally, chain your bike to something, and take a beach walk. At Sloat Boulevard, you can swing up and make friends with denizens of the San Francisco Zoo.

Continue along the Great Highway to its junction with Skyline Boulevard near Lake Merced, then return to your starting point, or slip onto our Bike Route No. 3, listed next.

3 Lake Merced Circle

Completely level; 4.4-mile loop.

Begin in Harding Park on Lake Merced's shore just off Skyline Boulevard. An asphalt biking-walking trail circles the lake. Follow it clockwise, making right turns to stay near the lakeshore.

Your route takes you east and then south on Lake Merced Boulevard, then you make a sharp right onto John Muir Drive, opposite the San Francisco Golf Club, and finally pedal onto Skyline and go north to your starting point.

It's a pleasant, traffic-free route (except for the Skyline portion), sometimes shaded by overhanging cypresses and eucalyptus. You'll pedal past Harding Park Municipal Golf Course, the back door of San Francisco State University, and the residential towers of Parkmerced. If you combine this with the Cliff House to Lake Merced route, the total distance is about eight miles.

4 Lake to Luxury

Mostly level, with some moderately steep but short hills; 3-mile loop.

Lake Street, which parallels California in the Presidio Heights area, is one of the few city streets with a separate bike lane. The bonus is that it's in a beautiful neighborhood.

Start at Park Presidio Boulevard, near Mountain Lake Park, a little jewel of a greenbelt surrounding a pond. Pedal toward downtown on Lake Street, go left on Arguello, then left again into Presidio Terrace. This circular lane takes you past some of the city's most opulent homes, including the oversized Hansel and Gretel cottage of Mr. and Mrs. Richard (Dianne Feinstein) Blum at 30 Presidio Terrace.

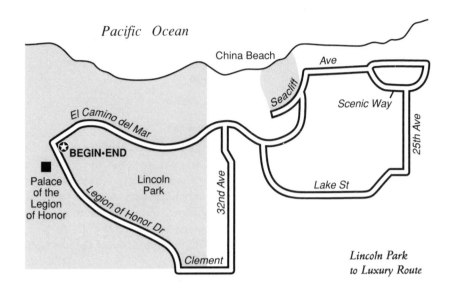

Lincoln Park
to Luxury Route

After wishing you could afford one of these mansions, pedal out of the terrace and down Washington Street, passing more upscale real estate. Turn right on Laurel for one block, right onto Clay, and return to your starting point. (Clay blends into Lake Street.)

5 Lincoln Park to Luxury

Somewhat hilly, but nothing terribly steep; 3-mile loop.

Sea Cliff rivals Presidio Terrace in opulence and offers ocean and bridge views as a bonus. To explore this haven of the rich, unload your bikes at the Palace of the Legion of Honor parking lot on Lincoln Boulevard, then follow the course we've outlined here. It's one of our prettier routes, with views of Pacific blue, golf course green, and all those stylish homes.

Our map doesn't attempt to show specific routes through the complex streets of Sea Cliff. Just pedal randomly until you've had your fill of envy, then pick up El Camino del Mar and return to the Legion of Honor. Pause to study the emotionally moving Jewish Holocaust Memorial just below the parking area.

6 Pedaling the Presidio

Some gentle hills and a couple of moderate ones; 5-mile loop.

Begin at a dirt parking area on Merchant Road near an old gun battery. Pedal down Merchant and merge right onto Lincoln Boulevard, then turn into the Presidio on Kobbe Avenue near a World War II monument.

By following our mapped route through the Presidio (mostly on Washington Boulevard), you'll pedal beneath pretty forests-in-the-city and catch some surprise vistas of cityscape, sea, and bay. The route takes you through the main part of the old military post. We suggest a pause at the Presidio Army Museum (see Chapter 17).

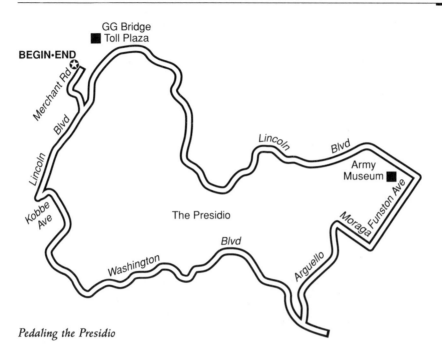

Pedaling the Presidio

7 Pedaling the Park

Level but busy with other bikers on weekends; 7.5 miles or more.

This is old stuff to Bay Area cyclists, but if you've just arrived from Madera, you'll enjoy pedaling in Golden Gate Park.

The main route, John F. Kennedy Drive, is closed to motor vehicle traffic on Sundays, but that doesn't mean it's deserted. You'll encounter legions of other cyclists, ghetto-blaster-toting roller skaters and roller bladers, skateboarders, striders, and runners. It's hardly a wilderness, but the park is beautiful. Start at McLaren Lodge near Stanyan and follow J.F.K. Drive to the Great Highway, then return along South Drive. That route will cover a bit more than seven miles.

Don't limit yourself to these two main routes. You'll find a dozen or so smaller roads and bike paths that zig and zag through the scenery and greenery. Of course you'll lose your way, but it's a pleasant place in which to go astray. The park is long but narrow; if you become totally misplaced, you'll shortly emerge onto a familiar street.

8 Across the Bridge and into the Willows

Mostly level, with one steep downgrade and upgrade; 8 miles round-trip. The Bay Model is open Tuesday-Friday from 9 a.m. to 4 p.m., weekends and holidays from 10 a.m. to 6 p.m., with shorter hours in the off-season; call 332-3870.

Sausalito means "little willows" in Spanish, and the ride across the Golden Gate Bridge into this pretty bayside town is one of the area's classic bike routes.

We start at the Golden Gate Bridge toll plaza and follow the bike route across the bridge. Pause at Vista Point on the far side, then take the marked bike route down Alexander Avenue, which blends into Bridgeway in Sausalito. Pedal along the handsome riviera-style bay front and past the town's cutesy boutiques, many in century-old buildings.

Our turnaround point is the Army Corps of Engineers' Bay Model at 2100 Bridgeway. The corps built a two-acre scale model of San Francisco Bay with its inflowing streams to study the effect of tidal action, silting, and such. An excellent graphic exhibit traces the development of life from the sea; a film on the model's function is shown on request.

9 Strawberry to Tiburon

Level; 5 miles round-trip.

Start at the Strawberry Shopping Center off U.S. 101 (take the Blithedale-Tiburon Boulevard exit), and follow Tiburon into the hidden hamlet of the same name. As you pedal along the boulevard, you'll pick up a walking/biking path near Greenwood Beach Park, and this takes you traffic-free into Tiburon. The village is just as cute as Sausalito, and it's generally less crowded.

A couple of good lunch stops are Sam's Anchor Café and Guaymas, both on Main Street and both offering decks with views of the distant San Francisco skyline.

10 Angel Island Amble

Level with some hills; 5-mile loop. The Red and White Fleet departs for Angel Island from Pier 41 in San Francisco; call 546-BOAT.

The funky old Angel Island Ferry offers service to the island from Tiburon; call 435-2131. Both operate daily in summer and weekends only in the off-season, and both can accommodate bikes. For general information, call Angel Island State Park at 456-1286.

Angel Island is that large green 758-acre lump in the northern corner of San Francisco Bay, off the Tiburon peninsula. It's a state park with hiking trails, picnic areas, abandoned forts, exhibits in the "Ellis Island of the West"—a former Asian immigration center, and an exciting 360-degree view of the bay.

The main route around the island is very bikeable. This is one of the most popular rides in the Bay Area, so it's best to avoid it on summer weekends, if possible.

Chapter 22

THE GOOD, THE GOOFY, AND THE STRANGE

Lists of Things that Fail to Fit into Other Lists

Toto, I have a feeling we're not in Kansas anymore.

—Dorothy, in The Wizard of Oz

The Ten Best Places to Snuggle with Your Sweetie

Feel a romantic urge? Want to slip away with someone special for a few moments, a few hours? Here are our favorite hidden corners.

1 **THE BEST PLACE TO SNUGGLE TOGETHER IN THE CITY**
The Huntington Hotel

1075 California Street (at Taylor on Nob Hill); 474-5400 or (800) 652-1539 in California and (800) 227-4683 outside. See detailed listing in Chapter 19.

The Huntington's "Romance Package" offers an intimate getaway in the middle of the city, complete with a bottle of champagne, formal tea or sherry service when you check in, and the use of the hotel's chauffeured limo. The price for this cozy opulence, when we last checked, was $189 per couple for an elegant room, with an upgrade to a suite for another $50.

You can continue your romantic mood as you explore the city, since those charming little cable cars pass right in front of the hotel. Or you can stroll—hand in hand, of course—about Nob Hill, exploring the grand lobbies and cozy cocktail lounges of the other elegant hotels. If you'd like to dine in, Huntington's staff will reserve a candlelit table in the hotel's Big Four restaurant. After dinner, you can sit beside a crackling fire—brandy glasses in hand—in the intimate and clubby cocktail lounge. All rooms have a view of the city or the adjacent Huntington Park. But aren't you supposed to be staring into one another's eyes?

2 **THE BEST PLACE FOR AN INTIMATE DINNER**
Fleur de Lys

777 Sutter Street (at Jones); 673-7779. Dressy, jackets for gentlemen. See detailed listing in Chapter 5.

Settle into a plush booth at a candlelit table, beneath the sensuous fabric canopy of this posh French restaurant, and let romance happen. Fleur de Lys is not only a romantic spot. We rate it as one of the city's ten best restaurants in

Chapter 5, and it was voted by café executives and celebrity chefs as the city's best restaurant in our other book, San Francisco's Ultimate Dining Guide. The menu is pure French, but in a lighter nouvelle style, so you won't doze off as you flutter your eyelashes at your partner.

3 THE BEST PLACE TO SIT AND SIP WITH SOMEONE SPECIAL
Mason's Cocktail Lounge at the Fairmont Hotel

950 Mason Street (at California); 392-0113.

Mason's, on the arcade level of the Fairmont, offers all the ingredients for an intimate cocktail lounge: soft lighting, table candles, overstuffed sofas piled with throw pillows, and a tinkling grand piano. Mason's also is an upscale restaurant, although the cocktail lounge is completely sheltered from the tinkle of silverware. It's an elegant little bar and gentlemen are requested to wear jackets.

4 THE BEST PLACE TO SHARE THE SUNSET
Marin Headlands

See Explore Marin Headlands Outer Limits in Chapter 1 for directions to the area.

The turnouts along the Marin Headlands road can get awfully cluttered with camera-clutchers during the daytime, but they're surprisingly uncrowded at night. The view of the sun slipping into the Pacific, the bridge standing below you, and the lights of the city beginning to twinkle will stir the romantic soul in anyone.

5 THE BEST PLACE TO GREET THE SUNRISE TOGETHER
Atop Tank Hill

East end of Belgrave Street.

This is a little-known promontory below Twin Peaks, which we nominated as the city's best vista point in Chapter 3. It's a wonderfully private place to greet the new day. The air may be chilly at that hour; all the more reason to snuggle.

To get there, drive up Market Street to Castro, and veer slightly to the right onto Seventeenth Street; follow this to Stanyan, turn left, and go up a steep grade to Belgrave. Go left again and, still climbing, drive a few blocks to the end of the street. Before you, on the left side of the street, is a trail sloping upward to Tank Hill. Take your partner's hand and walk toward the new day.

6 THE BEST PLACE TO BE ALONE TOGETHER IN A DARK THICKET
Sutro Forest

West end of Belgrave Street.

This thick stand of eucalyptus on the steep flanks of Mount Sutro is surprisingly remote. It's a nice place to walk hand in hand; you can climb to high viewpoints and gaze down at the city. To find it, follow the directions to Tank Hill above, but turn right onto Belgrave and follow it to the end of the road. There before you is your trail into privacy.

7 THE BEST PLACE TO SIT AND SIMMER WITH YOUR SWEETIE
In a Rental Hot Tub

*Grand Central Sauna and Hot Tub, 15 Fell Street (at Market), 431-1370;
Hot Tubs, 2200 Van Ness Avenue (at Broadway), 441-TUBS. Or look under
"spas and hot tubs, rentals" in the Yellow Pages.*

Can't afford to have a hot tub installed in your crabgrass patch? These two
companies rent hot tubs and sauna space by the hour, in cozy private rooms.

8 THE BEST THEATER IN WHICH TO SNUGGLE & IGNORE THE MOVIE
The Balboa

3634 Balboa Street (at Thirty-eighth Avenue).

The handsome old art deco Balboa Theater has rocking-chair loges for two,
high up in the back rows. They're great places to cuddle, so pick a dull movie.

9 THE BEST PLACE FOR A ROMANTIC BEACH STROLL
China Beach

Below Sea Cliff.

Situated below the cliff-hanging homes of Sea Cliff, China Beach is a pretty
little rock-bound cove offering striking views of the Golden Gate Bridge and San
Francisco's craggy coastline. Although it's busy with sunbathers on warm summer
days, it's practically deserted when it's windy and cool—the perfect time to bundle
up and stroll arm in arm. Sea caves and rocky overhangs offer places to snuggle
against the wind.

Although this small cove is hemmed by rocky cliffs, you can amble for about
a third of a mile when the tide's not too high, perhaps pausing to study a starfish
or gaze at the mist-shrouded bridge in the distance. Since it's outside the Golden
Gate, China Beach is washed by a modest surf. It earned its name during the California Gold Rush, when Chinese fishermen camped here to provide seafood for
the growing young city.

To reach China Beach, drive out Geary Boulevard to the Richmond District,
turn right onto Twenty-sixth Avenue and follow it until it T-bones into Sea Cliff
Drive. Go left to the end of Sea Cliff (veering right at a Y-intersection). You'll find
a small parking area and a set of railroad-tie steps leading down to the beach.

10 THE BEST PLACE FOR AN OUT-OF-TOWN ESCAPE
Claremont Resort and Spa

Ashby and Domingo avenues, Oakland; (510) 843-3000.

With its fully equipped spa, night-lighted tennis courts, bay view restaurant,
and modern rooms furnished with antiques, the Claremont has become the hidea-
way resort in northern California. Romantic souls can percolate in a hot tub, get
an "aromatic massage," dance to a fantastic Bay Area vista, and stroll the twenty-
two-acre grounds. It's just half an hour from San Francisco.

All this happens amid the historic ambiance of a resort hotel dating back
to 1915. It has undergone a complete restoration, from its monumental lobby
to its spacious rooms tucked behind those wonderfully silly little cupolas. (See
Chapter 24.)

Driving Yourself to Distraction:
The Ten Best Motoring and Parking Tips

We prefer walking or riding Muni or BART in the city. If you must drive here, these Ten Best driver's pointers may save you a lot of grief. They're listed in no particular order.

1 The Best Places to Find Civic Center/Downtown Parking Spaces

On weekends, daytime parking around the Civic Center is rather open, and it's a short stroll or brief Muni or BART ride downtown. Catch BART at the Civic Center station, and Muni Metro at the Civic Center or Van Ness station. Parking also is available during weekends along Mission Street, south of Market. And you can find slots during evenings and weekends in the Financial District.

For weekday evening parking in the downtown area, use a trick employed by locals: Edge into one of the evening tow-away zones about 5:45 p.m. and spend a furtive fifteen minutes watching for the parking patrol.

2 The Best Places to Find Tourist Area Parking

Fort Point always has more parking available than the more popular Golden Gate Bridge view area just above it, and there are no meters. To reach the bridge, park at Fort Point and then hike a few hundred feet back along the entrance road to a small ranger station. Just opposite the station, a trail leads up through the wooded slope. (A trail closer to Fort Point was closed in 1993 because of possible lead contamination in the soil.)

If you're visiting the Marina Green and can't find a spot, drive into Fort Mason Center; it's just a couple of blocks away and it's also meter-free. If the Palace of the Legion of Honor parking lot is full, drive down along El Camino del Mar; there's plenty of legal parking along the shoulder.

3 The Best Times to Find Not-Quite-Legal Free Parking

The odds of getting an overtime parking ticket drop on weekends because the parking patrol ranks thin out. Most meters go to sleep after 6 p.m. Monday through Saturday and all day Sunday, but not in popular tourist spots. We've gotten occasional tickets for expired meters on Saturdays, but only once were we ticketed in an unmetered time-limit zone on weekends or evenings. (Be warned: This can change; please do not forward parking citations to the authors.)

4 The Cheapest Parking Garages

Most downtown hotels charge $20 a day parking fees for guests and even more for outsiders. And most parking garages nick you a dollar or more for every twenty minutes. Downtown street meters—when you can find one empty—demand two bits for ten or fifteen minutes. However, rates at Portsmouth Plaza Garage at Kearny and Washington on the edge of Chinatown, and at St. Mary's Square Garage on California just down from Grant Avenue are a mere dollar an hour. It's a short walk from either to Chinatown or the Financial District. An even better deal is Embarcadero Center, where free parking is available on evenings and weekends with validation of your ticket by a restaurant, shop, or other merchant in the shopping arcades.

5 The Best Streets on Which to Get from Here to There

During non-rush hours, drop over to Howard Street (westbound) or Folsom Street (eastbound) instead of struggling up Market or Mission streets. If you're headed into Chinatown or North Beach, the Stockton and Broadway tunnels cut out a lot of stoplights. The problem is, you can't find a parking place once you get there.

6 The Worst Streets on Which to Get Anywhere

The city Traffic Engineering Department says the most heavily traveled street is Van Ness Avenue between McAllister and Lombard. Franklin Street and Nineteenth Avenue aren't exactly speedways, either.

7 The Best Places to Experience Gridlock

The most congested intersections, says Traffic Engineering, are Lombard at Van Ness, the Broadway-Columbus-Grant confrontation, and Nineteenth Avenue at Lincoln.

8 The Best Driving Maps

The California State Automobile Association (150 Van Ness Avenue at Hayes) produces the best maps of San Francisco and other Bay Area cities and counties, but you have to be a AAA member to get one.

9 The Best Way to Make Freeways Work for You

The Central Freeway—an octopus tangle of I-80, I-280, and U.S. 101—can come in handy for hopping quickly about town during non-rush hours. Study your map and you'll see that the spaghetti sprawl does a rather good job of feeding into various areas. However, some sections damaged by the 1989 Loma Prieta earthquake were still shut down as of this writing, and other sections have been demolished, so make sure your map is current. And of course, the Embarcadero Freeway is gone for good.

10 The Best Way to Go Southbound Out of Town

Let's face it: going north and east, you've got two bridges between you and the rest of the world. If they're jammed, you're stuck. Avoid them during morning and evening commute hours, *particularly* during or shortly after a rain. If you're headed south, take I-280; it's less crowded and prettier than U.S. 101. You can pick up 101 again just south of San Jose, and also miss that growing city's traffic.

Tourist Busing: The Ten Best Muni Rides

If you grow weary of the quest for a place to park your Belchfire V-6, you can do considerable touring on the assorted buses, streetcars, and—of course—cable cars of Muni, the San Francisco Municipal Railway system.

Fares are $1 on buses for each line ridden (there are no free transfers) and $2 for cable cars. You'll likely save money by getting a one-day ($6), three-day ($10), or seven-day ($15) Muni Passport. Also, tokens can be purchased at 80 cents each. If you're going to be around for a while, get a Fast Pass for $35, good for a calendar month. These passes allow unlimited rides on the city's bus, streetcar, cable car, and Muni Metro rail system, and on BART and CalTrain within the city. They're available from the information booth in San Francisco City Hall, the Visitor Information Center in Hallidie Plaza (near the cable car turntable at Powell and Market), the Cable Car Museum at Washington and Mason streets, and the STBS ticket office on the Stockton Street side of Union Square. For transit information, call 673-MUNI.

You'll find Muni route maps to be valuable aids. They're $1.50, available at the pass outlets listed above and in some stores. Or you can order one for $2 through the mail: San Francisco Municipal Railway, 949 Presidio Avenue, San Francisco, CA 94115.

Okay, Muni pass and map in hand? Let's use public transit to play tourist. Here are our Ten Best routes (with helpful input from the Community Affairs Office of Muni).

1 76–Marin Headlands

This special bus, which runs Sundays and holidays only, takes you across the Golden Gate Bridge to the outer reaches of the Marin Headlands. The terminal is at the Fourth Street and Townsend CalTrain depot, south of Market Street.

2 J–Church

The Muni Metro system travels under Market Street, then emerges to rumble through the Mission District on Church Street. You can jump off at Church and Sixteenth Street and walk a block down to Mission Dolores. The train travels on its own scenic right-of-way between Eighteenth and Twenty-second streets, and delivers you to the shopping district of Noe Valley on Twenty-fourth Street. Note the nice city views from Dolores Park, between Eighteenth and Twentieth. The terminal is at the Embarcadero Muni/BART station at the foot of Market. You can catch it at any Muni/BART station along Market, or at the Market and Van Ness Avenue Muni station near the Civic Center.

3 L–Taraval

If you're into tunnels, the L-Taraval takes you through the Twin Peaks tunnel and out to the San Francisco Zoo and Ocean Beach, where you're within walking distance of Lake Merced. Like the J-Church, it's part of Muni Metro, running beneath Market Street. Both share subway stops with BART at the Embarcadero,

Montgomery, Powell, and Civic Center, then they continue up Market Street while BART swings out along Mission, headed for Daly City.

4 18–46th Avenue

You can travel to Sutro Heights, the Cliff House, along the edge of Golden Gate Park, down the Great Highway, and around Lake Merced on this run. A good place to catch this bus is at the Palace of the Legion of Honor parking lot in Lincoln Park.

5 29–Sunset

Take this bus through the Presidio, along Lincoln Boulevard with ocean and Golden Gate Bridge views, across Golden Gate Park, and down Sunset Boulevard to Lake Merced and the Stonestown Shopping Center. Catch it in the Presidio on Lombard, near DeWitt Road.

6 30–Stockton

The popular "Orient Express" travels through Chinatown into North Beach, terminating in the Marina at Broderick and Beach. From there, it's a short walk to the Palace of Fine Arts and the Exploratorium. En route, it passes close to the Cannery and Ghirardelli Square on the edge of Fisherman's Wharf. (The 30 is not an express, but earned its nickname because of its service along Stockton Street through Chinatown.) If you're in the downtown area, a good place to catch it is at Stockton and Sutter, just before it enters the Stockton Street Tunnel.

7 37–Corbett

Panoramic views are the lure on this bus, which travels through the hilly Buena Vista Park/Haight-Ashbury neighborhoods, then climbs up into the Twin Peaks area. It passes quite near the Twin Peaks lookout, and you can hop out for a view. A good place to catch it is at Market and Church.

8 38–Geary

This bus serves the heart of downtown, then roams out Geary Boulevard past Japan Center to Ocean Beach, within a short walk of the Cliff House. It launches from the Transbay Terminal at Mission and First streets, or you can catch it any-where downtown along Geary. On weekdays, take a 38-Geary Limited, which delivers you to the Forty-eighth Avenue and Point Lobos terminal. On weekends, make sure your bus is marked "48th Ave. & Point Lobos," since all 38's don't go the full distance.

Incidentally, to reach Golden Gate Park by bus, catch the 5-Fulton or 21-Hayes along Market Street.

9 42–Downtown Loop

We think of this route as the San Francisco "sampler" because the bus wanders around a good part of downtown, skirts briefly along the Embarcadero, passes through Fisherman's Wharf, follows Van Ness Avenue through the Civic Center, then prowls south of Market. Catch it downtown on Sansome at California, or at Fremont and Market, or anywhere along Van Ness Avenue between Bay Street and Market. It runs in a continuous loop, with a layover at Fourth and Townsend.

10 44–O'Shaughnessy (via Glen Park BART station)

This is an interesting cross-town route that winds through a pretty ravine in Glen Canyon Park, passes landscaped homes of the Twin Peaks area, then crosses through Golden Gate Park near the major museums, Japanese Tea Garden, and Academy of Sciences. To catch it, take a Daly City-bound BART train to Glen Park station, then board the 44 on Bosworth Street, headed uphill.

Easy Listening: The Ten Best Radio Stations

If you insist on herding your car through San Francisco's busy and often complicated streets, you might want to tune in to your favorite music or talk show.

1 BEST TALK RADIO
KGO at 810 AM

2 BEST NEWS RADIO
KCBS at 740 AM

3 BEST SPORTS RADIO
KNBR at 680 AM
Wall-to-wall sports talk, mixed with news, plus San Francisco Giants broadcasts.

4 BEST MORNING MOUTH
KSFO at 560 AM
With Gene Nelson.

5 BEST CLASSIC ROCK & POP
KFRC at 610 AM AND 99.7 FM

6 BEST JAZZ
KJAZ at 92.7 FM

7 BEST ROCK
K101 at 101.3 FM

8 BEST COUNTRY
KSAN at 94.9 FM

9 BEST CONTEMPORARY EASY LISTENING
KBLX at 102.9 FM and 1400 AM

10 BEST CLASSICAL MUSIC
KKHI at 95.7 FM and 1550 AM

Chapter 23

THE BOTTOM TEN

Lists of the Least of the Best

I never give them hell; I just tell the truth and they think it is hell.

—Harry S. Truman

For twenty-two chapters we've verbalized the virtues of San Francisco. We aren't suggesting that it's flawless, only that it's wonderful. There are a few things up with which we'd rather not put. Much of it is centered on Fisherman's Wharf, which has become a sorry shadow of its former self. A few other areas could use a bit of brushing up as well.

The Tacky, the Tawdry, and the Tolerated

1 THE TACKIEST TOURIST AREA
Fisherman's Wharf

What once was a charming visitor attraction of friendly Italian seafood restaurants and a working fishing fleet has become a shoddy collection of wax museums, cheap souvenir shops, and trinket peddlers passing themselves off as street artists. The cafés and some of the fishing boats are still there, and the smell of the crab pots is still wonderful in the morning air. But junk shops, wax museums, and other contrived tourist attractions have turned the place into a cheap carnival.

2 THE LARGEST CLUTTER OF USELESS SOUVENIRS
Only in San Francisco

Pier 39, near Fisherman's Wharf; 397-0122.

Only indeed! This souvenir parlor at Pier 39's entrance epitomizes the gimmickry of much of the rest of this tourist stronghold. It has replaced the Bay Company at Fisherman's Wharf—which we nominated in the first edition of this book—as the ultimate supermarket of schlock. Both places have upgraded their merchandising images, incidentally. We noted a definite decline in trinkets of poor taste since our first survey nearly a decade ago. Lots of silly stuff, but not as crude and bawdy.

3 THE TACKIEST SHOPPING CENTER
Pier 39

Off the Embarcadero, at Fisherman's Wharf.

When Pier 39 was opened in 1978, many observers judged it to be rather tawdry and garish, with its architecture of used pier pilings, noisy video game parlor, and a carousel with plastic horses. It's more carnival than character—a jarring extension of Fisherman's Wharf's growing tackiness.

Yet, despite its touristic excess, the joint's beginning to grow on us. It's the best place in northern California to buy refrigerator magnets, Chip 'n' Dale Rescue Ranger logo products, and other obtuse treasures. We like the sea lions that have taken over part of Pier 39's boat slips, and we admire the pier management for letting them stay. They've even issued a brochure heralding the barking beasts as "Pier 39's natural attraction."

4 THE MOST BORING TOURIST ATTRACTION
Ripley's Believe It or Not Museum

Jefferson Street (at Jones), Fisherman's Wharf; 771-6188.

"Three-ball Charlie could put three balls in his mouth and whistle at the same time." It'll cost you $7.25 for the privilege of walking by a collection of freaks, distortions, gimmicks, and wax figures, and learning the good news about Charlie.

5 THE SADDEST STREET
Market Between Powell and Van Ness

Market Street should be our Champs-Elysées or Canal Street, with its brick sidewalks, polished granite benches, and designer trash cans. For many visitors, arriving by bus or cab from the airport or wandering from their downtown hotels, it provides one of their first impressions of the city.

But middle Market, from the Powell Street cable car turntable to Van Ness Avenue, remains a sad gathering place of the unwashed and unwanted, the despairing and disturbed castoffs of society. They shuffle about aimlessly, extending soiled hands for coins, sipping from bottles in brown paper bags, and upending the fancy trash cans in search of some grubby treasure.

The homeless sleep in littered doorways here, or stretch out on the dirty bricks, sometimes startling our clean-scrubbed visitors from Kansas.

6 THE UGLIEST BEACH
Ocean Beach

With scalloped breakers washing over miles of broad strand, Ocean Beach should be a pretty place and a haven for families. Instead, it attracts bands of scruffy types who look like rejects from outlaw motorcycle gangs. Their idea of a day at the beach is to perch on the graffiti-ridden seawalls, turn up their ghetto-blasters, and guzzle beer. The beach has been cleaned up somewhat in recent years, although it still falls sadly short of being a proper sandy doorway to the West's most beautiful city.

7 THE WORST NEIGHBORHOOD
The Tenderloin

There is hope for this scruffy downtown neighborhood wedged between O'Farrell, Market, and Larkin streets. Vietnamese and other immigrants are opening up decent stores and restaurants, trying valiantly to upgrade the area—and gradually succeeding. However, it's still a haven for pimps, their prostitutes, and dope peddlers. You should think twice before venturing through here late at night.

8 The Worst Places to Find Parking

Parking is nearly impossible in Chinatown, North Beach, Nob Hill, and Russian Hill at almost any time; downtown and the Financial District are difficult during working hours. Next time, take the bus.

9 THE MOST CROWDED PARKING GARAGE
Portsmouth Plaza Garage

On the edge of Chinatown, this is one of the least expensive garages in the downtown area (see Chapter 22) and bargain seekers line up around the block on Friday and Saturday nights and most weekday afternoons. To avoid the mob, try the garage about midmorning, after commuters have settled in, or during the day on weekends.

10 THE WORST TIME OF THE YEAR
Summertime

San Francisco's summer weather doesn't arrive until fall—from September through early November. The normal July-August summer is marked with unpredictable weather and crowded streets. You try to guess how to dress but the elusive sun always fools you. You hope for a nice weekend; Saturday dawns brightly and you head for Baker Beach, but a cloud bank is just offshore, lurking and smirking. At noon, the wind blows the clouds ashore, casting dark shadows over your day at the beach.

Back in the city, tourists in shorts and halter tops wear goose pimples and puzzled expressions. Come on, September, hurry up!

The Ten Tackiest Tourist Trinkets

What do folks do with all those pointless made-in-the-Orient souvenirs that overflow the curio shops? In traveling about the city to compile this guide, we gathered this list of the silliest of the silly.

1 **Bare fanny coffee cup,** labeled Bottoms Up from San Francisco, $6.99; the Mug Tree, Anchorage Shopping Center, Fisherman's Wharf.

2 **Penholder** with cable car and Golden Gate Bridge, brass on wood, $29.99; the Bay Company, 211 Jefferson Street, at Fisherman's Wharf.

3 **Plastic salt and pepper shakers** depicting Alcatraz convicts, $1.25 each; Beach and Taylor Gift Shop, at Fisherman's Wharf.

4 **Plastic "snow dome"** with a cable car that slides along a groove when you tilt it, $3.99; Shandini's Gifts, Columbus Avenue at North Point, Fisherman's Wharf.

5 **Leaded glass window hanging** of The Crookedest Street in the World, $19.95; Only in San Francisco, Pier 39.

6 **Sweatshirt** labeled Hard Lock Café: Alcatraz Penitentiary, $19.95; Only in San Francisco, Pier 39.

7 **Half a coffee cup** labeled San Francisco Was So Expensive I Could Only Afford Half a Cup, $4.50; Only in San Francisco, Pier 39.

8 **Plastic back scratcher** with a cable car, 95 cents; Kwon Sen Lung Co., 943 Grant Avenue, Chinatown.

9 **Fortune cookie** containing a condom, with the message: You Are Going to Get Lucky; Be Prepared, $1.99; Gifts Unlimited, 835 Grant Avenue, Chinatown.

10 **Polished cedar paddle** labeled Bald Man's Hair Brush, San Francisco, $2.99; Seal Rock Gifts at the Cliff House.

The Ten Dumbest Things You Can Do in San Francisco

1 Parking in a Tow-Away Zone During Rush Hour

Now, that's dumb! The fine is $40, but that could be just the beginning of your misery. If you're towed, you'll have to pay $50 or more to liberate your Belchfire V-6 from the towing company's garage, plus a daily storage fee if you don't pick it up right away. The only good news is that, periodically, a moratorium is called on tow-aways because the city often has trouble negotiating contracts with towing companies. But don't count on it.

2 Parking Anywhere Without Reading the Signs

San Francisco has an amazing assortment of parking restrictions, with an aggressive troupe of meter maids—sorry, parking enforcement officers—to back them up. Garage space is scarce, so residents can get car stickers allowing them to park on their neighborhood streets. If you leave your car in one of these zones for more than two hours without a permit, you're out $33. Also, watch for signs designating street-cleaning hours. Block the sweeper and you're short another $20. In addition to conventional yellow zones, there are special loading zones; avoid these or pay the man $30. And don't double-park while you're looking for a place to park. That's the toughest ticket of all—$50. Bus stops and particularly handicapped zone violations also carry a hefty fine.

San Francisco has a fine public transit system, and special discount passes for visitors (see Chapter 22). Maybe you'd better leave your Belchfire V-6 home.

3 Failing to Curb Your Wheels

This law may not exist where you come from, but there's a $20 fine for failing to tuck your car's wheels against a curb on a steep street—to keep your car from going somewhere without you. The law says the wheels must touch the curb, and the city's Traffic Engineering Department defines an "enforceable hill" as one that's steep enough for a pencil to roll down; specifically, it's a 3 percent grade.

4 Trying to Reach the Bay Bridge During Rush Hour

The commute rush, incidentally, starts around 4 p.m. If you'd like to experience terminal gridlock, try getting onto the bridge at rush hour during the first rainstorm of the season.

5 Entering an Intersection Just Because the Light Turns Green

San Francisco drivers are notorious for nipping red lights, apparently enjoying a game of chicken with waiting cross-traffic. After the light has changed, look both ways, count to three, fondle your St. Christopher's medal, and *then* start across. This is particularly important if you're a pedestrian. An encounter with a Marin-bound BMW probably will ruin both your day and your shoe shine.

6 Trying to Park at Fisherman's Wharf on a Sunny Weekend

Fisherman's Wharf parking is virtually impossible on good-weather weekends, particularly in summer; don't even attempt it. The same holds true for the Coit Tower parking lot.

7 Driving Along Chinatown's Grant Avenue on Friday or Saturday Night

Friday and Saturday are banquet nights for the Chinese, who come from all over California to attend catered affairs in Chinatown's restaurants. It's back to gridlock again. And don't even try to get into Portsmouth Plaza Garage.

8 Arriving at a Popular Restaurant on Friday or Saturday Night Without a Reservation

As we established in Chapter 5, San Franciscans love to eat out. They virtually swamp favored restaurants on weekends. And if you *really* want to spend the evening staring at the maître d's desk, try one of the trendy new places without advance notice after it's been plugged in Herb Caen's *San Francisco Chronicle* column. Until the novelty wears off, some of popular new places require several days' advance notice.

9 Wearing a Dodger Cap...

at a San Francisco Giants game.

10 Calling it 'Frisco

What's wrong with that? For one thing, the city is named for a saint—Francis of Assisi—so it's in poor taste to abbreviate it. For another, only sailors on shore leave and southern Californians use that awful abbreviation. It is never used by a true San Franciscan. However, it's trendy to call it SFO, the official airport destination. If you're *really* a San Franciscan, you simply refer to it as "the city."

After all, is there any other?

Chapter 24

AN ODE TO OAKLAND

Spending a Day Across the Bay

Gertrude Stein was misquoted.

—*Robert Maynard,* Oakland Tribune

It's difficult enough living in the shadows cast by San Francisco's appeal, but living with the memory of Gertrude Stein's famous quote makes it even worse. She wrote in her autobiography: "Anyway what was the use of my having come from Oakland... There is no there there."

The late *Oakland Tribune* publisher Robert Maynard once commented that Stein hadn't intended to knock the East Bay metropolis. She simply meant that when she returned to the Oakland neighborhood where she grew up, after forty years' absence, she found that everything had changed. Her childhood home was gone, and there was nothing there to which she could relate.

We'll let historians argue over Gertrude's intent. Oakland does offer some interesting lures. Also, local tourist promoters claim that hotel rooms are less expensive, suggesting that visitors can stay in Oakland and commute quickly by BART to San Francisco. I can say from personal experience that Oakland has a far superior and less crowded airport and generally—dammit—a better baseball team.

The visitor bureau in the Trans Pacific Center in downtown Oakland (1000 Broadway) can tell you more about the city's objects of intrigue. Call or write: Convention and Visitors Bureau, 1000 Broadway, Suite 200, Oakland, CA 94607-4020; (510) 839-9000. Tell them Gertrude sent you.

Here then, with considerable help from that bureau, are the Ten Best attractions in Oakland and neighboring Berkeley. (*Note:* The East Bay telephone area code is now 510.)

The Ten Best Attractions in Oakland and Berkeley

1 The Oakland Museum

1000 Oak Street (at Tenth Street), Oakland; (510) 238-3401. Open 10 a.m. to 5 p.m. Wednesday-Saturday, and noon to 7 p.m. Sunday. Free; charges for some special exhibits.

The Oakland Museum is California in a capsule, reflecting the history, art, culture, life-styles, and natural science of the Golden State. It's the only major museum in the world devoted exclusively to the state of California.

No musty collection of bric-a-brac and butter churns, the museum features innovative, full-dimensional exhibits. A focal point is the Cowell Hall of California History, which ingeniously carries out a "California dream" theme with tableaux of life styles through the generations. Equally intriguing are the dioramas and environmental displays depicting California's various biotic zones, in the Natural Sciences Gallery. They graphically depict the climate, geology, flora, and fauna of this incredibly complex state, from the Pacific to the Great Basin. The Gallery of California Art showcases photography, paintings, sculptures, and crafts from 1830 to the present.

The museum also is an architectural landmark. The structure looks like it emerged from the earth instead of being built upon it. Covering four city blocks, it is a three-tiered complex with hanging gardens, terraces, and lily ponds. Your first impression is that you've come upon a park instead of a museum. In fact, visitors are encouraged to picnic on the grounds.

2 Claremont Resort and Spa

Ashby and Domingo avenues, Oakland; (510) 843-3000.

The Claremont is the Bay Area's only full-scale resort, with a $6 million spa, tennis courts, Olympic-sized swimming pools, and elegant rooms. It's also one of the East Bay's Ten Best attractions, worth a visit even if you aren't planning to stay. This great white castle snuggled against the Berkeley hills has been a landmark since its completion in 1915. With a recent $27 million restoration, it's even more opulent than before. The château-like main building is massive, eight hundred feet long and more than a hundred feet high. The look is both regal and whimsical, with a grand entry and curious little cupolas popping out of the steeply raked roof.

Stroll about the monumental lobby and the twenty-two acres of manicured grounds; have a cocktail or meal and enjoy awesome views of the Bay Area. For a fee, you can use the spa and other resort facilities without an overnight stay.

3 East Bay Regional Parks

Headquartered at 2950 Peralta Oaks Court, Oakland; (510) 635-0135.

Alameda and neighboring Contra Costa counties got together back in 1934 to form a joint parks district. It has grown to a complex of fifty parklands covering more than seventy-five thousand acres, scattered over the two counties; many are linked by hiking or biking trails. Some of the largest and woodsiest preserves are in the Oakland and Berkeley hills, offering commanding Bay Area views.

A trip to Tilden, Redwood, or Chabot park provides instant wilderness relief from the pulsating urban sprawl below. For a stunning panorama, drive along Skyline and Grizzly Peak boulevards, which pass through these parks as they follow the twisting ridgeline of the East Bay hills.

To get there, head southeast through Oakland on I-580 until you hit the Golf Links Road turnoff. Go east (inland) on Golf Links for about two miles, then swerve left onto Grass Valley Road. This blends into Skyline Boulevard. Just keep following it north along the ridge; it eventually becomes Grizzly Peak Boulevard,

4 Jack London Square and Village

Along the Oakland estuary; (510) 465-9006.

The story is that hell-raising author Jack London used to run with the oyster pirates off Oakland's estuary. He also sailed from here on many of his worldwide adventures. As a teenager, he'd hang out at a rat-trap saloon called Heinhold's, sipping beer and thumbing through Johnny Heinhold's thick dictionary, shaping his future as a writer.

The square today is an attractive area of landscaped gardens, bayside walks, parks, curio shops, and seafood restaurants. More than the memory of London lingers here. Heinhold's First and Last Chance Saloon survives, and the barkeep sometimes regales visitors with tall tales of the wild young writer. Jack London's Cabin, where he wintered during the Yukon gold rush, was discovered in Canada's wilds a few years ago, and its logs were shared with the people of Oakland and Dawson City. Oakland's share has been reassembled on the square, with additional logs added to make it whole again.

Jack London Village, a themed shopping center built in the manner of an old waterfront hamlet, is just south of the square.

5 Lake Merritt and Lakeside Park

In downtown Oakland.

Resplendent in its Necklace of Lights, which rims Lake Merritt, Lakeside Park is to Oakland what Golden Gate Park is to San Francisco. It's a city retreat for strollers, picnickers, joggers, cyclists, roller bladers, and folks who just like to sit on cool grass with their backs against real trees.

This park has a bonus: saltwater Lake Merritt with small-boat sailing, canoeing, and a shoreline where you can feed Wonder bread to the ducks. Old-fashioned Sunday afternoon concerts are held in Edoff Memorial Bandstand. You can ride around the lake on a silly old stern-wheeler or hop aboard a kiddie train. There's a large playland with fairy-tale structures for curtain-climbers.

The Necklace of Lights is a string of five thousand small bulbs supported by Florentine lampposts circling the lake. It was removed during World War II, then restored in 1987 to return a dazzling nighttime glitter to the park.

For those who love trivia: This is the "largest saltwater lake lying wholly within the boundaries of an American city," and it's the nation's oldest bird sanctuary. The nicest thing about Lake Merritt is that it's smack in the middle of downtown Oakland.

6 Lawrence Hall of Science

Centennial Drive near Grizzly Peak Boulevard, Berkeley; (510) 642-5132
(taped information) or (510) 642-5134. Open 10 a.m. to 4 p.m. Monday-Saturday,
and noon to 5 p.m. Sunday; adults $5, seniors and students $4, ages three to six,
$2. Two-hour lab tours available by appointment.

Perched on the rim of the University of California campus in the Berkeley hills, Lawrence Hall is a science museum with a focus on computers and state-of-the art research. It offers a variety of interactive exhibits, discovery laboratories, participation planetarium shows, and special events and exhibits.

Among its many intriguing displays are a two-story computerized periodic table of the elements, a thirty-foot robotic dinosaur, a seismograph, a sixty-foot replica of a DNA model, and artifacts focusing on the lives and works of Nobel Prize winner E. O. Lawrence.

And once you've finished fiddling with scientific intrigue inside, you can step outside for a spectacular bay view.

7 Mormon Temple and Genealogy Center

4766 Lincoln Avenue (near the Warren Freeway), Oakland; (510) 531-1475 or (510) 531-3905 for the genealogy center. Grounds open 9 a.m. to 9 p.m. daily. A free guided tour includes a visit to the imposing Christus statue and a video presentation. Genealogy center open 9:30 a.m. to 9:30 p.m. Tuesday-Thursday, 9:30 a.m. to 5 p.m. Friday, and noon to 5 p.m. Saturday; closed Sunday and Monday.

This modern granite temple is one of the city's most visible landmarks, with golden spires thrusting skyward from a shelf high in the Oakland hills. It's particularly striking with its nighttime illumination. The grounds are carefully manicured, and the Bay Area view from this high niche is impressive.

You can use the facilities of the genealogy center to trace your roots. After all, you might be kin to someone famous. Or, more interesting, perhaps a horse thief.

8 Oakland Zoo and Knowland Park

9777 Golf Links Road (take the Golf Links Road-98th Avenue exit from I-580 and go east); (510) 632-9525. Open 10 a.m. to 4 p.m. daily (until 5 p.m. in summer); $4.50 for adults, and $2 for kids and seniors. Park admission is $3 per car; free first Monday of the month; always free to pedestrians.

Greatly improved in recent years, the Oakland Zoo exhibits scores of critters in realistic habitats built into the Oakland hills. Highlights are a one-and-a-half-acre African lion exhibit, an extensive African elephant exhibit, and the tropical Siamang Island, which opened in the fall of 1993. Also featured are a sky ride that provides a bird's-eye view of the zoo and the Bay Area, a children's zoo, kiddie rides, and picnic areas.

9 Paramount Theatre of the Arts

2025 Broadway, Oakland, (510) 893-2300; box office, (510) 465-6400.

Once a lavish 1930s art deco movie palace, the Paramount was rescued from redevelopers a couple of decades ago and meticulously restored. It now functions as a major performing arts center and home of the Oakland Ballet.

You can peer at the wonderful detail of its Egyptian and art deco motifs without catching a concert. Guided tours are conducted the first and third Saturdays of each month at 10 a.m. for $1 per person; reservations aren't necessary.

10 University of California at Berkeley

Visitor Information Center at 101 University Hall. Ninety-minute campus tours depart weekdays at 1 p.m.; (510) 642-5215.

The senior campus of the University of California occupies a sloping 720-acre site above Berkeley. More than a major learning center, it's a repository of museums, gardens, and other things worthy of visitor interest. Here's a partial list:

UNIVERSITY ART MUSEUM   *(510) 642-0808, Bancroft Avenue near College.* The museum exhibits oriental and contemporary art and is open Wednesday through Sunday from 11 a.m. to 5 p.m.; adults $2; kids and seniors $1.

PACIFIC FILM ARCHIVE   *In the University Art Museum; (510) 642-1412.* The archive shows classic films nightly from its extensive collections. Adults $4.25; less for kids and seniors.

CAMPANILE   *(510) 642-3666.* This slender observation tower in the center of the campus provides imposing Bay Area vistas. An elevator ride to the top (daily between 10 a.m. and 4 p.m.; closed second Tuesday) costs an entire fifty cents.

PHOEBE A. HEARST MUSEUM OF ANTHROPOLOGY   *(510) 642-3681, Bancroft Avenue at College.* The museum features excellent exhibits on the study of mankind, and particularly California Indians. A special exhibit focuses on Ishi, "the last free native Californian." He was found in Oroville earlier in this century and brought to San Francisco for observation and study. The museum is open weekdays except Wednesdays 10 a.m. to 4:30 p.m.; weekends noon to 4:30 p.m. Admission is $1.50.

The Next Ten Best Attractions in Oakland and Berkeley

1 Berkeley Municipal Rose Gardens

Euclid Avenue and Bayview, Berkeley; open during daylight; free.

Go sniff more than four thousand kinds of roses. The blooms are best from late spring to September.

2 Bret Harte Boardwalk

Fifth Street, between Jefferson and Clay, Oakland.

Author Bret Harte grew up here, and the area's Victorian homes have been refurbished and fashioned into boutiques and restaurants.

3 Greek Orthodox Church of the Ascension

4700 Lincoln Avenue, Oakland; (510) 531-3400. Open 9 a.m. to 4 p.m. Monday-Friday; free.

The copper dome of this Byzantine-style church is a dramatic Oakland landmark. Inside are biblical mosaics and a twelve-foot Baccarat crystal cross.

4 Dunsmuir House and Gardens

2960 Peralta Oaks Court, Oakland; (510) 562-0328. Open Sundays only, from Easter to September, noon to 4 p.m. Guided tours scheduled at 1, 2 and 3 p.m.; small admission charge.

This thirty-seven-room colonial revival mansion in the East Oakland foothills resembles a relic of the antebellum South, with its thick white columns and second-floor balconies. The surrounding forty-acre garden contains more than seventy types of trees and shrubs hauled in from all over the world. Hiking trails curl around the borders of this large estate.

5 Kaiser Center

Lakeside Drive at the edge of Lake Merritt, Oakland. Art gallery open weekdays 8 a.m. to 6 p.m., (510) 271-2351; roof garden Monday-Saturday 7 a.m. to 7 p.m.; both free.

Once the largest office building west of Chicago, the dramatically curving Kaiser Center provides two reasons for visitors to enter: the second-floor art gallery and an attractively landscaped roof garden with pleasant views of the city and the bay.

6 Mills College

MacArthur Boulevard and Seminary Avenue, Oakland; (510) 430-2255. Art gallery open Tuesday-Sunday 10 a.m. to 4 p.m. during the school term.

Mills College occupies a comely wooded campus in the Oakland hills; the art gallery offers a variety of changing exhibits.

7 Morcom Ampitheater of Roses

700 Jean Street, Oakland; (510) 658-0731. Open during daylight; free.

Landscaped pools and walks set off this garden. Late spring through summer is the best blooming time for its eight thousand rose bushes.

8 Oakland-Alameda County Coliseum Complex

Hegenberger Road off I-880; (510) 639-7700.

Home to the Oakland Athletics and Golden State Warriors, this modern complex hosted more pro sports champions during the 1980s than any other in the nation. The A's, the Warriors, and the now-departed Raiders won eleven world titles during that decade. It's also the birthplace—perhaps unfortunately—of the "human wave," started here on October 15, 1981, by A's cheerleading mascot "Crazy George" Henderson.

9 Oakland Chinatown

From Eighth to Eleventh streets between Broadway and Harrison.

Although it lacks the glitter and dragon lamp posts of San Francisco's Chinatown, Oakland's version is every bit as ethnic. It brims with good restaurants, and they're generally less expensive than those across the bay.

10 Takara Sake

708 Addison Street, Berkeley; (510) 540- 8250. Open noon to 6 p.m. daily; free.

Sip a little sake and watch a slide show in California's only Japanese rice wine distillery.

The East Bay's Ten Best Restaurants

What the world is now calling California cuisine began in Berkeley with the inventive creations of Alice Waters of Chez Panisse. We consider it the finest East Bay restaurant, although there are many other excellent dining places across the water as well. Our selections are a mix of our own choices and those from *San Francisco's Ultimate Dining Guide,* a book we compiled from surveys of people in the food and hotel business.

1 Chez Panisse

1517 Shattuck Avenue (at Vine), Berkeley, (510) 548-5525. California cuisine; expensive; wine and beer. Dinner 6 p.m. to 9:15 p.m. daily. Reservations essential; MC/VISA, AMEX.

For years, Alice Waters and her chefs have created new taste sensations every night, with her simple philosophy of obtaining the freshest ingredients and combining them creatively. The *prix fixe* dinner may feature warm puff pastry with sweetbreads and artichokes; fennel, carrot, and spinach soup; blood orange salad; a foil packet of sea bass with *julienne* carrots, scallions, thyme, and lemon.

The Café at Chez Panisse, occupying the upper floor of Alice's simple shingle-sided cottage, is less expensive and equally creative. It focuses on California-Mediterranean items such as grilled fish and interesting salads, along with calzone and pizza from a wood-burning oven.

2 Bay Wolf

3853 Piedmont Avenue (Piedmont District), Oakland; (510) 655-6004. California-Continental; moderate; wine and beer. Lunch 11:30 a.m. to 2 p.m. weekdays, dinner 6 p.m. to 9 p.m. weeknights, and 5:30 p.m. to 9 p.m. weekends. Reservations accepted; MC/VISA.

With its inventive, constantly changing menu, Bay Wolf might be regarded as a more casual and modestly priced Chez Panisse. The food style is difficult to label, since entrées wander tastily from duck with apricots and lemon-honey glaze to French country *cassoulet* to sautéed lamb chops or Provenal fish soup. The wine list, like the menu, is both varied and moderately priced, featuring several lesser-known and excellent California wineries.

Bay Wolf's setting is sort of upscale mid-America. The restaurant is housed in a converted Victorian (with porch dining in warm weather) set in the old established neighborhood of Piedmont. Attentive yet casual service is appropriate to this low-key culinary climate.

3 Broadway Terrace Café

5891 Broadway Terrace (at Clarewood), Oakland; (510) 652-4442. California grill;
moderate; wine and beer. Dinner 5:30 p.m. to 10 p.m. Wednesday-Saturday,
and 5 p.m. to 9 p.m. Sunday. Reservations essential; no credit cards.

This is California cuisine done on a grill in a woodsy setting. Broadway Terrace Café specializes in mesquite-grilled fish, chops, and birds, accompanied with fresh salads, pastas, and desserts.

Restaurateur Albert Katz creates such tasty curiosities as Gorgonzola with romaine, fruit, and nuts; a corn and bell pepper custard *timbale;* and for dessert, chocolate soufflé cake with blood oranges. The restaurant seats only thirty-four, so reservations are a must.

4 Gertie's Chesapeake Bay Café

1919 Addison Street (at Martin Luther King Jr. Way), Berkeley; (510) 841-2722.
Seafood; moderate; wine and beer. Lunch 11:30 a.m. to 2:30 p.m. weekdays, dinner
5:30 p.m. to 9:30 p.m. weeknights, and 5:30 p.m. to 10 p.m. weekends.
Reservations advised; major credit cards.

If you're thinking that Oakland and Berkeley restaurants serve only nouveau cuisine, this pleasant little place takes us to the East Coast for crab cakes, Maryland crab soup, steamed mussels, and other regional favorites of the Chesapeake Bay.

It also features Down South specialties such as seasonal soft shell crabs, gumbo, and bayou *bouillabaisse.* The look of the place is art deco modern, and diners adjourn to a patio when the weather's right.

5 Hunan

396 Eleventh Street (at Franklin), Oakland; (510) 444-1155. Northern Chinese;
inexpensive to moderate; wine and beer. Daily 11:30 a.m. to 9:30 p.m. Reservations
accepted; MC/VISA.

We mentioned earlier that Oakland's Chinatown has some tasty and inexpensive places to eat, and this is our favorite. It specializes in spicy north China fare such as ginger crab, Mandarin braised fish, sizzling chili sauce prawns, and honey-glazed walnut shrimp.

Hunan recently moved from its original site on Eighth Street to these larger quarters. It features contemporary decor, carved cherry-wood chairs, wall hangings, and a large aquarium.

6 Juan's Place

941 Carlton Street (at Ninth Street), Berkeley; (510) 845-6904. Mexican; inexpensive; wine and beer. Open 11 a.m. to 10 p.m. weekdays, and 2 p.m. to 10 p.m. weekends. MC/VISA.

Locals like this casual little cantina for its basic California-Mexican fare, all created on the premises. The servings of chile rellenos, flautas, burritos and such are monstrous, and dinners average around $8. The decor is a bright blend of wonderful Mexican clutter.

7 Plearn Thai Cuisine

2050 University Avenue (at Shattuck), Berkeley; (510) 841-2148. Thai; inexpensive; wine and beer. Lunch 11:30 a.m. to 3 p.m. Monday-Saturday; dinner 5 p.m. to 10 p.m. daily. MC/VISA.

San Francisco *Chronicle* restaurant critics have called Plearn the best Thai restaurant in the Bay Area, and we're inclined to agree. Its tasty fare is served in a modern, attractive environment, instead of a scruffy Formica café typical of many inexpensive ethnic places.

Entrées include a variety of barbecued satays in peanut sauce, fresh seafood seasoned with lemon grass, and assorted spicy curries.

8 Santa Fe Bar & Grill

1310 University Avenue (at San Pablo), Berkeley; (510) 841-4740. American regional, specializing in smoked meats; moderate to moderately expensive; full bar. Lunch 11:30 a.m. to 3 p.m. weekdays; dinner 5 p.m. to 10 p.m. Sunday-Thursday, until midnight Friday and Saturday; Sunday brunch 10 a.m. to 3 p.m. Reservations essential; major credit cards.

Fazio Poursohi, whose smoked meats and brick-oven fish created raves at Faz in San Francisco, has taken his talents to Berkeley's Santa Fe. Some of the original Southwestern menu remains as well, and the place also offers homemade pastas and pizzas.

Its appearance is rather striking: sort of Southwestern Byzantine with Spanish arches, a domed roof, and an outdoor patio.

9 Skates

100 Seawall Drive (at University), Berkeley; (510) 549-1900. American regional; moderate; full bar. Open 11 a.m. to 11 p.m. daily. Reservations essential; MC/VISA, AMEX.

Folks go to Skates for the scene as much as for the food. It's an upscale, trendy palace of noise perched on piers at the Berkeley Marina, with glass-walled views of the bay. In fact, the ambiance is probably better than the food. The menu tries to cover all the trendy styles: California cuisine, Southwestern, Cajun, sushi, kiawe-wood grilled, and yuppie *nouveau*. At times, the fare at this corporate creation is rather good, and the scene is always fun.

10 Sorabol

372 Grand Avenue (at Perkins), Oakland, (510) 839-2288. Korean; moderate; full bar. Open 11:30 a.m. to 9:30 p.m. daily. Reservations accepted; major credit cards.

We've had several pleasing meals at this handsome place near Lake Merritt. Much of Korea's fare, like the notorious *kim chee,* is hot and spicy, apparently to get citizens through those cold Korean winters. But one can balance a Sorabol meal with milder dishes. Try the gentle *bul-gokee* (thin-sliced ribeye steak), fluffy *beandu duk* (egg pancakes), and spicy *sengsun guyee* (whole rock cod). Incidentally, beer is the best accompaniment to Korean food.

Sorabol is styled to resemble a royal Korean courtyard, with carved wooden panels, Korean prints, and a ceramic tile false roof.

Chapter 25

BEYOND PARADISE

The Ten Best Reasons to Get Out of Town

San Francisco has only one drawback—'tis hard to leave.

—Rudyard Kipling

We've done San Francisco and even Oakland. Perhaps it's time to slip away for a few days. If you're new to northern California, just about any area of the Golden State will be a discovery. But if you're a Bay Arean, you've probably grown tired of Tahoe, and you've been to Yosemite so many times you're beginning to recognize some of the bears. The art colony of Mendocino is old hat, and nobody goes to Carmel anymore because it's too crowded.

What follows is a list of places you may have overlooked. They're all within long weekend or minivacation range, from a two- to seven-hour drive from the Bay Area. Other than selecting Columbia as our favorite, our nominees are listed in no particular order.

1 Rediscover the Gold Rush in Historic Columbia

A three-hour drive from San Francisco. Contact Columbia State Historic Park, P.O. Box 151, Columbia, CA 95310; (209) 532-4301. For Fallon Hotel or City Hotel reservations, contact City Hotel, P.O. Box 1870, Columbia, CA 95310; (209) 532-1479.

Tucked into the woodsy foothills of California's Sierra Nevada range, Columbia is a historic jewel, a living museum of the great California gold rush.

A Wells Fargo stagecoach rumbles and squeaks along Main Street while gingham-gowned ladies sell scented soaps and homemade candies in iron-shuttered stores. You can sleep amidst eighteenth-century finery in the City or Fallon hotels, dine in 1860s splendor at the City Hotel Restaurant, or enjoy fine Mexican food in a converted nineteenth-century home at El Sombrero.

Dramatists perform in the Fallon Theater; a blacksmith hammers visitors' names into hand-forged horseshoes; miners demonstrate gold-panning and take visitors on mine tours. Western bands twang happily away in the St. Charles Saloon, as elbow-bending good old boys raise a little harmless hell. It's a place where yesterday still happens.

Gold was discovered here in early 1850. By the time the mines ran dry, $2 billion in bullion (at today's prices) had been taken from the ruddy soil. During its rowdy heyday, Columbia was one of the largest cities in California, ranking behind San Francisco, Sacramento, and Stockton. Then it shriveled to a sleepy, scruffy hamlet. The state bought many of its sagging buildings in 1945, and restoration began. Through the years it has become a fascinating one-of-a-kind place: part living-history museum and part lively community, where residents buy groceries at the corner Mercantile and pick up their mail at a century-old post office.

The people of Columbia dwell in a gentle time warp, living for today but cherishing yesterday. They welcome visitors the year around, and particularly during their old-fashioned festivals. Come celebrate the Fourth of July with greased-pole climbing and watermelon-eating contests. Experience a country Christmas with the scent of pine boughs and a grand gold rush feast at the City Hotel.

Columbia folks like to think they've found paradise, and, as a matter of fact, they have. The town was used as the historic model for the "Paradise" television series.

2 Wander Northern Sonoma's Wine Lands

A two-hour drive from San Francisco, north on U.S. 101. The best guide to the area is a brochure called Russian River Wine Roads, listing wineries, lodgings, and annual events. Send a stamped self-addressed business-sized envelope to: Healdsburg Area Chamber of Commerce, 217 Healdsburg Avenue, Healdsburg, CA 95448; (707) 433-6935.

The vineyards of the Napa and Sonoma valleys are beautiful and the wineries are fun to visit; but, good grief, the weekend crowds! Next time, explore the wine lands of northern Sonoma County. The area isn't much farther, the countryside is equally attractive, the wines are excellent, and the wineries aren't as busy.

Northern Sonoma wine lands begin in the Russian River Valley north of Santa Rosa; most are centered around Healdsburg and Geyserville. This region has more wineries than the better-known Sonoma Valley and—except for some summer and fall weekends—they're rarely crowded. If you plan a couple of days for this vineyard country ramble, you'll find that bed and breakfast inns and good restaurants are cropping up like crocuses.

Here are some of our favorite northern wineries:

J. PEDRONCELLI WINERY *A mile north of Geyserville at 1220 Canyon Road; tasting daily from 10 a.m. to 5 p.m.; tours by appointment; (707) 857-3531.* John and Jim Pedroncelli continue a tradition of fine wines started by their father, who must have been the original Italian optimist. He established the winery during Prohibition. Generous sips of their award-winning varietals are poured in a comfortable tasting room.

FERRARI-CARANO WINERY *8761 Dry Creek Road, Healdsburg; tasting daily from 10 a.m. to 5 p.m.; tours by appointment; (707) 433-6700.* This new facility is a striking blend of manor house, castle, and leading-edge winery. The large complex is fronted by a formal entry and rimmed by billiard-green lawns. Its tasting room and gift shop are as stylish as a Rodeo Drive boutique.

HOP KILN WINERY *6050 Westside Road, Healdsburg; tasting 10 a.m. to 5 p.m. daily; informal tours; (707) 433-6491.* Hop Kiln's tasting room is located in the loft of an impressive triple-towered 1905 hop-drying barn. Art exhibits brighten the walls of the tasting room, and picnic tables outside invite visitors to linger.

KORBEL CHAMPAGNE CELLARS *13250 River Road, Guerneville, along the Russian River west of Santa Rosa; tasting 9 a.m. to 4:30 p.m. daily; tours 10 a.m. to 3 p.m. daily; (707) 887-2294.* This handsome vine-covered stone winery complex looks like a transplant from the Rhine. Korbel specializes in champagne and brandy, and the tour provides a good study of the champagne-making process.

Some places to stay:

HOPE-MERRILL AND HOPE-BOSWORTH HOUSES *21253 Geyserville Avenue (P.O. Box 42), Geyserville, CA 95441; (707) 857-3356.* These two nicely restored and elegantly furnished Victorians are across the street from each other. They feature whirlpool baths, a swimming pool, and a gazebo suitable for sitting and wine sipping.

MADRONA MANOR *1001 Westside Road (P.O. Box 818), Healdsburg, CA 95448; (707) 433-4231.* This is a beautifully restored 1881 Victorian mansion on several wooded, landscaped acres. Its twenty-one rooms feature antique and modern furnishings; there's an excellent restaurant here as well.

RIDENHOUR RANCH HOUSE INN *12850 River Road (next to Korbel Winery), Guerneville, CA 95446; (707) 887-1033.* This ranch-style bed and breakfast furnished with antiques is located near Korbel Champagne Cellars. Offerings include a hot tub, old-fashioned lawn croquet, and a full breakfast.

3 Sample Shakespeare in a Hamlet

A seven-hour drive from San Francisco. Write Oregon Shakespearean Festival, P.O. Box 158, Ashland, OR 97520-0158; or call (503) 482-4331 for a thick brochure listing the current season's events, plus hotels, motels, and restaurants. For general information on the area, contact the Southern Oregon Reservation Center, P.O. Box 477, Ashland, OR 97520; (800) 547-8052. For information on music festivals in neighboring Jacksonville, contact Peter Britt Festivals, P.O. Box 1124, Medford, OR 97501; (800) 882-7488.

Quick quiz: Where is America's largest annual drama festival held? Not in some major cultural bastion. It occurs in the small lumber town of Ashland, Oregon, just across the northern California border. This village of fifteen thousand souls lures more than *three hundred thousand* visitors a year to its Oregon Shakespear Festival.

The drama fete runs from late February through October, with about a dozen plays in repertory, ranging from Shakespeare and his contemporaries to modern classics to *avant-garde* to brand-new works. The professional company, which has won a Tony Award and other accolades, performs in two indoor theaters and on a large outdoor Elizabethan stage (which operates in summer only).

The entire town has taken up Shakespeare's tune, with fluttering banners, cross-timbered buildings, madrigal singers, and Elizabethan dancers. The festival began in 1935, the brainchild of local drama teacher Angus L. Bowmer.

About fifteen miles down the road, visitors can prowl along the funky nineteenth-century main street of Jacksonville, a gold rush town that's been designated as a national historic landmark. Like neighboring Ashland, Jacksonville has a cultural tilt: It presents the Britt Festivals each summer, with outdoor music programs of classics, jazz, and bluegrass.

4 Drop Anchor in Avila Beach

A six-hour drive. For information, contact the neighboring San Luis Obispo Chamber of Commerce, 1039 Chorro Street, San Luis Obispo, CA 93401; (805) 781-2777. For San Luis Bay Inn accommodations, contact San Luis Bay Inn, P.O. Box 189, Avila Beach, CA 93424; (805) 595-2333.

Flanked by more popular Pismo Beach and Morro Bay, Avila Beach is a scattering of old homes and a few stores on a sloping hill next to a pretty crescent bay. The weathered main street shops and old concrete beach promenade are right out of the thirties. The wide, clean strand is rarely crowded, although it gets busy on sunny summer weekends.

Most travelers on nearby U.S. 101 bypass this small enclave on San Luis Obispo Bay. Its ominous neighbor, the Diablo Canyon nuclear generating plant, is much better known. The town is certainly worth a stop; it's charming and suitable for a weekend retreat, with its oak-thatched, rumpled hills sloping down to peaceful beaches.

There's little to do here, and therein lies the area's appeal. It's a place to stretch out on or stroll along the strand and scuff at seaweed, and perhaps wander over to the old pier at Port San Luis, about a mile away. San Luis isn't a town; it's a harbor and pier with a couple of seafood restaurants. Nearby San Luis Obispo also is worth a look, with its old mission, pretty creekside park, and a couple of rustic-themed shopping centers.

You can lounge in luxury at the San Luis Bay Inn, a handsomely appointed resort with its own golf course and sea-view rooms on a bluff above Avila Beach.

5 Cool It in Capitola

A three-hour drive. Contact Capitola Chamber of Commerce, 410 Capitola Avenue, Capitola, CA 95010; (408) 475-6522. For Shadow-Brook Restaurant reservations, call (408) 475-1511; American-continental; weeknights from 5:30 p.m., weekends from 4:30, Sunday brunch from 10 a.m.; major credit cards.

If Avila Beach is too much of a stretch for your weekend, hop down to Capitola, one of our favorite northern California seaside cities. This gem of a town is built along a wooded ravine and a small harbor at the mouth of Soquel Creek in Santa Cruz County. Like Avila Beach, it's only a few miles from a much more famous resort—Santa Cruz in this case—and it's less crowded.

Beach seekers have a choice between freshwater dipping in Soquel Creek lagoon or the salty sea just beyond a sandbar. We like the town for its fine examples of Victorian homes, its art and crafts galleries, and a pretty sheltered walkway along Soquel Creek. This is begonia country, and the town celebrates with its Begonia Festival every September.

Our favorite restaurant here is the Shadow-Brook, snuggled against a shaggy hillside above Soquel Creek. Patrons reach it by parking above and taking a tiny red funicular down to the dining room.

6 Climb through a Lava Cavern

A seven-hour drive. For information, contact Lava Beds National Monument, P.O. Box 867, Tulelake, CA 96134; (916) 667-2283; and Klamath National Wildlife Refuge, Route 1, Box 74, Tulelake, CA 96134; (916) 667-2231.

On its busiest days, Lava Beds National Monument is practically deserted. Yet this intriguing area has three major lures. It's a place where Mother Nature tortured the earth's crust with a volcanic fury that left a barren world of broken lava, cinder cones, and dozens of lava caves. It's home to hundreds of thousands of birds of Klamath National Wildlife Refuge. And it's the site of one of America's last Indian wars. Since it's tucked into a remote corner of northeastern California, most of the world passes it by.

Visitors to this dark, tumbled land can prowl through a score of lava tubes, created when rivers of liquid basalt hardened on the surface but continued flowing beneath to leave natural tunnels. These aren't "developed" caves with guided tours and fancy indirect lighting. To explore the tubes, you should first stop by the monument's visitor center to borrow a strong lantern. And you can buy, for about $3, a hard plastic "bump hat" that will prevent the low, jagged ceilings from giving you an Excedrin headache.

Just over a century ago, a Modoc Indian named Captain Jack liberated his people from a hated reservation and led them into the Lava Beds wilderness, where he defied the U.S. government to root them out. Using the natural fortifications of caves and lava trenches, he held off the army for five months in a miserable war that one park ranger described as "an American Indian Vietnam." Fewer than sixty Modocs defied an army of six hundred soldiers, inflicting two hundred thirty-seven casualties while losing only sixteen of their own. Finally, chilled and starved by a merciless winter, the band was rounded up; Captain Jack was hanged.

In a natural lava fortress called Captain Jack's Stronghold, numbered markers help visitors reconstruct those fascinating days of 1872 when—for a brief and angry moment—a band of frustrated native Americans kept the government at bay.

More than a million birds visit nearby Tule Lake and the Klamath Lakes across the Oregon border, making Klamath National Wildlife Refuge one of the busiest bird sanctuaries in the country. More than four hundred species have been identified here. Peak viewing time is early November, when migrating and resident birds mingle. For a brochure and self-guiding auto tour, ask directions to the refuge headquarters, just north of Lava Beds. It's open weekdays 8 a.m. to 4:30 p.m., and weekends 8 a.m. to 4 p.m. A small visitor center has stuffed versions of local critters, wildlife photos, and exhibits on preservation efforts.

The Lava Beds area isn't a resort. The camping crowd can feel at home here, but the national monument has no lodging, no stores, and nothing to drink but water. The nearest town with a reasonable assortment of motels and restaurants is Klamath Falls, Oregon, about fifty miles north. You'll find a couple of motels and restaurants in tiny Tulelake, California, just north of Lava Beds.

7 Seek Shangri-La in the Sierra

A five-hour drive. Contact the Sierra County Chamber of Commerce, P.O. Box 222, Downieville, CA 95936; (916) 289-3560. For Sierra Shangri-La reservations, contact Sierra Shangri-La, P.O. Box 285, Downieville, CA 95936; (916) 289-3455.

You've noticed that our theme here is to find fascinating but uncrowded places. One of the least-visited and prettiest parts of the great Sierra Nevada is in the northern end of this rugged mountain range, in Sierra County. If you like swift-running streams, untrammeled hiking trails, funky old gold rush towns, and pine-clad mountains that reach for the stars, this is your place.

To find this undiscovered land, head east on I-80, then turn north onto State Highway 49 at Auburn. Stay on 49, the historic Golden Chain highway, and you'll eventually find yourself in a beautiful river canyon in the uppermost reaches of the Gold Country. Here, you can fish, wade in chilly waters, camp, picnic, and even pan for gold. (In 1993, *Newsweek* magazine reported a mini-gold rush as modern-day prospectors rushed to sift the runoff from record winter snowfalls.)

Downieville, with four hundred residents, is the Sierra County seat, sitting in a narrow, wooded valley at the confluence of the Downie and Yuba rivers. It's one of the prettiest settings for a town in the entire West. A few years ago, it took a major step toward yesterday when utility lines were sent underground and board-walks replaced sidewalks. With its iron-shuttered, rough-cut stone stores and stee-pled churches, it looks little changed from the 1850s, when it was a thriving mining camp.

A bit farther upstream is Sierra City, a slightly smaller version of Downieville, and just beyond that, an excellent historic park called the Kentucky Mine Museum. Above Sierra City, you can hike, backpack, fish, and generally explore the wilds and alpine lakes of Tahoe National Forest. Particularly appealing are the Gold Lakes area and a rugged outcropping called the Sierra Buttes.

One of our favorite hideaways is Sierra Shangri-La, a resort perched above a rocky gorge in the Yuba River between Downieville and Sierra City. It offers kitchen cabins with potbellied stoves and smaller bed and breakfast units. Most have their own decks, some right over the roaring river.

8 Saunter through Sacramento

A two-hour drive. For details, contact Convention and Visitors Bureau, 1421 K Street, Sacramento, CA 95814; (916) 264-7777.

We aren't suggesting that Sacramento is a little-known place. But you may not know that it has several major tourist lures. So all right, it isn't Carmel or Mendocino. However, our capital city, spraddled over the flatlands of the Sacramento Valley, can keep the visitor occupied for a weekend or even a week.

Begin with Old Sacramento, a gathering of boutiques, shops, and galleries in carefully restored, century-old brick and clapboard buildings along the Sacramento

River. Clump along boardwalks, clatter across cobblestone streets, and pretend you just got off a riverboat. Spend some time at the California State Railroad Museum, with one of the largest collections of trains and railroading memorabilia in the world. Through the ingenuity of modern museum-makers, you'll hear the lonely call of a distant whistle and the rumble of voices in a 1930s train station. You'll even feel the rhythmic sway of a 1929 sleeping car as you stroll past its curtained compartments.

Reserve most of an afternoon for a tour of the impeccably restored State Capitol, about a mile from Old Sacramento. Several years ago, at a cost of $68 million, the domed French revival structure was carefully returned to its 1874 elegance. More than two thousand craftsmen labored five years to complete the most expensive and meticulous restoration of a public structure in the country's history.

Pause a while at Sutter's Fort at Twenty-seventh and L streets, a re-creation of the civilian fortress built in the 1840s by Swiss fortune hunter John Sutter, one of California's first colonizers. It was his plan to construct a sawmill in the Sierra Nevada foothills that led to the discovery of gold by his mill foreman, James Marshall.

9 Stand in a Sequoia's Shadow

A five-hour drive. For general park information, contact Sequoia/Kings Canyon National Parks, Three Rivers, CA 93271; (209) 565-3134. For lodging, contact Sequoia Guest Services, Inc., P.O. Box 789, Three Rivers, CA 93271; (209) 565-3381.

If you're a Californian, you know that you practically have to take a number to get into Yosemite National Park these days. Sequoia National Park, only two hours farther from the Bay Area than Yosemite, is equally intriguing and not nearly as crowded.

Offering a wonderful nature's brew of giant Sequoia trees, cascading streams, aspen-rimmed meadows, and the high granite splendor of the Sierra Nevada, this is a park for all seasons. You can hike in the summer, photograph golden aspen in the fall, snowshoe or cross-country ski beneath cinnamon-barked sequoias in the winter, and watch wildflowers dance across spring meadows.

Although less crowded than Yosemite, the park does get busy in summer, so arrange for reservations well in advance, particularly if you plan a weekend visit.

Sequoias, should you wonder, are a different species than the redwoods of Muir Woods and other coastal areas near San Francisco. They're shorter but fatter and heavier. Sequoia National Park's General Sherman Tree is the largest living thing on earth, weighing an estimated 2.8 million pounds.

10 Shop Until You Drop in Solvang

A six-hour drive. Contact Solvang Chamber of Commerce, P.O. Box 465, Solvang, CA 93464; (805) 688-3317.

Solvang is another of the state's unexpected delights: a re-creation of a Danish village in the green farmlands of south central California's Santa Barbara County. Danish immigrants settled here in 1911 to establish a farming community and school. It has since become a tourist-oriented Danish village, complete with cross-timbered houses, Scandinavian folk dancing, and enough smorgasbord to feed the Danish navy.

It's a major shopping area, with more than three hundred stores offering imports and tasty Danish pastries. The town is particularly popular with credit-card clutchers during the holiday spending period. Solvang also fosters a Danish Days celebration the third weekend of September and an outdoor theater festival in the summer.

Interesting, too, from quite another ethnic world, is Solvang's Mission Santa Ines, established in 1804 as one of a chain of Spanish outposts in California. The surrounding Santa Ynez Valley features an expanding assortment of wineries, many with tasting rooms open to visitors.

Index